SEXUALITY, EQUALITY AND DIVERSITY

Sexuality, Equality and Diversity

Diane Richardson

Surya Monro

palgrave
macmillan

First published 2012 by
PALGRAVE MACMILLAN

Palgrave Macmillan in the UK is an imprint of Macmillan Publishers Limited, registered in England, company number 785998, of Houndmills, Basingstoke, Hampshire RG21 6XS.

Palgrave Macmillan in the US is a division of St Martin's Press LLC, 175 Fifth Avenue, New York, NY 10010.

Palgrave Macmillan is the global academic imprint of the above companies and has companies and representatives throughout the world.

Palgrave® and Macmillan® are registered trademarks in the United States, the United Kingdom, Europe and other countries.

ISBN 978–0–230–27557–7 hardback
ISBN 978–0–230–27558–4 paperback

This book is printed on paper suitable for recycling and made from fully managed and sustained forest sources. Logging, pulping and manufacturing processes are expected to conform to the environmental regulations of the country of origin.

A catalogue record for this book is available from the British Library.

A catalog record for this book is available from the Library of Congress.

10   9   8   7   6   5   4   3   2   1
21   20   19   18   17   16   15   14   13   12

Printed and bound in Great Britain by
CPI Antony Rowe, Chippenham and Eastbourne

*For Audrey La Roche and Clara Quien, my freethinking,
independent, non-gender normative grandmothers*
Surya Monro

For Lillian
May she grow up to live in a more equal and just world
Diane Richardson

Contents

Tables

Boxes

Acknowledgements

We would like to thank the two Research Associates who worked on the project: Dr Michaela Fay, who worked on the project for the first nine months and conducted the majority of fieldwork in the north-east of England, and Dr Ann McNulty, who undertook fieldwork in the south of England and Northern Ireland and also carried out data analysis, dissemination and writing up. Ann's contribution to the project was invaluable and it was a great pleasure to work with such an accomplished and committed researcher. Dr Angie Scott also deserves a big thank you for her contribution to the project, in particular for her role in conference organization and data preparation for the ESDS data archive. Others have supported the project in various other ways along the way. In the School of Geography, Politics and Sociology at Newcastle University, Newcastle upon Tyne, UK, we would like to thank Sue Tatah, who provided administrative support to the project; Sue Mitchell, research manager in the Faculty of Humanities, Arts and Social Sciences; Ingrid Young, who provided IT support and facilitated workshops at the end-of-project conference; and Dr Edmund Coleman-Fountain and Dr Rachel Wilde-Jones, who also provided conference support. In the School of Human and Health Sciences at the University of Huddersfield, Huddersfield, UK, we would like in particular to acknowledge Professor Jim McAuley for his helpful comments on the chapter about LGBT Equalities in Northern Ireland. We would also like to thank supportive staff at the universities where Surya Monro was previously located (Sheffield and Leeds Metropolitan). We also extend thanks to those who have provided helpful input on the project at various stages of development, including our advisory group members, and in particular thanks go to Davina Cooper and Chris Creegan. And, of course, most importantly we thank all those who took part in the research for sharing their experiences, thoughts and feelings with us. This book is in part a measure of their invaluable contribution to moving forward our understandings of equality in relation to sexual and gender diversity, and of what drives or, in some cases, impedes the implementation of the sexualities and trans equalities agenda. Finally we are grateful to the Economic and Social Research Council (ESRC) for funding the project in the first place (ESRC grant no. RES-062–23–0577 'Organisational Change, Resistance and Democracy: Lesbian, Gay, Bisexual and Transgender Equalities Initiatives in Local Government').

Surya: I am extremely grateful to colleagues at the University of Huddersfield, Huddersfield, UK, who allowed me the time to write and provided a supportive academic environment for the co-production of this book.

I have been spurred on by the many interactions I have had with people committed to LGBT equalities – academics, policymakers, practitioners and activists – and the international dimension of this work has been a particularly exciting development. My students have engaged well with the emerging material, reminding me of the need for an accessible text addressing issues of sexuality/gender diversity and themes such as intersectionality. I would like to thank family and friends for their support, in particular Tom – at the time of writing he was too young to understand the book, but he already had a strong interest in fairness and social justice.

Diane: For myself, a great deal of the writing was done during the time I was Visiting Scholar at Columbia University, New York, USA, based at the Institute of Research on Women and Gender (IRWaG), and I would like to thank staff there for a stimulating and enjoyable visit. Lastly, as ever, my thanks go to family and friends who have good-naturedly supported me in the particular vicissitudes that are entailed in the journey of 'making a book', in particular to my mum, Nina, Cynthia, Chris, Ol, Rachel, Sue, Jackie, Ann, Jane, Hazel, Loren and Lillian.

Introduction

In recent years there has been an explosion of interest in the field of equalities and diversity, fuelled by many legislative changes, as well as broader demographic trends concerning migration and citizenship. Sexualities and transgender (trans) equalities issues, which have for many years been marginalized, have now gained social and political currency and visibility. There is wide variation concerning the equality and human rights of lesbian, gay, bisexual and trans (LGBT) people internationally, and human rights abuses are still commonplace in some countries (International Lesbian and Gay Association 2010). However, over the last few years there has been a shift towards LGBT people's equality and normalization in some countries ('normalization' refers to processes of social acceptance, so that LGBT people are not seen as different from anyone else). The changes associated with this normalization of sexual minorities and gender diversity can be critically examined from a range of conceptual positions.

In countries or states which are pro-equality, broad shifts in understandings of the 'good' sexual citizen contrast sharply with the processes of marginalization that some sexual and gender minorities experience. More broadly, there are a range of forces which shape sexualities and transgender equalities internationally, including postcolonialism (the social and material legacy of colonialism), neoliberalism (a market-driven approach to economic and social policy, which emphasizes individual choice) and democracy (there are a wide variety of forms of democracy, but free and fair elections of the government are a cornerstone).

This book is structured around the following themes:

- Equality and Diversity
- Intersectionality
- Sexuality and Citizenship
- Democracy and Representation
- Organizational Change
- Processes of Organizational Resistance and Compliance

This introductory chapter begins by outlining some key concepts concerning gender and sexuality, and then places the book in relation to existing literature in the field. The chapter describes the empirical study which is drawn on in different places throughout the book, and it discusses the terms used in the book and its scope. Lastly, the chapter provides a snapshot of the content of each of the chapters in the book.

Gender and sexuality

Scholarship in the field of gender and sexuality studies has developed substantially over the last two decades. This work builds on the writings of first- and second-wave feminists (see, for example, Jackson and Scott 1996; Richardson 2008), and engages with other approaches, such as interactionism (see Calhoun 1994) and reflexive modernity (see Giddens 1991; Heaphy 2008). It includes Black feminisms (Davis 1981; hooks 1984; Hill Collins 2000), queer theory (Sedgewick 1991; Warner 1993), masculinity studies (Connell 1995) and poststructuralism. Poststructuralists, who take a range of different approaches, share a critique of the idea that we make decisions rationally on the basis of a unified sense of self, and they reject the idea that there is an essential self or a biological basis to our identities. Instead, subjectivity (our sense of ourselves) is seen as socially constructed; this includes our gendered and sexual identities. The work of Judith Butler (1990, 1993, 2004) has been particularly important to the development of gender theory. Butler sees physiological sex, as well as gender, as being socially constructed phenomena (1990). Although we perceive these parts of our identity as being 'real', they are actually constructed by the repetitive processes and discourses (sets of ideas which are tied to social practices and structures) that are part of our everyday lives, and hence 'identity is performatively constituted by the very "expressions" that are said to be its results' (Butler 1990: 25). The social construction of sex, gender and sexuality is of importance to understanding LGBT equalities issues. For example, Stephen Whittle and Lewis Turner (2007) have analysed the way in which the United Kingdom (UK) Gender Recognition Act 2004 destabilizes biological sex as a basis for gender attribution, because people can seek to be socially and legally recognized as a particular sex on the basis of gender identity rather than genital configuration.

Mark Blasius and Shane Phelan (1997: 2) argue that 'same-sex love is a phenomenon common to almost every culture, one occurring throughout recorded history', although, of course, the ways in which this is socially constructed and the extent to which it is linked with identities (such as the relatively recently developed identity categories of LGBT) vary widely. Anthropological and historical studies of sexuality support this view. Although there is some disagreement between writers as to precisely when the idea of the homosexual person emerged, the general belief is that in Europe at least, this is a relatively recent notion having its origins in the seventeenth to the nineteenth centuries (Foucault 1979; Weeks 2009). The use of the term 'lesbian' to designate a certain type of person, it is argued, emerged somewhat later than that of the male homosexual (Faderman 1981; Weeks 2009).

The contemporary dominance of heterosexuality can be seen to stem from the division of people into two discrete categories, male and female, and the norms of heterosexuality which assume attraction between people in these categories. The social construction of heterosexuality and gender binarism (the assumption that there are only two sexes and genders – male and female) as foundational (or natural) (see Prosser 1998; Monro 2005; Richardson 2008), means that alternatives become seen as abnormal or deviant, fuelling homophobia, biphobia and transphobia, and impeding the equality of LGBT people.

The construction of heterosexuality is bound up with normative notions of masculinity and femininity. R. W. Connell's (1995) notion of hegemonic masculinity continues to be important in understanding the way in which there are different forms of masculinity that are hierarchically structured, and hence an effeminate white gay male would be constructed (within mainstream society) as being lower down the gender hierarchy than a normatively masculine white heterosexual male. Notions of hegemonic masculinity have been revised since the term was originally introduced, and a more complex model of gender hierarchy which includes attention to women's agency and the interplay between local, regional and international levels has developed (Connell and Messerschmidt 2005, see also Richardson 2010).

The poststructuralist or 'cultural' turn in gender and sexuality studies has been followed by another, more recent development, in which scholars have questioned the deconstruction of gendered and sexed identities and have pointed to the ways in which our realities are structured by material forces, including physical processes associated with the body (such as aging and the effects of hormones) and economic inequalities. This 'material' turn (see, for example, Hines and Sanger 2010) builds on the earlier work of Marxist and other feminists, but incorporates aspects of poststructuralism and recognizes gender and sexual diversity and fluidity. There is a parallel trajectory, in which the importance of identities for political activism is recognized, so that a 'strategic essentialist' position is taken (see Wilchins 1997; McCall 2005 and Chapters 1 and 2). 'Strategic essentialism' means the adoption of certain identities *as if they were real* for the purposes of social interaction, identity politics and so on. The development of identity politics has been an important feature internationally over the last 50 years, and this has included the LGBT movements (see Adam 1987; Bristow and Wilson 1993; Blasius and Phelan 1997; Currah et al. 2006). Identity politics, where people organize on the basis of a particular aspect of shared identity, will be one of the themes which weave through this book.

Situating the book

This book contributes an interdisciplinary perspective to the literature on sexuality and trans equalities. It speaks to the large body of US, Canadian and other scholarship which has developed primarily within the discipline of political science and also in other disciplines such as sociology and psychology (see Stryker and Whittle 2006; Wilson and Burgess 2007). Relevant literature includes the work of Jay Barth and Janine Parry (2009), Mark Blasius (2001), Patrick Egan and Kenneth Sherrill (2005), Jyl Josephson (2005), Shane Phelan (1989, 1994,

2001), Ellen Riggle and Barry Tadlock (1999) and Riggle et al. (2009), Joe Rollins and H.N. Hirsch (2003), Miriam Smith (2008), Joseph Bristow and Angelia Wilson (1993) and Wilson (2000). The book also builds on approaches which have been more sociological, including for instance the work of Ken Plummer (1995), Diane Richardson (2000a, 2005), Steven Seidman (1996) and Jeffrey Weeks (2000, 2008a). It also complements work in other disciplines, including politics and critical legal studies (for instance work by Davina Cooper (1994, 2004), Carl Stychin (2003, 2004), Stephen Whittle (2002, 2006) and Paisley Currah et al. (2006)), politics and political sociology (such as Louise Vincent and Bianca Camminga's (2009) analysis of South African transsexual people's equality), psycho-social approaches (Rostosky et al. 2007) and studies concerning social policy and LGBT issues in the US (for example Cahill and Tobias 2007).

This book explores some of the key debates of relevance to LGBT equality, grounding discussions primarily via a case study based in a particular set of locations (England, Wales and Northern Ireland). By conducting qualitative research at the level of the individual and on a local scale, new understandings of global processes can be developed (Burawoy 2000). Indeed, the advantage of using a case study approach is to illuminate the general by looking at the particular (Denscombe 2003). The grounding in a particular set of locations provides the depth that is needed to understand key aspects of the bigger picture regarding equalities. The UK situation is in some ways not that dissimilar to what is happening in many parts of the world, where equality initiatives that seek to recognize and support specific types of collective rights have been rolled out, for example, in Andean countries (see, for example, Andolina et al. 2009) and in New Zealand (see, for example, Larner and Craig 2005). Although the book draws on material from the UK situation, illustrative examples from a range of countries are given, specifically the US, Nepal and South Africa, in order to provide international comparisons. These were selected for inclusion in our discussions because, alongside the UK discussion, they provide some range across the global north and south. The US is important not only because of its global influence on the literature and sexual politics of the age, but also because, as 'the most neoliberal of states' (Weeks 2008a: 192), it has been one of the most hostile of western nations to LGBT equalities (see Canaday 2009). In this sense, it affords interesting comparisons with other neoliberal states. Our choice for including Nepal and South Africa is both personal, as these are places where we have conducted research, and political, in the sense that these are two countries from the global South which have 'new' constitutions that bear upon the making of new forms of citizenship. We also draw briefly on illustrative material from other countries at different points throughout the book where relevant, including for example Russia and Spain. It is worth noting that LGBT activism, and other activism concerning the rights of gender and sexual minorities, is becoming increasingly globalized, and hence it is important to address international dimensions even when focusing attention on a particular country.

The book addresses large gaps in the literature concerning the interfaces between sexual and gender minorities and the 'mainstream', as well as the ways in which legislation and the statutory sector implementation can shape sexualized and gendered subjects and contain dissent. In other words, people living in particular societies are affected by legislation and social policy initiatives during the course of their daily lives (even if they are not always aware of this), and part of this patterning concerns the ways in which they manage their sexual and gender identities in relation to the status quo. The book examines the ways in which policies concerning sexual and transgender equalities are resisted by organizations, with institutional processes being mobilized in ways which support or block implementation, sometimes in a fragmented fashion. It explores the expression of sexualities and transgender equalities initiatives in relation to the other equalities strands, in particular the topical and important relationship between faith equalities and sexuality equalities. The book provides insight into the broader ways in which social constructions of sexuality and gender are changing, and the impacts that these may have on the equalities field. It also contributes to the literature on sexual and transgender citizenship, including debates about issues such as whether the increasing citizenship rights of sexual and gender minorities alter models of sexual and non-transgender citizenship. Lastly, the book provides a discussion of issues concerning participatory democracy and the difficulties it raises for equality in the representation of minority groups. Local authorities (local government in the UK) provide an ideal case for the examination of these key debates, sited as they are at the interstices of central government, which has driven change, and local communities, which engage with – and subvert – local authority activities in varied, sometimes conflicting ways.

The study

The empirical content of the book is based on anonymized findings from a study of local authorities in the UK funded by the Economic and Social Research Council (see McNulty et al. 2010). Previous research (for example Cooper 1994, 1997; Cooper and Monro 2003; Carabine and Monro 2004; Monro 2005) has tended to focus on local authorities in which a substantial amount of work concerning sexualities equalities was taking place. In the UK, local authorities are funded by taxes on the local population and by central government; they have locally elected members (councillors) as well as paid workers; they manage infrastructure and welfare provision and they play an important role in local and regional affairs and in managing the interface between local people and central government. The research sought to include data from local authorities that were relatively inactive and/or resistant to conducting work in this field. The study is also distinguished from earlier work in that it was conducted at a time (2007–2010) when the field of LGBT initiatives in UK local government and equalities work more generally was going through a period of rapid change, including the establishment of the Equalities and Human Rights Commission (EHRC) in 2008 and the introduction in 2010 of the single Equality Act. Due to practical constraints, Scotland was not included in the study (see Carabine and Monro (2004) and Rahman (2004) for developments in Scotland).

The study employed qualitative research methods, including a participative action research approach (PAR) (see McNiff 2001). Qualitative PAR approaches can be included under the 'action research' umbrella to describe 'approaches to enquiry which are participative, grounded in experience, and action-orientated' (Reason and Bradbury 2001: xxiv). The study tracked the implementation of sexualities equalities policies in four local authorities: Wales, Northern Ireland, Northern England and Southern England. These sites were purposely sampled to select authorities of different types according to political party, type of authority (size and structure), levels of deprivation, activity concerning equalities (using the Equality Standard), location (urban/rural) and levels of performance via Comprehensive Performance Assessment (the Comprehensive Performance Assessment was the precursor to the Comprehensive Area Assessment; the points given were the means by which the performances of local authorities were externally assessed in the period up until May 2010). English authorities were sampled using Equality Standard grades 1–5 (with 5 being the highest) as criteria; we purposefully selected one with a low Equality Standard. In Wales (which does not use the Equality Standard) we sampled via scoping interviews with local authority and national representatives in order to find an authority which had only recently become active in this field. We adopted a similar approach in Northern Ireland, whilst also taking the existing Equality Impact Assessments into account. Semi-structured interviews were carried out with a sample of 37 strategic level and frontline local authority officers (focusing on two different service areas for each authority to enable examination of policies through different levels) and their partners in statutory sector and voluntary or community sector agencies in four local authorities located in the case study areas. A further 20 interviews with key national stakeholders and councillors across the three countries were also conducted.

The PAR aspect of the research involved running Action Learning Sets (ALS) in each of the four case study areas. An Action Learning Set is a facilitated series of meetings between stakeholders, in which stakeholders define the focus of discussions and in which mutual support enables the identification of organizational problems and possible strategies for dealing with them. Action Learning Sets are now used in a variety of settings including local authorities, where groups meet regularly to discuss issues and problems with the potential for learning arising from the process (Dilworth 1998). In our study, each ALS met four times over a period of six months, 16 group meetings in total, with members of the ALS representing different local authorities, community organizations and partner agencies across each region. Qualitative thematic analysis was conducted on both interview and ALS data. In quoting individuals who took part in the case study interviews we have listed their organizational role and the area of the UK where they worked; other quotes highlight whether they were stakeholder interviewees or ALS members. The majority of quotes refer to different individuals in each case; however, there are a few instances where a single individual is quoted more than once.

Terminology and scope

In this book, the terms 'transgender' and 'trans' are used to mean gender-variance; gender-variance occurs when people's gender identity or expression differs from that ascribed to them at birth (see Currah et al. 2006). Trans and gender variant people may include those who are transsexual, cross-dressers, third or other gender people, androgynes, non-gendered people and people whose gender identity is fluid. It is important to acknowledge that transgender and trans are contested terms and that it is difficult to reach a definition that will be agreed on by everyone. The term 'cisgender' is now used in some sections of the gender-variant and trans community to mean people whose gender identity is the same as that ascribed to them at birth (non-trans people) and we utilize this term on occasion. The terms 'sexualities' and 'sexuality' are used to refer to what is commonly called 'sexual orientation' (the sex/gender of the person/people desired by a person/people). We avoid the term 'sexual orientation' because it may imply that the 'direction' of desire is fixed, or essential. However, in using the terms 'sexualities' and 'sexuality' we are focusing on issues of the human focus of attraction, and on related identities (such as LGBT or heterosexual), rather than on other aspects of sexuality, including sexual conduct, eroticism, transactional sexualities, sexual minorities other than the LGBT communities (such as the 'kink' community) and so on. It is also important to recognize that terms such as lesbian, gay, bisexual, transgender, queer, questioning and intersex (LGBTQQI) are now used in the US and elsewhere, but we employ LGBT because this is the most commonly used term. The benefits as well as the drawbacks associated with using this collective term are recognized by participants in the study, as well as by ourselves. For instance, in the UK, some people, including men who have sex with men (MSM) and swingers, do not relate to identities such as 'gay' or 'bisexual' even though they may engage in same-sex sexual activities. And, there are of course difficulties with the use of LGBT terminology on a global level, as these terms originate in the west and may not translate directly into other languages, or into the categories employed by people in other countries to describe their sexual and gender identities. For example, as Monro (2010a) has previously discussed, the sex/gender systems in India are different from those in the west, where LGBT identities operate alongside more traditional categories such as 'Kothi', which includes effeminate male-bodied people who engage in same-sex behaviour but do not necessarily identify as 'gay', or as 'trans'.

Another point concerning terminology is that we have not used the term 'queer' widely. This term is variously interpreted, depending on national context (see, for example, Essig's 1999 work on queers in Russia); and in countries such as the US and the UK the transgressive meaning associated with of 'queer' sits uncomfortably with the more assimilationist 'LGBT equalities'. However, we recognize the importance of work concerning queer identities and the political process (for example Rollins and Hirsch's 2003 US study).

There has been an historical tendency for scholarship about sexual minorities to focus on lesbians and gay men, whilst much of the progressive writing about gender assumes that gender is binaried and therefore focuses on women's equality. This book aims to include bisexuals and trans people (with the exception of the chapter on citizenship, which focuses primarily on lesbians and gay men), as a means of helping to fill the gap in knowledge about these groups. Moreover, analysis of the empirical material about bisexuality and transgender contributes to developing the understandings of complexity that are needed concerning themes such as intersectionality, democracy and organizational processes. However, because trans – and in particular, bisexuality – are so often erased in both the scholarship and in the research data, there are places in the book where some of the discussion is more specific to lesbian and gay than to bisexual and trans communities. It is also necessary to point out here that the study did not include analysis of intersex, and the discussion reflects this. Intersex people are those who are born with gender-ambiguous or gender-complex genitalia, chromosomal, or gonadal characteristics (see, for example, Dreger 2000).

The chapters

Chapter 1 explores the trend towards the normalization of LGBT equalities in the UK and in many European countries, as well as elsewhere in the world, including in Canada, Australia and parts of the US. It looks at normalization in relation to the processes taking place in other countries, for example, South Africa. The chapter also examines the frameworks of equality underpinning demands for LGBT 'equality', and how political rhetoric has moved towards 'equality in sameness', rather than 'equality in difference', arguments. It explores the institutional recognition of same-sex partnerships, which function in a similar fashion to heterosexual marriage, in terms of associated duties and legal and economic privileges. Related to this, the chapter considers the relationship between equality and diversity, two concepts that are often discursively tied together but, as the chapter goes on to show, often pull apart in practice.

There has been a flurry of scholarly interest in the field of intersectionality studies in recent years. Intersectionality theory provides a means of understanding identity complexity, and the ways in which different social characteristics such as gender and race, for example, are routed through each other. However, limited work has been published to date on sexualities, trans and intersectionality. Chapter 2 begins by unpicking the tensions within the LGBT acronym, tensions that concern the ways in which LGBT people differ in terms of their gender and sexuality. It then discusses the ways in which LGBT people are diverse in terms of a range of different social characteristics: race and ethnicity, nationalism, faith, socio-economic class, age, ability and geographical space. The discussions of faith, ethnicity and nationality indicate some directions for the development of postcolonial, non-Eurocentric analysis of LGBT equalities (and the equality of people with other diverse sexualities/genders). In addition, the chapter flags up some of the more challenging issues for equalities work concerning LGBT people on an international level, such as the interface between faith groups and LGBT communities and the increasingly important problem of climate change. The chapter draws on a range of works in its attempts to outline some of the broad dynamics associated with intersectionality, sexualities and gender diversities. It weaves in empirical material where this is relevant, given the ways in which UK equalities work is a site for raced, gendered, able-bodied, spatial and other intersections with sexuality.

LGBT citizenship in the UK has shifted from one of exclusion to inclusion, and to notions of being 'ordinary citizens', at least for some LGBT people. These changes are associated with discourses of rights and responsibilities, as well as with shifting public/private boundaries concerning citizenship. Chapter 3 explores some of these issues and considers what they may tell us about the relationship between sexuality and citizenship. In particular, the concept of sexual and intimate citizenship and how it has been variously imagined is examined. Practices of sexual citizenship in the UK are contested in various ways, and these processes of contestation are also evident internationally. To illustrate this, examples of Nepal and South Africa are used as a contrast to the UK situation. Finally, the limits to, and limitations of, sexual citizenship are considered conceptually, politically and in terms of implementing equalities. Though the focus of the chapter is on sexuality and citizenship, it addresses some of the key themes and debates within citizenship studies more generally, including universal versus particularist approaches to citizenship (models of citizenship that appeal to/seek to include everyone as opposed to those framed in relation to particular groups), processes of normalization and the costs of new forms of belonging.

There are various strands of literature that can be drawn on in developing our understandings of LGBT democracy, and Chapter 4 outlines and builds on the substantial existing scholarship concerning sexuality and democracy. The chapter then places discussions about LGBT democracy in a global context. LGBT politics are increasingly shaped by processes of globalization, because of the effects of global infrastructure organizations, the new social media and transnational pressure groups (both pro- and anti-LGBT equalities). Moreover, the assertion, by homophobic stakeholders in the global south, that the movement for LGBT equalities is a western phenomenon forms a significant impediment to equality internationally and within western countries with significant immigrant populations. Having situated the discussion internationally, the chapter moves on to address LGBT equalities in the UK in relation to, firstly, representative democracy and, secondly, participative democracy. These sections of the chapter allow the examination of some of the key issues concerning democracy, such as the issue of majoritarianism and minority group rights, in relation to LGBT politics.

Organizational studies have, until recently, overlooked sexuality, and there is a substantial gap in the literature concerning trans. However, there has been a mushrooming of interest in organizational sexualities during the last few years, including some scholarship about LGB issues and the operation of heterosexuality in organizations. Chapter 5 seeks to contribute in a critical way to the organizational studies literature, and to draw concepts that are useful in understanding the ways in which organizations construct, mediate, and reflect LGBT equalities from it. The chapter begins with an overview of organizational theory before looking at the literature concerning gender and sexuality in organizations. It draws on the findings from the UK study using concepts drawn from this literature, looking at the role of factors such as organizational culture in shaping LGBT equalities work, and the ways in which organizational cultures can change. The chapter demonstrates that inequalities concerning sexuality and gender can be addressed at an organizational level using mainstream management techniques, which do not have – in themselves – a particularly pro-equality agenda.

Chapter 6 goes on to examine the ways in which progressive constitutional and legislative frameworks concerning sexualities can be subverted, resisted or erased (in other words, in countries where there is state support for LGBT equalities, there are various ways in which the institutions in those countries negotiate pressures to support equalities). The chapter addresses tensions and divergences within local government in terms of the types of barriers and various forms of resistance to change that are manifest. It describes a continuum of approaches or narratives of resistance that are influenced by intersecting factors such as cultural knowledge, beliefs and norms about sexuality and gender, organizational cultures and issues of visibility of LGBT people and LGBT inequalities. The chapter goes on to explore where resistance occurs not only in terms of the spatial aspects of resistance, but also in relation to the type of LGBT equalities issues involved, variations across different sections and levels within local authorities and differences within the LGBT cluster itself. Finally, it considers the individual actor as an agent of resistance through an exploration of constructions of the resisting subject in terms of various characteristics that may be perceived as potential barriers to a person endorsing LGBT equality.

Northern Ireland has a tranche of progressive legislative drivers that support sexualities equalities, including in particular Section 75 of the Northern Ireland Act 1998. Recent years have seen a cultural shift towards greater tolerance of LGB identities (there is less of a change regarding trans people, who still appear heavily marginalized). Whilst infrastructures have been developed to facilitate LGBT equalities work, there are ongoing tensions regarding the interface of sexualities equalities with equalities concerning the faith communities, and these play out in the political arena. Chapter 7 explores some of the key themes of the book via the prism of Northern Ireland, paying attention to the specificities of the Northern Ireland context, the intersections of faith, ethnicity, locality and sexuality. It also examines the complexities of LGBT democracy in Northern Ireland, demonstrating some of the ways in which Northern Irish democratic politics – including participative democratic politics – are being used to push LGBT equalities forwards. It explores the sectarian nature of LGBT equalities work in Northern Ireland, and documents the way in which prejudice is institutionalized within some of the political parties, as well as changes at the party political level.

The book finishes with a brief concluding chapter which addresses some of the key ongoing issues for the equalities agenda in relation to sexual and gender diversity. This book is set in a particular historical period in which diversity is increasing, making discussions about equality at international, national and local levels increasingly important.

This introductory chapter has sought to outline the remit of the book, describing the methods used for the empirical study that we carried out and providing a snapshot of the content. The next chapter goes on to address the first of our key themes: equality and diversity.

Equality and Diversity

1

This chapter explores the trend towards the normalization of LGBT equalities that has taken place in many parts of the world including the majority of European countries, Canada, Australia and parts of the US. Historically, lesbians and gay men have had ambiguous citizenship status, neither fully accepted nor totally excluded they have been marginal citizens. For LGBT people to be recognized and accepted as 'ordinary citizens' who deserve equal rights suggests, therefore, that there has been a profound shift in the meanings attached to sexuality, gender and citizenship. The reasons for these changes are complex and may be different in different countries. However, what *is* clear is the importance of social movements who have fought for social change in relation to gender and sexuality in bringing about such shifts.

This is where this chapter begins, with an overview of the forms of political activism that have shaped our understanding of what it means to be a sexual and gendered citizen. This first section illustrates how there have been dramatic shifts in 'sexual politics' since the second part of the twentieth century. From the radical sexuality and gender politics of 1960s and 70s, the last two decades have seen the ascendancy of a very different kind of politics, one that seems to be more about reforming than transforming society. This is often referred to as a politics of normalization or assimilation. The next section of the chapter examines the frameworks of equality deployed in campaigning for LGBT 'equality'. It then goes on to look at how particular ways of framing equality are linked to the concept of diversity and notes that there are apparent tensions between advancing equality and recognizing diversity, despite the two often being conjoined. The discussion is illustrated drawing on the UK as a primary case study in the context of recent legislative and policy changes in relation to sexualities and transgender equalities. The themes that are addressed, however, are relevant to debates about equality and diversity more generally, at least in western democracies.

Sexuality and politics

The 1960s: New styles of protest

Over the last half century or more, LGBT people have formed groups and organizations that have been the basis for political action and engagement. Those growing up in the 1950s, for instance, lived through a time when homosexuality was defined as abnormal, unnatural and inferior to heterosexuality. Generally regarded as a medical disorder and as social deviance, homosexuality was seen as posing a direct threat to social and moral order that the state and other institutions sought to contain through criminalization and other measures (Terry 1999; Minton 2002; Weeks 2009). Some people responded by organizing to advocate for tolerance and homosexual rights. For example, in the US and in parts of Europe a number of 'homophile' organizations – a term less contentious at the time than homosexual – were formed, often originating in large urban centres such as Los Angeles, San Franscisco and London (Katz 1992; Blasius and Phelan 1997; Epstein 1999). These organizations were, on the whole, conservative in their demands, seeking tolerance and civil rights for homosexuals; some argued that, as a psychiatric disorder, homosexuals deserved treatment not punishment, while others aimed to reverse the medical model by claiming that homosexuals were normal people *like heterosexuals* (Richardson and Seidman 2002).

By the late 1960s and early 70s a very different kind of sexual politics was in evidence. The liberal social and legal reforms sought by most activists a decade earlier were replaced by a more militant and radical lesbian, gay, bisexual and trans politics that was highly critical of society in general and the way it treated people who diverged from heterosexual norms in particular (Weeks 1990; Adam 1997; Eaklor 2011). This was a time of protest in the US and Europe, of anti-war movements, civil rights and students demonstrations, and the emergence of women's liberation. High on the political agenda of the gay liberation movement (which included bisexual people and gender-diverse people in the early stages) was to rid society of negative ideas about homosexuality, in particular that it was abnormal and unnatural (Weeks 2008a). This early movement fragmented to a degree soon after it was formed, and hence by the early 1970s a shift towards autonomous lesbian organizing took place (D'Emilio and Freedman 1988). This was prompted not only by political differences between lesbians and gay men, but also tensions within the women's movement that led some lesbians to set up lesbian feminist groups on their own (Phelan 1989; Jackson and Scott 1996). As well as the gay/lesbian split, both trans and bi people were increasingly excluded by lesbian feminist and gay movements with consequences for political organizing (Ault 1994; Highleyman 2001; Monro 2005). The bisexual and trans movements took different (although sometimes overlapping) trajectories, however, with the bi-community developing as a grassroots-based community with an emphasis on lifestyle politics and political visibility (Angelides 2001; Hemmings 2002). The trans movement (as it is known today as opposed to the movement which developed in the 1950s, which was similar in political orientation to the homophile movement discussed above) grew from its roots in the Stonewall riots in New York in 1969 and the early gay liberation front (GLF) in response to rejection by some gay men and lesbians associated with the GLF and lesbian organizations (Kirk and Heath 1984; Stryker 2008), and manifested in organizations such as the Street Transvestite Action Revolutionaries in the US (Wilchins 1997).

The lesbian and gay movements that developed in the 1970s and subsequently appeared on the surface to have similar goals to earlier 'homophile' organizations. Significantly, however, lesbian and gay liberationist attacks on constructions of sexual and gender 'abnormality' were neither associated with seeking to be 'normalised' or 'assimilated' through incorporation into mainstream culture, nor with a form of liberal toleration based on the expectation of privatized lives lived in the closet (Epstein 1999). Although rights claims were part of claims for sexual liberation, including specific demands such as an equal age of consent for gay men and parenting rights in the face of lesbian mothers' custody battles, this was a politics that was about much more than civic acceptance and was expansive in its goals and ambitions. There were those who still advocated assimilationist approaches to change, but the dominant political rhetoric was one of lesbian and gay liberation, a movement whose aims were not to assimilate into, or seek to reform society, but to challenge and transform it. It was about establishing an egalitarian society and overthrowing capitalism and patriarchy (Weeks 2008a; Moore 2010). In other words, this was not a politics of seeking equality through similitude, of 'fitting in', but rather of proclaiming the right to be different and to be proud of it. The language it spoke was voiced not in the name of what was seen as a highly negative hand-me-down category 'the homosexual', but in self-chosen positive terms that represented new social and political categories and associated identities: *lesbian and gay*. Most of all, it was about emphasizing difference *and* visibility. It was about coming out and publicly declaring oneself 'glad to be gay' (Blasius and Phelan 1997; Rimmerman, 2001; Eaklor, 2011).

As a consequence, from the 1970s the notion of 'the homosexual' as 'troubling' to society was closely connected with the view of lesbian and gay as *politicized* identities, constituted as counterculture and *actively* seeking to bring about radical social change. Certainly, as noted above, these new social movements contested many core institutions and cultural values in fundamental ways. Critiques of traditional gender roles and 'the family', including marriage as a social institution, were at the fore (Altman 1993; Jackson 2008; Weeks 2008).

The 1980s: The AIDS crisis and a scaling-up of politics

The impact of HIV/AIDS during the 1980s worked to both 'revitalise' and professionalize the gay (less so lesbian) movement, especially in the US (Watney 1994; Brown 1997; Epstein 1999; Richardson 2005). It brought a new focus on gay rights in terms of health and welfare rights and policy making. In its inclusion of bisexual men, the practical work that was done in response to the HIV/AIDS crisis also opened the door to greater inclusivity of people of diverse sexualities. AIDS also helped to re-establish ties between gay and lesbian communities and, in the early stages at least, led to greater collaboration in political organizing (Vaid 1995; Epstein 1999; Engel 2002).

HIV and AIDS was inclusive in another important sense; it was an international issue. Linked with this, it is perhaps unsurprising that the 1980s was a period that led to the development of lesbian and gay movements at an international level through organizations like the International Lesbian and Gay Association (ILGA), which now includes bi, trans and intersexed people, and the International Lesbian and Gay Human Rights Commission (IGLHRC). Alongside this, a globalization of lesbian, gay, bisexual and transgender organizing and advocacy has occurred (see Adam et al. 1998), with the establishment of transnational networks as well as international organizations (Kollman and Waites 2009), which is associated with a professionalization of LGBT politics as political organizations have scaled up their activities from local to national levels and drawn upon mainstream funding (Chasin 2000; Richardson 2005).

These developments have raised new issues and questions about the wider implications of such changes. For instance, although there are culturally specific domestic factors in the regulation of sexualities and gender, it is important to recognize broader effects associated with the work of transnational organizations and the globalization of human rights discourse (Stychin 2003, 2004). Recent legislative changes in the UK, for instance, can be seen as part of wider policy processes within Europe including the establishment of the European Union (EU) Charter of Fundamental Rights (2000), which is discussed later in Chapter 7. This has led some to argue that processes of international influence and social learning fostered through transnational networks have led to policy convergence in Europe (see, for instance, Paternotte and Kollman (2010) on same-sex unions policies). However, a recent EU report found that legislation and practice in relation to LGBT rights is taking place at a different pace and unevenly throughout the European Union (FRA 2010). This is further supported by the findings of the first comprehensive study of discrimination on the grounds of sexual orientation and gender identity covering all 47 member states in the Council of Europe, which reported that while there is progress on the human rights situation of lesbian, gay, bisexual and trans people in some countries, in others discrimination and human rights violations against LGBT people are continuing (see the Council of Europe report (2011), which contains a number of specific recommendations on how the situation can be improved).

At a broader level, there is concern that international human rights organizations use the terms lesbian and gay, and bisexual and transgender in ways that suggest these are universal terms rather than social categories that have particular local as well as global meanings. Dennis Altman (2001), for example, discusses this in terms of a tension between the 'global gay citizen' and local (homo)sexualities, arguing that global definitions are inadequate to represent local sexual practices, activisms and identities. Jasbir Puar (2002, 2007) has also addressed such issues in her work, arguing that in producing a new global lesbian/gay citizen, whose rights claims go beyond single nation-states, there is a need to be attentive to what circulates as global definitions of lesbian and gay identities and politics. The charge is that it is definitions from the US and Europe that have colonized ideas of the 'universal' in relation to sexual and gender minorities, resulting in a 'Westernization' of LGBT identities *and* politics (see also Binnie 2004). However, as these writers also recognize, in highlighting the risk that local meanings and practices may be undermined by this 'colonising process', it is important to be careful not to ignore the complexity of interactions between local sites and global contexts (Cruz-Malavé and Manalansan IV 2002). This complexity is often referred to as a process of 'hybridization', where interactions between the local and global can be productive of new 'hybrid' identities and political goals. At the same time, we need to acknowledge that in some parts of the world lesbian and gay rights continue to be subject to harsh critiques as western 'exports' (see, for example, Massad (2002) on Arab gay male identities), and that describing LGBT equality as an 'imperialist plot' can be a powerful narrative of resistance. (See also Chapter 2, Chapter 4 and the discussion later in this chapter on 'Africaness' and lesbian and gay rights.)

The 1990s: Queerly different or just like you?

Fuelled initially by organizations and groups involved in AIDS activism such as ACT UP, the 1990s also saw the emergence of a new queer perspective on sexuality and sexual politics. Queer was put forward by activists 'as a replacement for labels such as "gay" and "lesbian" ' and the 'modes of community and self-expression associated with them' (Epstein 1999: 61), rather like the terms gay and lesbian had 20 years earlier been put forward by gay liberationists to replace homosexuality and the meanings and identities associated with this social category. Queer was about 'a politics of difference' that sought to be more inclusive of sexual and gender diversity, including bisexual and transgendered people, than mainstream lesbian and gay culture was perceived to be. In this sense, in putting forward a new, unifying term that included all sexual and gender minorities – even queer straights (Thomas et al. 2000) – queer saw itself advancing an anti-identity politics that displaced the categories lesbian and gay, *and* heterosexual (Gamson 1995; Richardson 1996). Influenced by postmodern understandings of identity as more complex, fluid and fragmented than can be adequately expressed in the notion of a shared group identity such as 'gay', queer represented a rejection of the 'identity politics' of the 1970s and 80s. It did, nevertheless, echo many of the radical aims of lesbian/feminist and gay liberationist movements in critiquing dominant culture and the 'heteronormative' order deeply embedded within it (Seidman 1993; Warner 1993; Richardson et al. 2012). Heteronormativity is a term that emerged out of queer theory in the 1990s (see Warner 1993), although it has links to earlier feminist work, in particular the notion of 'compulsory heterosexuality' (see Richardson 2012). It refers to the ways in which heterosexuality is both *naturalized* as universal and *privileged* as the 'norm', as a particular form of practice and identity, over other 'non-normative' sexualities.

Queer perspectives have subsequently been drawn on, and influenced by, people across the LGBT spectrum. For example, the transformational part of the trans movement has drawn substantially on queer theory and postmodernism in developing critiques of binary gender systems (the idea that 'male' and 'female' are the only gender categories) as well as heterosexism (Bornstein 1994, 1998; Wilchins 1997).

Since the 1990s, a different form of sexual politics has emerged alongside queer that has been highly influential in re-defining the goals and strategies associated with LGBT activism. This is a politics whose aims are more reformist than transformist, seeking incorporation into the mainstream rather than critiquing social institutions and practices as did gay and lesbian/feminist activists in the 1960s and 70s, and the queer and trans activists of the 1990s; a politics which eschews the earlier political language of women's, lesbian, gay and trans 'liberation' in favour of an 'equality' rhetoric in demanding equal rights of citizenship. The use of the abbreviation/term LGBT to refer collectively to lesbian, gay, bisexual and transgender people is associated with these shifts, although it is also driven by the changes that have taken place within the communities under discussion over the last 20 years. (Variants on the LGBT acronym include LGBTQ, where Q stands for queer or those 'questioning' their sexuality, and LGBTQI which is also inclusive of intersex people.) An acronym that over the last 20 years has become increasingly mainstreamed in the west, though not exclusively so, LGBT is now adopted by many organizations and groups as well as by governments, policy makers and the media.

The strategic use of the term LGBT is contested on a number of grounds including the collapsing of specific issues within and across the L, G, B and the T (see also Chapter 2). Also, as is well documented (Monro 2005), there have been long-standing historical tensions between all of the groups included within the acronym LGBT. Firstly, as noted earlier, within GLF early splits led to women leaving (Moore 2010) and the development of specific forms of lesbian/feminist politics, which included lesbian separatism. There continues to be ongoing friction between some lesbians and some gay men, concerning for example resources and space, set against a backdrop of lesbian feminist criticisms of gay male privilege (Epstein 1999; Casey 2004). Secondly, there are issues concerning the inclusion or not of transgender and bisexual people within the label LGBT that relate to earlier exclusions of trans and bisexual people from what became the lesbian and gay movement. The exclusion of trans people was partly because one of the prerequisites during the early stages of treatment for transsexuality was that transsexuals would become heterosexual after surgery (Monro 2005). It was also because of the impact of feminism, in which certain early writers such as Janice Raymond (1980) and Mary Daly

(1984) critiqued trans identities, framing transsexuality as a patriarchal means of enforcing gender stereotypes. Subsequently, trans activists and authors (see, for example, Feinberg 1996; Currah et al. 2006; Stryker 2008) and feminist authors (for example Monro 2005, 2007a; Hines 2007) have provided coherent critiques of the work of feminists like Raymond, opening the conceptual ground for alliances to be built.

The exclusion of bisexuals was linked to the development of biphobia (in which the existence of bisexuality is denied and/or bisexual people are stigmatized). This exclusion had other (related) sources, including:

- The way that bisexuality challenges discrete sexual 'orientation' categories because bisexuals feel desire for people across these; this can be unsettling for lesbians and gay men who build their identities in opposition to heterosexuality (see Dunphy 2000)
- Notions of purity concerning sexual orientation (Hutchins and Kaahumanu 1991)
- Various types of stereotyping, for example bisexuals being framed as promiscuous, apolitical or parasitical to the lesbian and gay communities (Monro 2005)
- Bisexuality being seen as 'fence-sitting' or a 'cop-out' by lesbian feminists in the 1970s and 80s (George 1993)
- Early bisexual authors such as Ochs (1996) traced biphobia to the ways in which some bisexual people can access heterosexual privilege, which lesbians and gay men resented

The research into LGBT equalities initiatives in local government in the UK showed that issues concerning the differences between lesbians, gay men, bisexuals and trans people are still very relevant. For example, notably there were tendencies towards the erasure of the visibility and interests of both bisexuals and trans people by the generally more prominent gay and lesbian communities. There was also some evidence that community organizations seek to de-link LGB and T, which tended to be seen as a gender rather than a sexuality issue in many cases.

There are also tensions within as well as between L/G/B/T communities around issues such as internal hierarchies (for example, historically, the trans community had noticeable internal hierarchies based on identity and appearance, see Bornstein 1994) and intersectional differences such as age and socioeconomic class (see Chapter 2). These tensions within the different groups of lesbians, gay men, bisexuals and trans people also include political divisions over the question: What should LGBT politics do? (For instance, between those seeking to advance rights claims through assimilation arguments ('fitting in') and those who want to change society through destabilizing or abolishing heteronormative categories and institutions like 'marriage' (Rimmerman 2005).) Our findings demonstrated that there is general awareness of the tensions and differences amongst and between the groups amalgamated under LGBT, as illustrated in the following quotes.

> The LGBT community are not one happy family under a rainbow banner. They are a lot of people grouped together, maybe not through choice, maybe because it's easier to define people who are not straight. Bit of a hodge podge, mish mash, [a] cobbled together term.
>
> (Local Authority Officer, Northern Ireland)

> ... the grouping of lesbian, gay, bisexual, transgender etc, etc, there's a multitude of different issues within, within those groups, be they physical, be they psychological, emotional what have you, which will suggest that actually they will, that they will expect very different things from our services.... so I think if you put gay, bisexual, transgender together it's a, it's a very blunt instrument and if you then overlay things like age and faith and that sort of stuff, then again there's a, that brings into consideration even more differences by individual.
>
> (Manager, Southern England)

The wider adoption of the LGBT acronym may owe something to the 'ease factor', where people are not comfortable with 'having to say the individual words'. In terms of LGBT politics, however, its use reflects a growing emphasis on diversity and a scaling up of political organizing. For instance, several participants saw the value of the LGBT cluster in terms of establishing 'critical mass' and thereby having a more powerful voice.

It is important to acknowledge in the context of this 'clustering' that the growth of a visible, politically efficacious trans politics has occurred more recently than the development of lesbian and gay movements, and that the bisexual movement is still relatively underdeveloped for a number of reasons, including the history of marginalization, and a tendency for some bisexual people to move in and out of heterosexual and lesbian/gay social/political spaces, thereby diluting the bisexual community as a political force (Angelides 2001). As outlined earlier in the chapter, the 1960s and 70s was undoubtedly one of the most important periods in the history of sexual politics. In terms of transgender however, the 1990s was a particularly significant period associated with the growth of trans activism and organizations as well as academic interest in trans issues, in part associated with the rise of queer (Monro 2005; Stryker and Whittle 2006; Valentine 2007). This different political timeline is captured in the following quote from a transwoman, who thought trans organizations were on a different learning curve compared to lesbian and gay communities in some respects.

> We can learn a lot from them [LG communities]. 'Coming out', being accepted, changing the legislation, fundraising, producing their own communities and then expanding that to encompass the wider community.
>
> (Transgender Community Representative (A), Wales)

A new politics of belonging?

The language of citizenship is central to this new politics of belonging in a way that it was not in the 1970s and 80s. This is often referred to as a 'politics of assimilation', in so far as it emphasizes 'wanting in' to the mainstream (D'Emilio 2000). The demands are for acceptance of sexual diversity and equality with heterosexuals, rather than a more fundamental questioning of how society is structured and organized. This rights-based approach represents a shift in the politics of recognition, where non-recognition or mis-recognition are understood to be central to questions of social justice (Honneth 1996, 2002, 2004; Taylor 1994). Although the kind of sexual and gender politics articulated by the lesbian and gay movements of the 1960s and 70s was alert to the issues arising from non-recognition, evidenced by the emphasis on the importance of being more visible through coming out, a primary focus was on *mis-recognition*. This took the form of contesting the regulation and categorization of lesbians and gay men in terms of pathology, criminality and immorality. More recently, the emphasis has shifted to addressing the problems of *non-recognition* manifested in the desire for public recognition and legitimate presence, through civil partnerships for instance. This raises questions of what counts as 'equality' in recognition, how categories of recognition are constructed and what practices are deployed through which particular recognition claims are acknowledged (McLaughlin et al. 2011). These questions, as well as different understandings of citizenship, are addressed in Chapter 3.

Opposition to assimilationist politics takes a variety of forms and makes strange bedfellows of feminist and queer critics, and those who are anti-gay. Feminist and queer critiques of this 'sea change' in sexual politics have contested the normalizing politics that forms the basis of mainstream lesbian and gay movements organized around claiming 'equal rights' (Seidman 1996, 1997; D'Emilio 2000; Richardson 2005). These include criticisms of a model of citizenship that reinforces both normative assumptions about sexuality and gender, and the desirability and necessity of monogamous marital-style sexual coupledom, privileged over other forms of relationships of care and support, as a basis for many kinds of rights entitlements (see, for example, Duggan 1995, 2002; Berlant 1997; Warner 1999; Bell and Binnie 2000). Such criticisms are particularly important for LGBT people whose lifestyles and identities do not fit with dominant norms concerning gender and sexuality (including the notions that our genders and sexualities are fixed, and that monogamous relationships are the ideal).There are some people and groups who are not able to claim equal rights within current rights frameworks, because these rights frameworks are insufficiently broad. These include people whose gender identities are fluid or who identify as third or multiple sex/gender or as androgynous or non-gendered, as well as people who have multiple relationship arrangements (the latter is termed polyamory). Inclusion of these groups would challenge some of the basic assumptions of the normalizing politics around sexuality and gender, whether or not these people have a transformative or assimilationist political agenda. Overall, however, the challenges to an equal-rights-oriented assimilationist agenda have tended to be marginalized in mainstream lesbian and gay political organizations (Waites 2003).

Despite various forms of opposition, it would appear that LGBT organizations that favour following assimilationist strategies to achieve social change have been relatively successful. Certainly, it is the case that in many parts of the world gains have been made in relation to age of consent laws, to healthcare, rights associated with social and legal recognition of domestic partnerships, immigration rights, parenting rights and so on (Kaplan 1997; Stychin 2003; Graupner and Tahmindjis 2005). However, it is important to recognize that these trends are not matched by developments worldwide, with the acceptance of same-sex sexualities and gender diversity being unevenly spread, and profound discrimination and inequality existing in many countries (Amnesty 2001; Kollman and Waites 2009). Also where change does occur, as noted earlier, the context and consequences of change may be different in different countries. For example, South Africa's constitution supports lesbian and gay equality, and issues concerning normalization and resistances to this are parallel albeit different compared to those in other countries. However, LGBT equalities initiatives in South Africa have followed a very particular trajectory (see Box 1.1).

Box 1.1 LGBT rights: Focus on South Africa

There is considerable evidence for the existence of same-sex sexualities and various same-sex-relationship forms in Southern Africa historically in different eras (see for example Murray and Roscoe 1998). The movement for LGBT equalities in South Africa was forged through the South African experience of apartheid, the notorious system of racial discrimination which was the result of the double colonization of Southern Africa by the Afrikaans (originally mostly Dutch) and subsequently by the British. During the 1990s, gay activism in South Africa converged with western notions of human rights, a powerful women's movement, and the emancipatory goals of the anti-apartheid movement, so that:

> the discourse of diversity, the celebration of difference, and especially the right to freedom of sexual orientation was defined as part of the challenge of building a diverse, pluralistic society. The 'rainbow' [defined here as a broad-based rainbow of different races, genders, sexualities and other social groupings such as the rural poor] emerged (and remains) as a strong collectivist and inclusivist symbol defining unity among the diverse peoples of South Africa and a source of national pride.
>
> (Cock 2002: 36)

Jacklyn Cock describes the way in which the gay movement placed gay rights on the agenda of the anti-apartheid struggle. The African National Congress (ANC, a political party that was exiled by the apartheid state) did not have any policies regarding sexual orientation until after 1992. Change came about as a result of reactions to statements by Ruth Mompati, a senior member of the ANC, that lesbians and gays have a good quality of life and also that they are not normal. These statements provoked lobbying by the UK's Peter Tatchell and others, and the ANC formally recognized lesbian and gay rights in 1992. A development of key importance was the detention in 1987 of out gay man Simon Nkoli, of the Gay Association of South Africa, following the mass protests against apartheid in the black townships. After his acquittal he became a figurehead for the gay and lesbian rights movement; as Cock reports, Nkoli said, 'I'm fighting for the abolition of apartheid, and I fight for the right to freedom of sexual orientation ' (Cock 2002: 36). The forging of links between the anti-apartheid movement and the broader aims of the ANC was the key factor in the inclusion of the sexual orientation rights clause in the new South African Constitution (Gunkel 2010), which was brought in after apartheid was abolished in South Africa, in 1994, making South Africa the first country in the world to constitutionally guarantee non-discrimination on the grounds of sexual orientation in 1996. This advance did not go uncontested, with opposition coming from those attached to notions of 'African Tradition, Christianity', and 'normalcy'. Despite the extremely progressive constitutional support for lesbian and gay equality, homophobia remains a serious problem in South Africa, including homophobic rape and murder (see Cock 2002). What can be seen here, therefore, are strong parallels – and political connections – between lesbian and gay rights movements in the West and South Africa: opposition to equality stemming from appeals to traditionalism and faith, and a rights movement which had to lobby key political actors to achieve equality, drawing on broader notions of human rights. There are however profound differences, including the way in which apartheid-related inequalities structured the political processes, the political opportunity taken by activists in forging alliances pre-1994 which then translated into rights in the new democracy, and ongoing debates regarding the 'Africaness' or not of lesbian and gay rights (see Gunkel 2010 for an analysis of postcolonial homophobia). Both bisexual and trans activism appear to have been absent or at least not very visible during the 1990s developments, although there is now a trans movement and legislation, such as the Alteration of Sex Description and Sex Status Act (2004), to support trans equality (Morgan et al. 2009).

South Africa has a very specific history regarding LGBT citizenship; models of LGBT citizenship were forged in close alliance with the anti-apartheid movement, as shown in Box 1.1. As outlined in Box 1.2 Nepal provides a useful contrast; LGBT citizenship has a less-developed historical trajectory, but there have been recent innovative developments regarding gender variance and citizenship.

Box 1.2   LGBT rights: Focus on Nepal

In Nepal, models of citizenship have historically operated in ways that are sexualized as well as gendered (see p. 73 for further discussion of rights to citizenship), with heterosexuality configuring normative citizen status. Organizations such as the Blue Diamond Society, which was established in 2001 and is based in Kathmandu, have actively campaigned for equal rights for sexual and gender minorities. The Nepalese government legalized homosexuality in 2007, after the ending of the monarchy, and also passed a ruling that allowed the registration of Nepal's first transgender ('third sex' in the terms of the ruling) citizen. In 2008 the Supreme Court ruled in favour of laws giving equal rights to LGBT citizens including same-sex marriage, making it the first country in South Asia to approve same-sex marriage. It is hoped that under the terms of the new Constitution currently being drafted these recommendations will become law.

In a number of countries, including the UK and the US, Canada, New Zealand, Australia and many European countries, the changing policy landscape over the last decade reflects changes to the citizenship status of LGBT people. These developments in the legal regulation of sexual and gender minorities have prompted research and debate over the likely effects of such policies on social institutions like family and marriage (Weeks et al. 2001; Stacey and Davenport 2002; Meeks and Stein 2012) and on individual's sense of belonging and identity (Bech 1997; Seidman 2002; Richardson 2004), and prompted also analyses concerning governmentality, intersectionality and models of citizenship (Cooper and Monro 2003; Plummer 2003; Taylor et al. 2010). Underlying many of these debates, however, is the broader question of what is meant by the terms equality and diversity.

Equality

It is important to clarify the frameworks of equality that recent demands for LGBT equality are based upon. There are various ways of thinking about equality, for example equal opportunities which concerns meritocratic access – based on ability and talent rather than privilege or wealth – to social opportunities, and rests on a liberal individualism (see Bagilhole 1997). Equal opportunities approaches differ from the range of interventions known as 'affirmative action' in which group-based actions are taken to redress inequalities that exist at a structural level, for example quotas of underrepresented groups, or 'positive action', which retains the individualist stance of equal opportunities but involves extra action such as outreach work to marginalized groups. One of the most common interpretations of equality in contemporary neoliberal societies such as the US and the UK however is equality of resources and recognition (Fraser 1995, 2003; Phillips 2006). Furthermore, what is often implicit in such models is an emphasis on shared characteristics, the presumption that equality requires 'sameness' (Cooper 2004). This is also the dominant model deployed by contemporary lesbian and gay, and trans, rights movements. The case being made is for equality with the dominant group (heterosexuals) for a particular social membership (of lesbians, bisexuals and gay men and increasingly trans people), where the subject of equality is interpreted as equal entitlement to recognition and to resources, centred upon demands for civil rights, access to welfare and rights as consumers (Vaid 1995; Chasin 2000; Pellegrini 2002). This approach is exemplified in the following quote from one of the stakeholder interviews.

> It's about who you are not what you do, so we don't get into what you do. Whether we would in future, I don't know, but we are, I think we are an assimilationist organisation. 'We're just the same as you, and it's fine' is kind of part of our message.
>
> (Stakeholder, England)

More specifically, it is struggles over the civil recognition of domestic partnerships, including the right to marry, that has been an important focus of both lesbian and gay politics as well as wider political and legal debates, and also academic discussions (Cahill 2004; Egan and Sherrill 2005; Smith 2005; Rimmerman and Wilcox 2007; Weeks 2008a; Badgett 2010). On the one hand, it is understandable why 'marriage rights' are important to lesbians and gay men in their pursuit of full citizenship, 'in so far as it has a number of material consequences such as access to housing, health care, parenting rights, tax and inheritance rights, etc.' (Richardson and Seidman 2002: 9). However, this raises broader questions about the wider implications of these trends. For instance, it is important to note that the right to marry has different connotations for single people, who may face social and economic marginalization due to the social privileging of partnered people. Also, it is not available to some trans people. For example, in the UK the Gender Recognition Act 2004, which has been central to trans people's struggles, actually undermines trans people's partnerships because it requires trans people who wish to reassign their gender to annul existing marriages (for a broader discussion of transgender rights and in the US context, see Currah et al. 2006). The fight for monogamous partnership rights is also problematic for many bisexual people, who may have more than one relationship. For polyamorous people, the privileging of one of their relationships over others could impose an unwelcome hierarchy on their relationships, cause them to be adulterous before the law, and have various difficult ramifications in terms of childrearing, for example:

> Within bisexuality there are bi-people who want still to get married to somebody of the same sex, but there are quite a lot of people who would rather have recognition of maybe multiple relationships or some kind of questioning of whether relationships have to be a sort of one person for your whole life. I mean not to reinforce the stereotypes that everyone is having lots of different relationships, because there's certainly monogamous bisexual people and bisexual people who don't want a relationship at all; but you know there may be more of a tendency to want to fight for different relationship structures being recognised ... poly people in families can be in a really difficult position. I think it becomes a big issue when people have kids and up until that point there's less of an issue. You know maybe some things like

being recognised if your partner goes into hospital or something; but it's particularly around families, that people can feel very insecure because you know you could just have your kids taken away or you know you could have no access to kids that you've been looking after for your whole life if you aren't biologically related to them ...

(Bi Community Activist, England)

Looking at couple, as opposed to poyamorous, partnership issues, it is clear that there have been substantial advances regarding same-sex unions in a range of countries. There is an array of international policies which legitimate same-sex unions. In the US there is diversity of law on same-sex marriage. The Defence of Marriage Act (2005), a federal law sometimes referred to as DOMA and first passed in 1996, bars recognition of same-sex marriage by any of the states and enables states 'to refuse to give full faith and credit to same-sex marriages entered into in another state' (Franke 2006: 237). Although a number of states such as California, Maryland and New York do recognize same-sex marriages, many states have passed their own DOMA laws, known as 'little DOMAs', defining the institution of marriage as a relationship between one woman and one man and specifically banning same-sex marriages in that state. Any state with a DOMA law, even if it provides some form of legal recognition of same-sex unions, will not recognize a same-sex marriage from any of the states that allow it. States with so-called super-DOMA laws go further than this, and will not recognize same-sex relationships of any kind. For further discussion, see, for example, Gerstmann (2004) and Pinello (2006).

In Europe the first national same-sex union legislation was in Denmark in 1989, which allowed registered partnerships but, at that time, specifically denied same-sex couples the right to adopt children. Since then 22 European countries have implemented laws that variously legitimize same-sex couples, either though marriage, civil unions or 'registered partnerships', which involve the same or similar rights to marriage, or unregistered partnerships. These trends are also seen elsewhere in the world, with many countries adopting such policies in recent years. This is outlined in Table 1.1, which provides a few selected examples in each case.

A common justification of the provision of same-sex partnership rights and other demands for social inclusion, already noted, is that lesbians and gay men are 'ordinary', 'normal' citizens. This is exemplified in the arguments developed by neoconservative gay writers such as Bruce Bawer, who asserts that the 'lifestyle' of most gay people is 'indistinguishable from that of most heterosexual couples in similar professional and economic circumstances' (1993: 33–34). Andrew Sullivan (1995) advanced a similar argument, claiming that the majority of lesbian and gay individuals have the same values, aspirations and lifestyles as most heterosexuals and desire nothing more than to be fully integrated into society as it is. Earlier normalizing arguments are associated with the 1950s. More than 50 years later a different politics of normalization can be observed. This is a neoliberal politics of normalization that, although it

Table 1.1   Same-sex union laws worldwide (Year of implementation)

Marriage	Registered Partnership	Unregistered Partnership
Netherlands 2001	Denmark 1989	Israel 1994
Spain 2005	Norway 1993	Hungary 1996
Canada 2005	Netherlands 1998	Portugal 2001
South Africa 2006	United Kingdom 2005	Croatia 2003
Norway 2009	New Zealand 2005	
Argentina 2010	Czech Republic 2006	
Mexico (conditional - only certain states) 2010	Uruguay 2008	
Portugal 2010	Ecuador 2009	
	Hungary 2009	

Source: ILGA-Europe. (http:// www.ilga-europe.org accessed 1 February 2011)

too deploys 'sameness' with heterosexuals as a central aspect of its argument, differs in emphasizing the human rights of individuals rather than collective ('gay') rights and in seeking equality with, rather than tolerance from, the mainstream.

The UK case

In the UK, under the post-1997 New Labour government, greater emphasis on social inclusion, recognition of diversity and community cohesion, in the context of increasingly plural, complex and rapidly changing societies, were key themes in the development of a new era of equalities work (Colgan et al. 2007). However, this was not just about New Labour, such shifts reflected broader struggles across the US and Europe, in particular EU legislation on equality (Walby 2011). This new era represented an attempt to move beyond a non-discrimination regime towards a more proactive 'equality-seeking' approach, exemplified by the introduction of positive equality duties in the public sector as part of local government modernization (discussed in later chapters). This is an equality model that emphasizes 'fairness for all' within an understanding of equality as treating 'everyone the same' and having equality of opportunity. Tackling inequality under this rubric is about removing obstacles based on group status, as gendered or disabled for instance, so that people have equal access and chances to develop their individual potential. It is about establishing 'formal equality' in society, where the focus is on recognizing civil and political rights and inequality is largely understood in terms of individual prejudice and discrimination rather than institutionally embedded patterns of inequality. The latter invokes a broader conception of equality, 'substantive equality', where rather than civil and political rights the focus is on social and economic rights requiring governments to assume a redistributive role in remedying group disadvantage and inequalities.

It is in this context that moves towards addressing lesbian, gay, bisexual and trangender equalities need to be understood. As well as the repeal of Section 28 of the 1988 Local Government Act, which outlawed the 'promotion' of homosexuality in local authority schools, we have seen the introduction of a range of new legislation in the UK including the Adoption and Children Act 2002, Employment Equality (Sexual Orientation) Regulations 2003, Gender Recognition Act 2004, the Civil Partnership Act 2004, and associated changes in policy making and practice more generally that emphasize 'Equality and Diversity'. Commenting on this period of change one interviewee said:

> We've been fortunate with this last government over the last ten years that they've made the changes that are necessary and they've done it in such a way that...public resistance is minimal...[a] new agenda of equality and diversity, which is much broader and deeper I think than just gay and lesbians.
>
> (Local Authority Officer, North East England)

What this quote also highlights is that these recent policy shifts in relation to sexualities and transgender equalities are associated with a particular model of citizenship and 'politics of recognition', where there is an emphasis on individual and not group rights. As one of the stakeholder interviewees remarked: 'The human rights principles have to be the kind of bedrock on which we make sense of very complex areas of belief, of freedom, of justice...[in a] liberal economy and liberty, yeah' (Stakeholder, England).

Underlying human rights discourse is a neoliberal formulation of equality in which access to new forms of citizenship relate to claims of universal belonging and, connected with this, the belief that it is not the individual's belonging to a particular group that confirms 'worth' in terms of belonging and recognition as equal citizens, but the worth of every individual as an individual (Phillips 2006). Access to citizenship is framed not in terms of gay rights or transgender rights, for instance, but in terms of a broader human rights agenda. Also, within this model of universal citizenship, equality is rendered meaningful through constructions of 'sameness'. This is the point Wendy Brown makes in her analysis of the operation of tolerance in contemporary struggles over identity and citizenship, including campaigns for gay rights. As she argues: 'Liberal equality is premised upon sameness; it consists in our being regarded as the same or seen in terms of our sameness by the state, and hence being treated in the same way by the law' (Brown 2006: 36).

Following this argument, LGBT people can be viewed as 'deserving' citizens not because they are lesbian, gay, bisexual or transgender but *despite* this, deserving of the same treatment as other citizens. Here the premise of sameness that Brown refers is constructed at two levels: sameness with each other, within the LGBT cluster, and sameness with heterosexuals (and for trans people, with cisgendered people). A process that Plummer (2003) alludes to as the 'McDonaldization of intimacies'. Connected with this, several contributors made the point that 'anything else would be special rights' or, at least, could lead to LGBT people being seen as getting 'special treatment' that might have negative effects on driving forward the LGBT equalities agenda (see Nava and Davidoff 1995).

> Councils, I think, certainly here to my knowledge, are very proactive in try-ing to … show that people from the LGBT community are seen on equal terms to anyone else. They're not saying that you get special privileges; they're saying that you get equal rights.
>
> (Transgender Community Representative, Southern England)

A single equality?

Associated with this neoliberal formulation of citizenship is the emergence of a more integrated approach to equality. In the UK, for example, there has been a gradual shift over the last decade towards a *single* equality regime, looking at equalities as a whole. This saw the establishment of the Equali-ties and Human Rights Commission (ECHR) in England and Wales in 2007, unifying the Commission for Racial Equality, the Equal Opportunities Com-mission, and the Disability Rights Commission, with responsibility to promote equality in relation to age, disability, gender, gender reassignment, ethnicity, religion and belief, and sexual orientation. These legally protected equality characteristics are called equality 'strands'. In Northern Ireland this shift was apparent earlier, with the amalgamation of various anti-discrimination bodies into a single Equality Commission in Section 75 of the Northern Ireland Act (1998), with 'sexual orientation' becoming one of nine equality strands. The others are gender, ethnicity, age, marital status, disability, people with depen-dants, people of different religious beliefs, and people of different political persuasion. The situation in Northern Ireland is discussed in more detail in Chapter 7.

This move towards addressing equalities in a more integrated way was con-solidated for the first time in England and Wales with the introduction in 2010 of the single Equality Act, which replaced previous legislation in relation to specific forms of inequality and discrimination such as the Race Relations Act 1976 and the Disability Discrimination Act 1995. The Act provides a frame-work to protect the rights of individuals and its aims are articulated primarily in the language of promoting a fairer and more equal society. It places a new obligation or 'public duty' on public sector organizations to promote equality and foster 'good relations' on the grounds of sexual orientation and gender reassignment. Such duties were also extended, beyond gender, ethnicity and disability, to age and religion and belief. These changes in approaches to equal-ity represent, in part, recognition that in relation to inequalities we may be 'in more than one box'. That is, an acknowledgement, in other words, that a person can experience *intersectional* discrimination and inequality (Crenshaw 1991; Hill Collins 2000; Grabham et al. 2009; Taylor et al. 2010), as will be discussed in more detail in the next chapter.

Several participants, both in the Action Leaning Sets and in the interviews, were of the opinion that the recognition of intersectional dynamics was a positive move: one that could act as a 'catalyst' in embedding equality issues in relation to sexual orientation and transgender.

> If you actually say 'We are going to look at all the different equality strands, including LGBT', that is an immediate driver... you know, this is not making sense from the perspective of a citizen, people with all sorts of factors and facets, considering them only under a disability scheme, where is that taking us?... Why would you focus on one aspect of a person rather than look at them in the round?
>
> (Stakeholder, Wales)

Recognizing that LGBT equalities can be 'sensitive', work interviewees could (Stakeholder, Wales) see other possible advantages of adopting an integrated equality approach.

> The benefit that that has for areas that are more sensitive is that it means that employers and public authorities, by adopting an integrated approach can actively promote equality in all areas, but they do it through one medium in effect. That can make it easier for organisations, to take that wider approach and not be consumed by their own prejudice.
>
> (Stakeholder, Northern Ireland)

> ...we had to package it with another element of the training. Off the top of my head I can't remember, it may well have been something along the lines of disability or gender, the rationale being that, you know, we would acknowledge that in the Northern Ireland context it [LGBT equalities] is still a very sensitive subject area, and so to ensure that staff didn't feel under pressure by attending or not attending, we packaged it with another element of our equalities training.
>
> (Local Authority Officer, Northern Ireland)

Other participants, however, expressed a number of concerns over the move towards an integrated equalities approach, in some respects mirroring the critique that the use of the LGBT acronym dilutes the specificity of issues pertaining to different equality strands. This was captured nicely in one person's description of this integrated approach as 'sheep-dipping'. The tension between Equality and Diversity is discussed later in the chapter. For now, it is important to consider how this rhetoric of 'treating everyone the same' plays out in reality.

Inequalities within equalities

It would seem that despite the introduction of an integrated approach to equality there are equalities and there are equalities. A hierarchy of equalities strands, a 'pecking order' as one person put it, was very evident in our research, with LGBT equalities being described as a 'poor relation' to other equality strands, especially race, gender and disability. To some extent this can be explained in terms of the fact that LGBT equalities are 'still the new kid on the block' and also in terms of how strong the legislation is to drive forward certain equalities agendas. For instance, public duties around gender, race and disability have been in operation in the UK for some time, whereas a duty on sexual orientation and gender reassignment (along with religion and belief and age) was only established more recently with the introduction of the single Equality Act. This was the view that some of the Welsh Action Learning Set members took. For instance: 'The others [equality strands] tend to take precedence because they're more... because of legislation, there's a lot more status behind them.' Another ALS member said that '...some strands have the focus because that's where the law is strongest and because of the inequalities within equalities, it causes that issue'.

This latter quote raises something else, the prospect that some strands of equality may be considered to be more equal than others. Our research indicated that LGBT equalities work *was* seen as different compared to working on other equality strands in ways that could undermine its equalities status. Some of the interviewees, for instance, highlighted the tension for some people between their responsibility to promote equality in relation to sexual orientation and their practice of a particular faith or religion. Such tensions were identified as a potential source of conflict in terms of rights to freedom of expression that if not dealt with could impede the process of taking the LGBT equalities agenda forward.

> I think it is an area that people still feel a little uncomfortable around, um, particularly, you know, particular faiths that have a belief, you know, that somehow it's wrong to be gay, um, and the clash between the right to express your own faith and the right to express... I think that's where the, you know, the line is drawn, you hold your own beliefs fine but if that leads you to try and discriminate against somebody else then that's where we draw the line.
>
> (Local Authority Officer, North East England)

This issue of the relationship between sexuality and faith is something that is addressed in more detail in subsequent chapters. In addition to generally being seen as more 'sensitive' than many other equality issues, there was also a sense that LGBT equalities were seen as less important and were less sanctioned.

> You wouldn't be allowed to get away with similar prejudices towards other minority groupings, but they're just, there are some minority groupings that there's less of a, you know, you can get away with more I think around sexuality, and that's wrong, and it's something that should be fought at all levels really.
>
> (Local Authority Officer, Northern Ireland)

[Y]ou've always got your . . . approved of equalities. because it's not the fault of the disabled, but some people, you've chosen a certain lifestyle . . . you could be disabled because you fought for your country in the war, and it's because of you that we have freedom, so you can paint a picture there which no council will go against.

(Local Authority Officer, Wales)

In the latter quote there is a sense of a moral distinction between the deserving and undeserving citizen, where the legitimacy of rights claims appears to centre on the ontological status of being LGBT. During the late nineteenth century and the first half of the twentieth century, it was the theories of biologists, medical researchers, psychologists and sexologists that dominated understandings of sexuality and gender, with homosexuality regarded as innate or fixed in early childhood (Weeks 2009). However, a new canon of sociological work on sexuality and gender emerged in the 1960s and 70s, which critiqued these earlier *essentialist* modes of thinking and signalled a shift away from biologically based accounts of gender and sexuality to social analysis. The work of sociologists associated with symbolic interactionism, labelling theory and the sociology of 'deviance', along with feminist writers, contributed to developing such a sociological perspective (for example Gagnon and Simon 1967, 1973; McIntosh 1968; Plummer 1975). This led to what during the 1980s became known as the essentialism/constructionist debates (Fuss 1990; Stein 1993), and to a more general understanding of being gay as a 'lifestyle choice'.

Advocates for liberal reform have in the past often drawn on essentialist understandings to argue for social change on the grounds that people should not be discriminated against for something they are 'born like' and don't choose to be. A classic example of this is the 1967 Sexual Offences Act, which decriminalized consensual sexual acts between men over the age of 21 in 'private' in England and Wales (such practices remained illegal in Scotland until 1981 and in Northern Ireland until 1982). Although it is possible to identify forms of essentialism in the radical politics of the 1960s and 70s described earlier, the idea that gender roles and sexual identities are socially constructed featured strongly (Jackson and Scott 2010). Lesbian feminism in particular advanced the idea of lesbianism as a 'choice', and bisexuality is also commonly viewed in this way. By contrast, transgender has typically been understood not as a choice, but in more essentialist terms (Hines and Sanger 2010).

Contemporary lesbian and gay rights claims have frequently drawn more on essentialist than constructionist arguments to make their case; with lesbians and gay men conceptualized as a legitimate minority group having a certain *quasi-ethnic* status (Epstein, 1987; see also Lehring 1997). This kind of political practice does not necessarily mean adherence to essentialist theories. Recognizing that it 'plays well politically' has led some to argue for the deployment of a 'strategic essentialism' in political organizing and activism, in the belief that such an approach is more likely to get results than emphasizing the socially and historically constructed nature of sexuality. For instance, the idea of a person's sexuality being a choice can suggest a certain voluntarism that may undermine rights claims in the sense of lesbians and gay men being recognized as a legitimate 'fixed' constituency. More negatively, it can lead to arguments for the denial of rights of citizenship on the grounds that if it's a choice then you can always choose *not* to be lesbian or gay.

Questions over the social and political utility of social constructionist approaches have also been part of debates in relation to racial and gender equality. Indeed, the notion of 'strategic essentialism' is associated with the work of Gayatri Chakravorty Spivak (1988) and her contribution to feminist and postcolonial studies, referring to the process of adopting an operational 'essentialism' about women specifically for the purposes of social action. In her work on intersectionality, discussed in more detail in the following chapter, Kimberle Crenshaw (1991) considers the meanings attached to 'race'. Her argument is that the crucial point is not establishing the meaning of 'race', as socially constructed or otherwise, but rather attacking the uses of these varied meanings to support racial discrimination and subordination. In the same way we might extend her 'pragmatic' approach to sexuality and gender identification. That is, one could argue for the irrelevance of ontological debates in understandings of lesbian, gay, bisexuality and transgender on the grounds that it shouldn't matter. The key issue is on critiquing whatever understandings are being deployed to support discrimination of LGBT people. This perspective is illustrated in the following quote from an equality and diversity officer who took part in one of the Action Learning Sets. Although he conceded that it was easier to get the equalities agenda across using a 'born like it' model, he felt that this shouldn't really matter.

> It's easier if you can persuade people that, or you can make people believe that, other people are who they are, what they are, and it doesn't matter if it is a choice or if it's something that you are born with or born as, you should just respect that person for who they are, what they are and their differences.
>
> (ALS member, North East England)

There are two different meanings of sexuality operating here, recognition of sexuality as something that is socially rather than naturally produced and sexuality as something that is a natural property of the person. Where claims to normality and universality are at stake, it would seem that sexuality as a social construction can be 'eclipsed' by the latter. That is, legitimate claims to citizenship are often grounded in essentialist understandings of sexuality, 'strategic' or otherwise. Indeed, the term used in equalities policies is 'sexual orientation', itself an essentialist concept (Botcherby and Creegan 2009). This section of the chapter has looked at how equality is framed in terms of contemporary struggles for LGBT equality and responses to these demands. The next section examines how this framing of equality is linked with the concept of diversity (see also discussion in Chapter 5).

Equality and diversity

Recognition that we live in societies that are increasingly plural, complex and rapidly changing has been central to the development of a new era of policy making and practice that is encapsulated by the term 'Equality and Diversity' which is used to define and champion equality alongside recognition of and respect for difference. For example, in its report on *How Fair is Britain?* the Equalities and Human Rights Commission states: 'Our vision is of a society at ease with its diversity, where every individual has the opportunity to achieve their potential, and where people treat each other with dignity and respect' (EHRC 2011: 12). In addition to being a dominant theme in political and policy discourse, the relationship between equality and diversity is also increasingly an important area of academic debate. For example, drawing on contemporary cultural politics from Western Europe, the US and Canada. Seyla Benhabib (2010) has provided insightful analysis of the relation between these terms through the lens of varieties of multiculturalism. Sara Ahmed (2011) has also provided an examination of the relationship between new equality regimes and institutionalized racism, focusing on what it means to 'embody diversity'. Specifically, she argues that equality and diversity have become 'performance indicators' (something discussed later in this book) and, moreover, that they function as 'non-performatives', that is they do not bring about the effects that they name. Equality and Diversity is not then just a 'mantra', it is institutionalized as an area of work in many organizations. For example in UK local government at the time of writing there are equality and diversity officers in most regions and, as Ahmed rightly recognizes, this is part of performance management. This section considers the interpretation of recognition of difference in the context of a politics of equality that emphasizes the values of sameness and universality, and the tensions that can arise from this.

As was outlined earlier, a concern to have difference recognized (indeed celebrated) as both positive and legitimate was an important aspect of lesbian and gay movements in the 1960s and 70s, which was also reflected in the demands of other social movements including black and feminist political activism. The establishment of the United Nations, post Second World War, was also influential in establishing a broader global context in which recognition of difference came to be linked to notions of social justice and citizenship, in particular an appreciation of dignity and respect to all individuals (McLaughlin et al. 2011). More recently, respect for diversity has become a cultural norm and core aspect of good (global) citizenship underpinning rationales for 'tolerance' and 'acceptance' of new forms of inclusion (Seidman 2002). It is in the context of these citizenship discourses, along with processes of detraditionalization and pluralism, that LGBT communities have been enabled in advancing their case for equal rights.

Respect for diversity invokes group difference through valuing of difference. This discourse of valuing diversity draws on 'discourses of economic value (the business case for diversity) and moral value (the social justice case)' (Ahmed 2007: 604). This is a model of diversity as providing benefit to organizations and a basis for organizational pride. As Regine Bendl and Alexander Fleischmann (2008: 390) argue, it 'claims to value differences among individuals to achieve fairness and reduce discrimination which in turn generates other organisational benefits'. It is also a model that constructs 'difference' – in this case sexual and gender 'difference' – as something that is already in existence 'in' the people who constitute diversity. Within this framework it is possible to depict LGBT people as a 'resource' (Cooper 2006), and indeed purposefully use this as a strategic lever to implement equalities initiatives.

However, in the context of understandings of equality that emphasize an integrated approach there is an apparent tension in the extent to which differences and the complex social locations within group membership may be acknowledged. This may mean that intersecting inequalities such as those of gender, class, race and disability, for instance, are not addressed. Indeed, use of the acronym LGBT would appear to close down recognition of differences and diversity among lesbians, gay men, bisexual and transgender people, especially those who do not approximate the mainstream normalized 'LGBT citizen' (Heaphy 2008). The emphasis on sameness and universality associated with contemporary neoliberal approaches to equality, where individuals are supposedly granted the same rights to live 'ordinary lives', suggests that difference 'can no longer be seen as the only value from which people seek recognition' (McLaughlin et al. 2011). This was evident in our research. There was a broad trend within local authorities for actors to legitimate the use of the LGBT acronym in terms of 'common interests' between the groups. For example:

> We've kind of made the assumption in writing a policy and equality plan, that you know, there are sufficiently similar issues whether they are gay, lesbian or transgendered, for us to say, this is a plan that we hope is sensitive enough to meet the needs of a group in a society.
>
> (Councillor, North East England)

However, although participants did see value in categorizing various groups of people together, agreeing that it was part and parcel of policy making, some also identified this with the risk of losing sight of different issues and priorities associated with the groups represented in particular equality 'strands'.

> We like to box and categorise people because we think it makes it easier to deal with, but actually in reality and in practice, talking from an equality officer perspective it's, you know, we use them because it is easier to use collective terms, but when it comes down to it we need to bear in mind, or public bodies need to bear in mind, that actually each of those groups have distinctly different needs, you know all gay men are not the same and don't have the same needs, do they? ... All of us cross over these different strands

and have these complex individual sort of, you know, our make up is all different . . .

(Stakeholder, Wales)

It would appear that despite being neatly stitched together in the phrase 'Equality and Diversity', equality and diversity are actually often pulling in different directions. This is because there are specific tensions associated with seeking to play down group difference within the discursive construction of equality as sameness and recognition of group difference as cultural validation within the discursive construction of good citizenship as including respect for diversity. This is a tension that is also manifest in the establishment of different equality strands.

The pull of these tensions may be felt more in some areas than in others. For instance, the research demonstrated that bisexuals and transgendered people were the more marginalized groups within the LGBT acronym and that, associated with this, issues distinct to these communities were more at risk of being obscured. For example, one person discussed the way that the tension between equality and diversity could play out in the 'sexual orientation' equality strand delimiting difference where this was expressed as a 'choice' for bisexuality.

And in our training we have done some work around what is the differences between equality and diversity and, you know, try to be honest that sometimes they appear to be in tension and you have to make some careful judgements . . . In other words, there are some equality issues around sexual orientation, but there are also some diversity issues around sexual orientation, allowing people to be comfortable with the choices they are making, and not to feel restricted – bisexuality for instance.

(Manager, Southern England)

The same officer went on to say that they felt that similar tensions between advancing equality and recognizing diversity were also at work in the equality strand for transgender status.

I guess if you were transgender and most of the people active in the LGBT arena are gay, you might feel that actually you've been appropriated but without your needs actually been met. You know, you've been brought into the fold but you've been lost in that fold.

Diversity neutral

These tensions are connected to how diversity, as well as equality, is framed. Diversity is generally used as an 'umbrella concept' under which individual characteristics can be subsumed. The phrase 'diversity neutral' is how some chose to describe this. This is the idea that the mainstreaming of equalities and the policy shift to integrating different equalities strands under a single equality scheme will eventually lead to a situation where there is no need to highlight diversity. However, this raises the question of whether 'going diversity neutral' means erasing diversity? The following extracts from an interview with an LGBT community representative working in the South of England demonstrate how these tensions may play out in practice.

An issue that's just come up very recently is that I've been made aware that we've employed a company that basically we've handed over our advertising to. They seem to be quite a sort of up and coming company that are sort of snaffling quite a few contracts around the country. I've become aware that since we've employed them our advertising in LGBT press has dropped from ten adverts last year to two adverts proposed for this year, with a drop in spending of £5,000. Well, this is on the back of a previous concern that I had when they issued our new set of advertising campaigns, because there was nothing at all that indicated LGBT, there was nothing on there whatsoever and when I raised this with our recruiting department I was told 'Oh well they have decided that they're going to go diversity neutral', [pause], which I have no clue what that means, you know, my concern is when you, you know, if you go carbon neutral you remove the carbon, so is diversity neutral removing the diversity?

He went on to say:

I think, from what I gather, that what they are trying to achieve or what they're assuming is that we are far enough down the line, that diversity is so embedded in everything that we do, that we don't necessarily need to specifically highlight it, which, if that was the case, it would be absolutely fantastic but I think that's maybe ten, twelve, twenty years down the line. When people don't worry about diversity any more then fine, we can go diversity neutral, but to my mind I've taken ten years to get a place at the table to actually get listened to, and I'm not happy with suddenly going back to the vanilla approach of like one size fits all. And the comment was made, 'Well we're appealing to the masses'.

Here again this highlights some of the problems and risks associated with the process of mainstreaming equalities, where the focus is on recognition and inclusion based on rights as individuals – 'ordinary citizens' – rather than specific group differences – such as 'lesbian and gay rights'.

... so there has been ... a creative time of neutrality ... so we don't talk about being gay and we don't talk about gay rights and we don't talk about different races ... so we're closed in on neutrality.

(LGBT Group Representative, Northern Ireland)

Within this framework the term 'diversity' acknowledges difference 'while at the same time homogenizing it' (Zanoni et al. 2010: 18) through the inscription of difference within the model of equality as sameness. Here again the risk associated with becoming 'diversity neutral' is of losing a focus on experiences of inequality and discrimination that are specific to the lesbian, gay, bisexual and trans communities as well as, for instance, living with a disability, having a particular religious belief or belonging to a minority ethnic community.

Discussion

This chapter has examined the concepts of equality and diversity. It has considered the dominant framing of these terms, and their intertwined construction, through the lens of lesbian, gay, bisexual and transgender politics. The 'identity politics' which emerged in the late 1960s and 70s celebrated difference and diversity, though was open to the criticism of obscuring differences within the categories of 'gay' and 'lesbian'. This is a critique that has been levelled at other social movements and which has been productive of a large body of work, especially within feminist theory, on the difficulties of articulating a particular identity (black, woman, gay) in order to legitimate a particular (black/feminist/gay) politics (see Lloyd 2005). Now, in contemporary struggles for equality, the adoption of LGBT or LGBTQI acronyms suggests inclusivity and acknowledgement of diversity that the term 'queer' also sought (Seidman 1996; Sullivan 2003), although coming from a very different kind of politics. Yet, it is argued, different homogenizing processes are at work in this new politics of recognition where processes of 'normalisation' are productive of what Lisa Duggan (2002) has referred to as a new 'homonormativity' (see p. 97). While there are clearly importance differences within the category LGBT, these differences may or may not be mobilized. The dominant trend is for appeals to be made on behalf of an LGBT community that is cast, *and inscribed in the process*, as relatively homogeneous. In this context, the reference point to difference is not intragroup distinctions, but distinctions against another sexual grouping (heterosexual). In this context, the meaning of LGBT is effectively 'non-heterosexual'. This meaning is problematic, in particular for trans people. For instance, our research demonstrated that in some countries such as Northern Ireland there is a strong move to separate the T from LGB because trans primarily concerns gender. It is also problematic for bisexual people to a degree, because bisexuals straddle the hetero-homo binary, so that their identities are not specifically 'non-heterosexual', rather they are hybrid, queer or 'not exclusively heterosexual'. What this also highlights is how heterosexuality remains at the centre, as the default norm against which 'others' are constructed, *at the same time* as the rationale for LGBT equality is forged through political rhetoric that constructs an imagined sameness with heterosexuals and with cisgender people.

As this chapter has tried to demonstrate, many of the issues we have raised are relevant to wider debates concerning equality and diversity more generally. For instance, problematizing the concept 'woman' and highlighting differences between women was a key aspect of feminist debates in the 1980s (see Bhavnani 1997; Woodward and Woodward 2009), from which these more recent debates over LGBT issues might perhaps usefully draw upon. In particular, this chapter has highlighted a number of concerns with the discursive construction of equality and diversity associated with neoliberalism. For example, to the extent that communities are socially heterogeneous, an obvious problem with an approach to equality as 'sameness' is that differences and the complex social locations within that group membership (in this case LGBT) are obscured. This may mean that intersecting inequalities such as those of gender, class, race and disability, for instance, are also not adequately addressed. To some extent this tension is manifest in the UK context, in the policy of retaining different equality 'strands' within an overall single equality scheme. A further reason to question the dominant tendency to interpret equality through similitude is that central to the meanings of homo and heterosexuality is the notion of 'difference'. It is this hetero/homo binary that potentially troubles the claims to sameness that underlay the 'just the same as everyone else' model of inclusion and recent shifts in the policy landscape.

Such trouble is managed, in part, through a complex economy of 'seeing and not seeing' difference (Brown 2006), where two forms of recognition are in play. Recognition of the right to belong as 'ordinary citizens' and to be assimilated into public life as part of the 'common good' and, at the same time, recognition of difference that is typically through naturalizing and essentializing processes that construct sexuality and gender identification as something that is embodied: a part of an individual's make up. The marking of difference is here a matter of human nature, reflected in the use of the essentialist term 'sexual orientation' within equalities policies and organizations (see Mitchell et al. 2008).

The emphasis on shared norms and inclusivity also raises important questions about what constructions of lesbians and gay men, bisexual and transgender people are mobilized in order to establish the case for equality. What counts as 'equal' recognition? What are the values and norms through which recognition of LGBT people as the 'same' as heterosexuals, as well as with each other, takes place. These questions are considered in Chapter 3, which examines the relationship between sexuality and citizenship more broadly. In the next chapter, the discussion of diversity is extended through elaborating on the intersectional differences between and within lesbian, gay, bisexual and trans communities; outlining the ways in which the interstices between social characteristics, including race, socio-economic status, faith, gender and age, can usefully inform understandings of sexuality and gender.

Summary

This chapter has examined

■ How sexuality and gender politics has changed in its aims and strategies since the second part of the twentieth century, with globalization resulting in a scaling up of LGBT politics
■ The frameworks of equality used in seeking to end discrimination against LGBT people
■ The links between establishing the case for equality and assumptions made about sexuality and gender identification, in particular essentialist and social constructionist explanations of what is marked as 'difference'
■ The introduction of new equalities initiatives and the existence of hierarchies of equalities or 'pecking orders' within these
■ The connections made between concepts of equality and diversity and the apparent tensions between the two
■ The concept of 'diversity neutral'

Intersectionality

Why include intersectional approaches in the study of LGBT equalities? Intersectionality theory has been around for many years, emerging initially from Black womens' critiques of white feminists' failure to understand identity complexity. Intersectionality approaches can be used to examine the way in which we are not just defined by sexuality, or gender, or ethnicity, or social class, or ability; we are each a unique mixture of different social characteristics. Because society is structured by many forms of inequality, some people – and groups of people – have identities that combine two or more marginalized or stigmatized characteristics. Importantly, these marginalized identities do not just add onto each other, but rather intersect in particular ways.

What is intersectionality theory? Like many concepts, the term 'intersectionality' is a rather slippery one. US scholar Crenshaw (1991) introduced the term to mean a crossroads or intersection, where different identities (in this case, race and gender) intersected. However, other theorists have subsequently explored intersectionality as an axis of difference (Yuval-Davis 2006) or as a dynamic process (Staunaes 2003, cited in Davis 2009: 68). There are tensions within the field of intersectionality studies, relating to broader debates within sexuality studies and feminisms, concerning whether to pursue category-based analysis (in other words, whether to focus on specific social categories such as sexuality or race) or to develop analysis along a range of category axes (see Walby 2007; Weldon 2008). One of the fundamental problems is that if we focus only on the intersections our analysis becomes very individualistic because, as suggested above, each person is a unique combination of different intersecting characteristics. Activists and policy makers who are concerned with equality cannot deal only with individuals, because they need to be able to group people together in categories in order to be able to organize politically or to develop policy initiatives. This grouping together is a crucial part of the identity politics that have underpinned the LGBT movement (see Blasius and Phelan 1997, Blasius 2001, and Chapter 1). Monro has argued elsewhere (2010a) that we need to combine interstice (intersection-oriented) and category-based intersectional analysis, so that we retain some sensitivity to individual differences, but are able to work with groups and categories as well.

The inclusion of intersectionality in a book about LGBT equality is important for two reasons. As indicated above, identities are complex and it is
necessary to develop tools for understanding sexuality and gender in relation
to raced, classed and other identities. Intersectionality theory provides a way
of addressing complexity and also the different ways in which social characteristics are routed through each other, so that at one point discrimination
on the grounds of age and gender might shape someone's life chances, but
this person might simultaneously use class privilege to resist or circumnavi-
gate this. Another important reason for using intersectional approaches is that
intersectionality studies have focused mostly on gender, class and race; where
it is included, sexuality is often placed in a marginal position (see Crenshaw
1997; Hurtado and Sinha 2008; Shields 2008). There have been some exceptions, including Clare Beckett's (2004) study of the operation of heterosexuality
in the lives of lesbian and disabled women, and Julie Fish's (2008) research on
LGBT identities and health care; however, there is a need to bring sexuality
more fully into intersectionality studies.

This chapter uses tools taken from intersectionality studies in order to
explore LGBT equalities issues, with the aim of demonstrating some of the
complexities in the field, as well as providing insights that may be useful for
subsequent studies. It begins by examining the complexities *within* the LGBT
acronym (these complexities concern gender and sexuality differences, and the
relationships between these differences) using examples from the LGBT Equalities in UK Local Government project. It then goes on to look at the ways
in which LGBT identities *intersect with other forms of identity*, using a range
of international sources. In other words, looking at the ways in which LGBT
people are affected by issues of race and ethnicity (ethnicity is defined here as
the heritage of norms, values, practices and shared physiological characteristics that each individual has), faith, age, class and ability. It also provides an
indication of the spatial ordering of sexuality. This is explored in more depth
in the work of Gill Valentine (2007) and Monro (2010a); see also Chapter 6.
It is important to acknowledge the range of other characteristics and forces
that can act in a structuring way but that cannot be included here, for example
relationship status.

Intersections within, and between, LGBT identities

We have already outlined the way in which the term LGBT (and the identities contained within LGBT as an acronym of 'lesbian', 'gay', 'bisexual' and
'transgender') is socially constructed and becomes historically and culturally
contingent. To briefly recap, the identity categories of 'gay', 'lesbian', 'bisexual' and 'transgender', and others, such as 'homosexual' and 'transsexual', are
relatively recent constructs, forged via the interrelationship between western
medicine and the emerging communities and identity movements associated
with sexual and gender diversity. These historical processes of sex, sexual and

gender identity construction have been widely discussed, by authors such as Michel Foucault (1979), Lillian Faderman (1981), Blasius and Phelan (1997), Weeks (2000, 2009) and Whittle (2002). It is important to emphasize the way in which LGBT identities developed in the context of the western colonial and postcolonial era. They are being used as a basis for developing social movements and rights claims in many parts of the world, but they sit aside indigenous sexual and gendered forms of self-expression and identity. These indigenous ways of being may involve same-sex sexual expression that is not used as a basis for any form of social identification, meaning that the LGBT categories would not be seen as relevant. This hidden and mutable nature of some sexual (and gender diverse) expression is also a feature of some western sexualities, for example MSM (men who have sex with men) in the UK and the fluid sexualities that are found in some youth cultures. The LGBT acronym is therefore open to question, also because the specific and different experiences of the groups within it, and tensions between the groups. The differences and tensions within the acronym are explored in the next section of the chapter.

Why is it useful to look at the differences within the LGBT acronym? Authors such as Crenshaw (1997) and Ange-Marie Hancock (2007) discuss the importance of analysing within-group diversity. As Crenshaw (1997) says, the struggle over which differences matter is one of power; who determines whether and which intersectional differences determine will be addressed in activism or policy work. This section of the chapter uses Leslie McCall's (2005) notion of intracategorical intersectional analysis as an attempt to *engage with complexity,* rather than to either eliminate categories or maintain group boundaries.

As discussed in the previous chapter, there have been long-standing historical tensions between all of the groups included within the acronym LGBT, tensions that have continued in the sense that there is still misogyny amongst some gay men, as well as anti-gay sentiment amongst some lesbians. Of course, the gay and lesbian populations are themselves widely varied, partially due to the intersections of other social characteristics such as race and class (see below) and partly due to cultural variations such as lesbian notions of 'butch' and 'femme' – notions which themselves are linked to class (see Cvetkovich 2003). Gender intersects with sexuality in a structuring way, with a tendency for gay men to hold positions of greater social power and status than lesbians, reflecting broader gender inequalities. The positions of some gay men also illustrate the way in which people strategically manage their identities to access privilege. For example, a trans man who works with statutory sector organizations said that:

> The G agenda is they've got the loudest voice. They set the agenda. They're the chaps who have jobs because they are gay. I think, I mean I'm going to sound really bitchy now, but I'm beginning to feel that there are some chaps who got jobs with their local Primary Care Trust [government funded health organisation] doing sexual health work because of the AIDS crisis... they

have quite nice jobs, quite well paid jobs and they have the sort of authority and they only really think about themselves.

Another issue concerning the LGBT acronym is the way in which hegemonic masculinities and sexualities act to police gender and sexual boundaries in tandem, through each other, and hegemonic masculinities are constructed in opposition to perceived gay or bisexual ones (see Richardson 2010). The abuse and harassment of gay and bisexual men and boys – and concurrent policing of gender and sexual boundaries – often take a gendered, rather than sexualized, form. For example, this could include the use of terms like 'sissy' to discipline men who refuse to conform to masculine norms. This seepage of 'sexuality' and 'gender' as discrete categories does however spill over in a useful way, because there are also political allegiances between people across the LGBT acronym in terms of understanding and opposing heterosexism, biphobia and transphobia. The research findings indicated awareness of this, for example:

> I certainly think there would be a case for tying the LBGT issues with gender issues as well, because I think some of the discrimination that women can face is some of the discrimination that we face as well on a day-to-day basis ... the comments that you can sometimes get made about you, the comments that can be made about appearance, the comments that can be made when you're walking down the street, and sometimes you just think, gosh, I wonder if this is how it must feel for, you know, when a woman walks past on her own and is suddenly, you know, the name-calling, the wolf-whistles.
> (Local Authority Officer, Wales)

Tensions are also evident between the LG and B and T groups. B and T are marginalized, overall, within the LGBT acronym. The research findings showed that some lesbians and gay men attempt to disassociate from trans people, and/or refuse to accept that bisexuality exists, or are overtly transphobic or biphobic. Transphobia may also be gendered, for instance a trans man talked about the way in which he experienced gay men as being 'terrified' of trans men, but relatively comfortable with trans women. Findings from the research support the argument that there has been a shift towards the inclusion of trans people by community groups that were formerly LG or LGB, although this does vary, for example the campaigning groups Stonewall England and Stonewall Cymru both frame trans as concerning gender, rather than sexuality; so it is not included within their remit. In the UK, there continues to be a lot of debate around the inclusion (or not) of trans people, and there is some evidence that LG community members seek to de-link LGB and T (this was less the case with bisexuals, because of the prominence of notions of gender and sexual variance – as well as the substantial numbers of bisexual trans people – in the bisexual community). There was some discussion in the research of the problematic framing of trans as concerning gender, given the way in which sexual attraction for trans people is not necessarily heterosexual, as well as differences within the trans population. There are of course also debates amongst the trans communities regarding whether or not to include trans within the acronym, including desire amongst some trans people to distance from the supposedly stigmatized identities of LGB people, and homophobic and biphobic attitudes amongst some trans people (see Monro 2005). However, the inclusion of trans people in the LGBT acronym is also seen as strategically useful, for instance:

> ...people complain that the T in LGBT is the tail on the dog, I said, 'yes it is, but it's a big dog with teeth', you know, on our own we're a tiny little animal that people just ignore but if we're part of that grouping, it's much harder to ignore us 'cause we've got a much bigger organisation, erm (-)
> (Trans Community Member (A), Wales)

There has been a shift in recent years amongst some groups towards the use of the term 'trans' as an umbrella, covering any form of trans identities rather than distinguishing between transsexuals and transvestites. This support for diversity within the trans community is a fairly recent phenomenon, working in contradiction to rigidly gender binaried and sexuality-based forms of categorization and identity politics based upon them. Monro has theorized this gender variance (Monro 2005), and it maps onto the 'increasingly finely grained categories' described by McCall (2005) in her anticategorical typology. McCall's anticategorical typology forms one of three approaches to understanding intersectionality, and it involves criticizing and deconstructing homogenous forms of categorization (see Monro and Richardson 2010).

There is a history of marginalization of bisexuals by the lesbian and gay communities, and it is only within the last decade that bisexuality has been usually included within the LGBT acronym. There are a number of tensions around bisexuals and lesbian and gays (see Hemmings 2002; Monro 2005) with stigmatization being based on the notion that bisexuals are more privileged than lesbian and gay people because they can supposedly 'choose' their sexual orientation, are going through a phase, or are untrustworthy. As one research contributor said:

> 'Best of both worlds', and that's the kind of comments that you get, 'Oh they don't know what they want' and it's like 'Have you ever thought that someone might actually like males and females?' What's wrong with that? I think there always will be tensions between lesbians and bisexual women. There don't seem to be tensions between gay men and bisexual people [sic] for whatever reason, I don't know. But there is that culture in pubs and clubs and I still hear comments like 'Oh don't bother talking to her, she's bisexual' and its like 'It's 2009, hello, we're not in the bloody cave now', and I do, I go on one, and I think 'Oh here I go again', but I don't get it, I don't get it. 'Oh, don't trust a bisexual woman because they'll cheat on you with a man'. Well why trust a gay woman, they may cheat on you with another woman.
> (Union Officer, Southern England)

Why is there still so much prejudice concerning bisexuality amongst lesbians and gay men? It appears to be partly because bisexuality destabilises the discrete sexual orientation categories on which lesbian, gay and heterosexual identities are based, categories that are developed in opposition to each other (see Butler 1997), and hence fluidity and multiplicity can seem very threatening to people with 'monosexual' (attracted to people of one sex) identities (see Monro 2005). However, the bisexual population is also noticeably diverse. Bisexuals can be, for instance, single, monogamous with either a same-sex or opposite-sex partner, or polyamorous, and there are tensions between those who seek to assimilate into the mainstream and those who seek to destabilize or abolish categories. Another relevant issue is that the bisexual population in the UK appears to be less professionalized than the lesbian and gay populations. This will affect the ways in which bisexuals interface with both more professionalized organizations that predominantly represent the interests of lesbian and gay men, and bisexual engagement with civil society and the statutory sector more widely, perhaps making it harder to tackle biphobia.

Intersecting social characteristics

It is impossible to do justice to the many social characteristics that shape LGBT (and other) people's lives, or the multiple group identities which people may move in and out of. However, it is important to consider the ways in which sexual, gendered, raced and classed and other realms of experience come into existence in and through each other, 'if in contradictory and conflictual ways' (McClinton 1995: 5). This section of the chapter will map out some of the key social characteristics and categories that structure LGBT people's lives, showing that we are always not only LGBTQI or heterosexual, but also (for example) raced, classed and living in bodies that change over time. Sometimes our raced, classed or national identities (for instance) may be more important to us than our sexual and gender identities, and we often strategically manage our identities in order to advance ourselves, or simply to survive.

One of the most important things that intersectionality approaches can show us is that when people are managing multiple forms of disadvantage, the foregrounding of sexuality or gender may be less important than other identities. And, as was indicated above, people negotiate their identities in complex ways. For example, the Welsh trans women contributors were out as trans women (thus facing intersectional discrimination as both trans and female); they also described themselves to the interviewer as neither male nor female. These two contributors appeared to very effectively utilize professional and middle-class norms and opportunity structures to attain social acceptance and respect. However, they also conceded to certain heteropatriarchal structuring forces, specifically norms about presentation in public space, for instance: 'It's dressing appropriately, we say, "if you go out down the street, dressed in a short skirt, you're attracting attention and people are going to look at you, and then they'll realise that you're not a real woman, and that may throw up problems that they may have and that could cause you problems", so, you know, "dress appropriately" ' (Transgender Community Member (B)). These comments relate to the 'politics of passing', as discussed in the literature concerning transgender (Hines 2007).

McCall's (2005) term 'intercategorical' concerns the multiple relations of inequality between existing social groups, with the aim of explicating these relations and the ways in which they operate across and within analytical categories. Inequalities are not patterned in a homogenous way, as McCall notes. This section will not look at gender and sexuality, as these have been discussed above; it will focus on:

- Race and ethnicity
- Faith
- Class
- Age
- Ability
- Space

Race and ethnicity

As we have shown above, intersectionality theory stemmed from the work of authors such as Crenshaw (1991, 1997) and Avtar Brah and Ann Phoenix (2004), who were concerned to challenge the exclusion of black women from feminist thought and research. These authors focused on gender and race, overlooking heterosexuality and the experiences of lesbian, bisexual and trans women of colour, although there are some exceptions, including Lisa Bowleg's (2008) discussion of intersectionality and black lesbians, in which she critiques additive notions of inequality. Bowleg's work contributes to the literature about LGBT people of colour (in the UK the term Minority Ethic (ME) LGBT people is used). For example, in the US, Devon Carbido (1999) critiques the way in which the Black Civil Rights movement has tended to ignore the relationship between racism and homophobia, overlooking the experiences of black lesbians, who face both heteronormative Black anti-racist discourse and normatively white gay and lesbian discourse. Kristen Schilt (2006) describes the ways in which US trans men's workplace experiences are structured by race/ethnicity and body structure. This is because tall white FTMs (female-to-males) are more advantaged than short FTMs or FTMs of colour, because they appear to be the sort of man who is generally more privileged in society (white, advantaged because of having a particular sort of body which is ascribed high status) and because of this they can access systems of male privilege more effectively than other trans men.

Accounts of race and sexuality need to include the work of authors who examine the colonial underpinnings of racism, gender and sexuality. These colonial underpinnings are important to our discussion of LGBT equalities because the systems of categorization, and the social inequalities with which they are intrinsically linked, stem from a western colonial past which impacted in various ways in southern, as well as western, countries. For example, Anne McClintock (1995) explores the ways in which imperialism and the invention of 'race' were central to western, industrial modernity; it was within this context that western genders and sexualities, including LGBT and heterosexual categories, developed. It is from this perspective that critiques of universalizing notions of western LGBT rights and associated missionary-style tasks and organizations can be made (Rouhani 2007; see also Hacker 2007). In other words, a number of writers, politicians and activists from southern countries, many of which have experienced colonial rule or invasion by western countries such as the UK and the US, have interpreted the categories of LGBT as being a western thing. In homophobic hands, homosexuality has been labelled as a 'western disease'.

The southern critique of the LGBT equality and rights movement is extremely important internationally. This is because, on the one hand, there is a risk of recolonization and cultural imperialism that is associated with the LGBT movement (western LGBT people thinking that they know what is best for 'less developed' countries, where in fact gender and sexuality categories may be somewhat different in these countries compared to those used in the west). On the other hand, traditionalist patriarchal, and sometimes virulently homophobic, discourses are being used by actors in certain southern regimes to justify human rights abuses against indigenous non-heterosexual and gender variant people, and the suppression of indigenous LGBT-type support groups and activism. For example, David Kato, a Ugandan gay rights activist, was murdered in his home in Kampala, in January 2011, shortly after winning a court victory over a newspaper that called for homosexual (sic) people to be hanged. At the time of writing, Brenda Namigadde, a Ugandan lesbian seeking asylum in Britain, told the *Guardian* (newspaper) 'I'll be tortured or killed if I'm sent back to Uganda. They've put people like me to death there' (Butt 2011: 20). Politicians and religious leaders in Uganda have fuelled homophobic hate crime in Uganda, a country in which homophobia is also common amongst the wider population (Butt 2011).

It is necessary, in developing understandings of LGBT identities and race and ethnicity, to be aware of issues of sexuality and nationalism. In the chapter on Northern Ireland we explore the way in which Irish nationalist discourses have constructed Irish masculinities in a heterosexual manner. Other examples are available in the literature, for instance Laurie Essig, in her exploration of queers in Russia, discusses the ways in which 'nationalism is internationally and intranationally comprehensible because it relies on gender and sexual identities in a myriad of ways' (1999: 123). She describes the links between nationalism and queer identities in Russia. During 1990s public queerness legitimated itself via discourses of nationalism because certain forms of queerness were visible in nationalist rhetoric and imagery, but these were distinct from 'outsider', western forms of LGB identities. In other words, there were tensions existing between the westernizing queers and indigenous forms of queerness. These tensions had practical, material impacts. For example, Essig described how she witnessed US-sponsored organizations running workshops in Moscow and providing resources for people who identified as LGB in a way that excluded people with fluid identities and displayed ignorance of the realities of people's lives – including the real dangers they faced if they came out. These workshops, run by foreigners, exemplified the above-indicated type of difficulties associated with the international LGBT movement. This is because there was a colonizing element (nationals from a better-resourced foreign country coming into a country and imposing certain ways of doing things – indeed, certain ways of identifying – as a prerequisite to getting much-needed funds). As Cvetkovich argues, queer transnational politics are 'freighted by the histories of racism and colonialism' (2003: 13). However, there are also possibilities of resistance and the formation of local countercultures in response to these colonizing forces. For example, queer transnational support networks can foster creative responses to the trauma that can be associated with migration (Cvetkovich 2003: 121). Overall, in addressing LGBT equality in the international context, an understanding of the complex dynamics of postcolonialism, and the problematic imposition of western norms on the southern world, is crucial.

Another aspect of understanding race and sexuality concerns the interrogation of whiteness. This is important in moving discussions away from a focus on people of colour, in a way that might displace attention from the way in which racism and related inequalities are largely constructed by white people. Looking at whiteness displaces the idea that whiteness is 'universal', and anything else is 'marginal'. For example, there has been some work done around whiteness (Teppo 2009; see also White 2007) that looks at the intersections between whiteness, class, poverty and space in the context of a poor suburb in South Africa. Annika Teppo traces the genealogy of 'poor whiteness', so that the poor white populations that were spatially segregated and subject to heavy surveillance under apartheid became increasingly fractured post-apartheid, with different systems of stigmatization and privilege developing, strongly linked to the places of residence of the different ethnic and classed groups in South Africa. Teppo argues that: 'It is high time to start looking at a white identity as something that has many different levels and shades' (2009: 232).

In what ways do race and ethnicity intersect with sexualities and gender diversities? The work of Claire Beckett and Marie Macey (2001) provides a starting point for an examination of race and LGBT identities in the UK. Beckett and Macey note that 'Homophobia, racism and sexism are widespread in the UK and take overt, covert, and institutionalised forms' (2001: 309). They argue that multiculturalism and anti-racism, which support racial and ethnic diversity, have been open to hijacking by macho, quasi-ethnic nationalism, because of a failure to address the intersections of race, class, gender (and sexuality). In other words, there has been a failure to integrate LGBT equalities and anti-racist discourse and politics in the UK. This has meant that sexist and homophobic phenomena, including the violence against lesbians and gay men that is condoned by some minority ethnic groups, have not been sufficiently tackled. Beckett and Macey argue that:

> there are limits to a cultural diversity in democratic societies that seek to extend human rights on an individual basis. For there can be no doubt that some cultural and/or religious traditions are in direct conflict with the long, and ongoing, struggle for justice and equality' (2001: 316).

The intersections between race and ethnicity, and LGBT identities, are demonstrated in a number of UK studies. Mitchell et al. (2008) review the research addressing ethnicity and sexual orientation, and Stonewall (2010) lists research showing that black and ethnic minority LGB people can experience homophobia (and biphobia) within their ethnic communities, and racism from the gay (sic) community. These findings were reflected, to a degree, in the data from the LGBT Equalities in Local Government project. For example, there was some discussion of homophobia within the Caribbean communities and traveller communities (LGBT activist, Southern England) and a Northern Irish project worker discussed racism and xenophobia within the LGB community and homophobia within the local Polish community. However, this worker then went on to discuss strategies for tackling these problems:

> there's definitely a greater role for the council in working with minorities, I'm well aware as well you know we're not the only minority in the city and that there are a lot of commonalities for example on the protocol we would have people from the race group [name of group] people from the Polish association all sitting on the protocol and visa versa there's a racism protocol developed along the same lines and the gay community sit on that protocol so that kind of work is happening at that level, erm, but pretty much driven by the [name of organisation] and the policing partnership which is council run.

More broadly, it is important to point out that whilst racism and xenophobia are very real, ME/LGBT peoples' experiences are also diverse, and that the transnational and ME/LGBT and queer movements are in a process of development. For example, in the UK Stonewall actively supports UK Black Pride (ukblackpride 2010). In the literature, Berry et al. (2003) outline the development of varied public cultures, social and activist groups, newsletters, clubs and internet networks. In fact, aided by the Internet and the new social media, there are indications that international LGBT cultures that supersede national boundaries may to a degree be breaking down the western/southern divide that has been quite apparent in LGBT cultures' as well as the LGBT/queer equalities movements that are developing.

Faith

There is a growing body of literature about the intersections between LGBT identities and faith. In the US, this literature includes the work of authors such as Cynthia Burack and Jyl Josephson (2005), who analyse contrasting anti-gay discourses within the Christian Right. Some of these studies focus on particular parts of the US, notably Angelia Wilson (2000) explores the inter-relations between religion, sexuality and gender in southern US, where 'the proliferation of conservative Christian morality distinguishes the South as the Bible Belt...Southern boys know what it means to be a man and Southern girls know what it is to be a lady (sic)' (2000: 3). Wilson explains the way in which these rigid norms were disrupted by the sexual revolution and the civil rights movement, and that Southern Christian gays and lesbians are developing their own churches and interpretations of Christianity. This 'reclaiming' of religion by LGBT people is mirrored elsewhere, for instance in the US literature about Islam. Farhang Rouhani (2007: 169–70) looks at Al-Fatiha, the most prominent queer Muslim group in the US, and addresses the:

> Complex political processes through which non-heterosexual Muslim immigrant minorities are seeking to form new spaces and spheres of engagement, the challenges and constraints they face, and the possibilities for new assimilationist and radical identity formations...

Rouhani discusses the importance of transnational queer faith networks, the importance of progressive Muslim notions of equality and justice and the support that the international queer Muslim movement provides for the LGBT communities and human rights movements more generally. Scholarship is also emerging from the UK regarding Muslim LGB identities; for example, Momin Rahman (2010) theorizes gay Muslim identities using an intersectional approach. He argues that gay Muslims demonstrate problems with the idea that western and eastern cultures are mutually exclusive and oppositional. Andrew Yip (2004) has also written about British Muslims, criticizing cultural interpretations of same-sex sexualities as a 'western disease' and emphasizing the complexities of negotiating multiple social worlds.

In the US and the UK (as elsewhere), the intersections between faith and LGBT identities are complex. For instance, Jeremy Kidd and Tarynn Witten reported that a survey of US trans elders showed:

> religious beliefs of the respondents differed so dramatically from the normative Judeo-Christian-Islamic belief systems on which conventional psychometric instruments are based that many of the survey respondents had difficulty completing the religiosity/spirituality/faith component of the survey (2008: 29–30).

These non-normative forms of spirituality may have emerged partly because of the influence of trans authors such as Kate Bornstein (1998), who developed alternative worldviews and spiritual practices concerning gender identity. Some of the UK research findings complemented the picture of complexity regarding LGBT and faith/spirituality; for example, one of the bisexual community representatives discussed the wide variety of belief systems within that community, including Atheism, Buddhism, Paganism and Christianity. The complexities concerning faith and non-heterosexual identities are also present in some Southern countries. For instance, Tebogo Nkoana (2008) describes the way in which traditional African notions of spirituality incorporate gender diversity. Tebogo, who was born with a female body, is now a Sangoma (traditional healer) and trans activist.

It is also the case that there are LGBT networks and activists within the major faith groupings in many countries; for example, Gill Valentine et al. have documented the strategies used by pro-LGBT groups at the Anglican Lambeth conference in the UK (Valentine et al. 2010, see also Wilson 2000). Findings from our research project also demonstrated the way in which some LGBT contributors were involved in faith networks. Some of the Welsh LGBT community members were Christian and involved with their churches, with their Christian faith providing a major source of support. However, there was also the sense that the faith/LGBT intersection is quite fraught in the UK. At the local authority level, the existence of religious groups who have 'really solid beliefs that being lesbian and gay is wrong' (Manager, North East England) is used in some cases as a reason for inaction concerning LGBT equalities. Contributors to the research said for example:

> Don't touch sexuality because it might offend people who have strong Christian or Muslim views.
>
> (Local Authority Officer, Northern Ireland)

> I've enough of a problem dealing with bigots in my faith community, let alone having to deal with the bigots in the gay community.
>
> (Representative of LGBT Muslim Organisation)

> I think sexual orientation is a particularly thorny one for some people or a difficult one for some people to come to terms with . . . and anything that sort of deviates from that, you know, white middle class conservative sort of upbringing, Christian upbringing, albeit it's more an agnostic position on faith I would suggest, but it's anything that deviates from that I think is frowned upon.
>
> (Transgender Community Representative, Southern England)

The tensions around faith and sexuality were managed in some local authorities by people of different faiths and sexual orientations maintaining boundaries, not forcing their views on each other, and referring to professional norms and duties, and hence LGBT equalities work was framed as part of their professional duties regardless of private belief. The example of LGBT work in local authorities illustrates how intersectionality concerning faith and sexual and gender diversity can work out in real life. Of course, every location will have a different set of dynamics, and we have aimed to provide a snapshot of some of these dynamics in this section.

Class

Socio-economic inequalities are constructed in different ways in different countries, making it hard to generalize about class and sexual and gender diversity. In the US, for instance, the distinction between supposedly 'deserving and undeserving' poor people is racialized in a particular way (White 2007) that is different from that in other countries such as the UK or South Africa. Class remains a powerful primary structuring force in the UK, with persistent occupational and spatial divisions, and it continues to be a predictor of health and life chances. For example, Yvette Taylor examines the experiences of working-class lesbians in Scotland, looking at the way in which access to LGB and queer social spaces is impeded for some working-class lesbians due to a lack of material, cultural and social capital (resources), so that 'queerness may in fact only be accessible to those materially poised to occupy the position' (Taylor 2007: 13). The classed nature of LGBT social spaces is linked with globalized capitalism, and hence those LGBT people who have money are welcomed, whereas others are excluded. This is a trend that is apparent internationally, because of the way in which 'gay scenes' have sprung up in major cities. Access to these LGBT-friendly spaces is affected by the amount of financial and social resources (capital) that LGBT people have, and hence privilege intersects with class differences (Bell and Binnie 2004).

Class and material inequalities were evident in some of the research findings. For example, a representative of a national bisexual activist network discussed the way that the LGBT acronym is dominated by white, middle-class gay men. Other contributors discussed the way in which classed inequalities combined with other forms of inequality such as age, space and health; for example, an impoverished trans woman in a rural location was unable to access any of the trans networks or statutory support systems that would be otherwise available. There was also considerable discussion of the difficulties with finding resources for LGBT community groups and activism. There was also some discussion of the way that not all LGBT people want to take part in the commercialized gay scene. This discussion mirrors Taylor's discussion about ambivalence in the classed nature of lesbian identities; some working-class lesbians positively identified with their own, working-class localities. This cultural affiliation is of course not the same as wanting to be economically marginalized or socially excluded.

Age

LGBT people who are either young or those who are older than average face specific issues which may be less relevant to heterosexual young adults and middle aged people. This section of the chapter looks firstly at young LGBT people (LGBT identities and childhood are outside the scope of this book) and then at older LGBT people. Young people's experiences may be shaped by the many youth scenes and hybridized cultures, particularly given the growth of the Internet and social media, which can be used to bridge across dominant and subordinate social spaces at local, national and international levels (see Nilan and Feixa 2006). However, youth and the intersection with LGB identities can also involve experiences of rigid sex segregation in schools (Gagen 2000), homophobic bullying (Guasp 2007), or the material experiences of being young, and poor, and unable to access LGBT networks because of a lack of transport or access to technology. It may be difficult to find a gay scene; for example, in our UK study, a Local Authority Officer in Wales described the town he worked in as 'rough in terms of, you can get beaten up and there isn't really a gay scene here, for young people to be part of the sort of drinking culture, you know, it's not seen as particularly safe'. One of the young gay men who contributed to our study said that:

> One of the real problems where bullying can come from, within education especially, if it's not discussed in classrooms or anything else, outside of that, 'cause I had some major problems when I was there, with, and shortly after I'd come out round here, somebody from round here gave me a death threat.

LGBT young people do have specific vulnerabilities, because of their social position, and in particular when they experience marginalizing intersections, for example 'areas where young transgender people may face increased risk – if there is familial or economic marginalisation – include vulnerability to exploitation as sex workers, homelessness, and violence' (Monro 2006a: 314).

In terms of older age, it is important to note that 'gay men and lesbians have confronted a special challenge posed by the tumultuous sexual identity politics and related political events of the late 1960s and early 1970s' (Rosenfeld 2003: 160). This section outlines some of the ways in which older age intersects with LGBT identities, using literature drawn primarily from the US. It is worth pointing out however that experience of aging varies enormously by country and by race. For example, Helena Thornton and colleagues note that the life expectancy of a black South African female is 55 years, as opposed to that of a white female which is 77 years, and that the racialized class differences that were forged under colonialism and apartheid have affected the wealth accumulation of the elderly (2009). These inequalities fundamentally structure older LGBT people's lives in South Africa, probably overriding other characteristics such as sexual orientation, especially when people are black and poor.

There is a substantial US-based literature on LGBT and aging. This flags up a number of issues, including:

■ The generic erasure of older people's sexuality, which obviously impacts on LGBT people as well as heterosexuals (Kimmel et al. 2006).

■ The impact of bodily changes such as the menopause (again, this impacts on women more generally).

■ The effect of the historically specific experiences of stigmatization, which mean that the generation of LGBT people who are currently older have learnt to hide their identities in order to avoid discrimination.

■ A lack of visibility amongst older LGBT people (S. Butler 2004).

■ 'The unique concerns of older gays and lesbians challenge existing service delivery models, and prejudice and discrimination among service providers can create barriers to receiving quality care' (Anetzberger et al. 2004: 23).

■ The need for service providers to be aware of non-normative forms of spirituality amongst the trans (and perhaps also LGB) populations, especially when providing end of life care (Kidd and Witten 2008).

The literature suggests that being older and LGBT may be challenging in various countries and contexts, for example a study of US LGBT elders demonstrated issues of estrangement from families, isolation and childlessness (Rosenfeld 2003). Mark Casey (2007) in his discussion of the structuring of urban gay space in the UK suggests that youth is one of the markers of acceptability within this commercialized space, and that older LGBT people may be excluded. Thornton et al. (2009), reporting research findings from residents of old age homes in South Africa, describe homophobia within some of the homes, and the difficulties that same-sex partners may face when dealing with the death of a spouse as well as the hurdles they face when looking for a new partner, including ageism from within the lesbian [and gay and bisexual] community.

However, some authors suggest considerable diversity amongst older LGBT people (Cronin and King 2010). Georgia Anetzberger et al. (2004) argue that the US research suggests that older gay men and lesbians are living successful lives and that they may develop specific skills, such as the ability to foster support networks. LGBT older people may also develop positive attributes as a result of their experiences as LGBT, including a greater capacity than heterosexuals to adapt and to manage social perceptions of 'difference' (S. Butler 2004). There are of course variations across the LGBT communities regarding age; for example, whilst many older bisexual women continued to identify as bisexual, there was a tendency towards monogamous relationships with either a woman or a man, for reasons such as decreasing opportunities to find same-sex partners, pressures to fit into heterosexual culture and the desire for a simpler life – and some bisexual women decreased their involvement with the bisexual community over time due to the life changes associated with monogamous partnership (Garnet and Peplau 2006). Recent scholarship about LGB people and aging suggests that there is a need to go beyond focusing on this diversity, to address the multiplicity of identities indicated by intersectionality theory (Cronin and King 2010).

Ability

There has recently been an expansion of the literature and the concepts that are available to help us understand ability, disability and sexuality. The same is less true of gender variance and ability/disability, although there are conceptual overlaps (Parkes et al. 2006), and in the US there are discussions about pursuing protection for trans people via disability laws. This chapter aims to outline developments in disability and sexuality studies, which are clearly of relevance to intersectionality studies. It does not address the various issues that people with different forms of disability face; interested readers can refer, for example, to the works of authors who look at psychiatric disabilities (for example Cook 2000) and learning disabilities (Lofgren-Martenson 2009).

Michael Rembis (2010) provides a current overview of the development of the social model of disability and the field of disability sexuality studies. He starts by discussing the way in which the medical model of disability 'consider [s] disabled people to be not only broken or damaged, but also incompetent, impotent, undesirable, or asexual' (Rembis 2010: 51). Following Butler, he then traces the ways in which gender, sexuality and ability are inextricably intertwined, and 'embedded in systems of compulsory, yet unattainable, "heterosexuality" and "ablebodiedness"' (Rembis 2010: 52). Rembis discusses the social model of disability and its challenges to the socially dominant ableist (meaning prejudice by able-bodied people) assumptions about sexuality. He outlines the ways in which the social model of disability has been used both to interrogate the different forms of discrimination that some disabled people face and to highlight the sexual pleasures and satisfactions that increasing numbers of disabled people experience. He notes that lesbians, bisexuals and gay men are amongst the groups most marginalized in the literature and in terms of lived experience. Although some early attempts were made to map possible alliances between disabled and lesbian and gay people in the UK using the social model (see Corbett 1994), overall the subfield of the social models of disability was imbued with heterosexism, and:

> much of the social research on disabled sexuality and many of the pronouncements of disabled subjects, both of which have been concerned with 'defying sex/gender stereotypes' and challenging powerful cultural myths concerning disabled people, have served to reinforce, rather than challenge the heterosexual matrix.
>
> (Rembis 2010: 54)

Queer approaches to disability studies, including the work of Dominique Davies (2000) and Tom Shakespeare et al. (1996) in the UK, and Robert McRuer (2006) and Michael Rembis (2010) in the US, map out approaches that go beyond medical and social models of disability. These emphasize:

- Developing notions of crip theory. Crip theory is a form of theory which critiques ableist and heterosexual models of sexuality, and the ways in which these shape and constrain sexuality (see, for example, McRuer 2006).

■ Destabilizing binaries between able and disabled, developing new – more fluid and diverse – discourses of sexuality and gender, and reclaiming dis/abled bodies (McRuer 2006).

■ The use of counterdiscourses, and coalition politics, as a means of challenging the normative values and erotophobia that affect oppressed groups (Wilkerson 2002).

In the UK, approaches that can be related to queer and crip theory are evident in some of the LGBT communities, although as pointed out above there is also a trend towards certain people (those who are able bodied, young and perceived to be attractive) being valued more highly than others (Casey 2007). Martin Mitchell et al. (2008) review a number of studies about UK disabled LGB people indicating that people in this group experience discrimination both from heterosexual people and within the LGB community. Some communities do however welcome difference concerning ability, including the sections of the transgender (see Box 2.1).

Box 2.1 Case study: Inclusivity of disability in transgender communities

Interviewee 2: I mean we do, one of the people who came to the weekend (–)

Interviewee 1: Was disabled.

Interviewee 2: Disabled.

Interviewee 1: But she just mixed with (–)

Interviewee 2: She needed a couple of sticks and things (–)

Interviewer: Yeah.

Interviewee 2: It's just a case of sort of thinking, 'Right, she said she was disabled', we made sure she had a ground floor room when she stayed overnight, and when we came in, we said, 'Would you prefer . . .', 'cause she's got like a little wheelie thing that she pulls her luggage around and sat in sometimes, we said 'Would you prefer us to move the chair so you can sit up?', and she said, 'Oh no, I'm happy on a chair', it's just, and another group that we belong to, it's a nationwide group for transgender Christians, and one of the girls that comes to that is in a motorized wheelchair (Transgender Community Members, Wales).

Overall, there have been developments in both scholarship about LGB (and to a lesser extent T) people and disability, and within the communities themselves in the UK. The development of queer crip politics has enabled the heterosexism of both mainstream and social models of disability to be criticized. It has also formed a basis for ableism (prejudice against disabled people and assumptions regarding able-bodiedness) to be challenged within the LGBT communities, and in some parts of these communities there is in any case an emphasis on diversity and inclusion. However, ableism is still apparent within sections of the LGBT communities, as part of the hierarchical intersectional structuring that positions some LGBT people as more 'desirable' and hence more privileged than others.

Space

There has been a considerable amount of scholarship about the geographies of sexuality, the trajectory of which is well rehearsed (see, for example, Phillips et al. 2000; Wilson 2000; Collins 2004; Browne et al. 2007). The role of space in structuring LGB peoples' lives was strongly evident in the UK research findings. The findings substantiated the assertion that 'sexuality – its regulation, norms, institutions, pleasures and desires – cannot be understood without understanding the spaces through which it is constituted, practised, and lived' (Browne et al. 2007: 4).

Our research findings showed a tendency for LGBT communities, and local authority LGBT equalities initiatives, to be concentrated in urban areas, with further differentiations being apparent across various cities. Although there is clear evidence for the spatial structuring of prejudice in rural areas and small towns, and for the operation of heterosexist regulatory and normative forces, it is important to point out that there were also some counter-indications. As one UK infrastructure representative said: 'you cannot assume that people will be narrow-minded, some are welcoming to everyone'. The findings indicated that there is a paradox concerning communities that are perhaps rather parochial, but are also experienced as a source of support for those (LGBT) people who are part of them. A number of contributors discussed the way that local communities included their local lesbian and gay people in the everyday affairs of the community, although this inclusion appeared dependent on keeping their sexual identities fairly closeted. For example, one contributor mentioned the 'lesbian aunties' who lived in one village and were generally liked.

The research findings indicated the importance of the social and cultural patterning of different spaces in shaping LGB peoples' lives. Prejudice against LGB people appeared to be heightened in rural or small town localities, with a number of contributors making comparisons between these localities and large cities, where there is more diversity generally, a finding which reflects the work of queer geographers such as Jon Binnie (2004). For example, there was a considerable amount of evidence for overt homophobia in rural and small town Wales, including hate crime (see Chapter 6). For instance, a community member said that the first stall ever dealing with LGB issues at a national Welsh cultural event was smeared with excrement. A number of contributors to the research discussed the way in which the geographical dispersal of people, into small, close-knit communities, means that people know each other's business, and that there is a strong sense of community support, but often a concurrent lack of understanding of diversity.

These findings complement the assertions of authors such as Gill Valentine, who, in her case study of a deaf lesbian's life, discusses the way that dominant groups construct and occupy specific spaces (home, work, the community) such that 'they develop hegemonic cultures through which power operates to systematically define ways of being, and to mark out those who are in place and out of place' (2007: 18). It appears that in rural and small town Wales, heteronormative cultures predominate, strongly shaping and constraining sexual identities in intersection with spatial forces. Such power dynamics were apparent in the small town setting in which the case study authority was located. Prejudice was structured in particular ways in this locality, with homophobic violence and displays of machismo serving to performatively shape heteronormative space (see Brown et al. 2007). Perceived effeminacy and gay masculinities were utilized in marginalizing ways, as demonstrated by a gay community member who described the locality as:

> an old mining community, where men have got to be men, you have got to act in a certain way, its abnormal to say you're gay; masculinity means strong, heterosexual, you know, going through the so-called norms of life, getting married, working hard, be a family.

Overall, space forms an important factor in the way that LGBT people's lives are structured, both within countries and internationally. Whilst there appears to be a tendency for rural areas in countries such as the UK to be more homophobic, there are also counter-tendencies towards the inclusion and tolerance of people whose ties to their neighbours are based on characteristics other than being LGBT.

This chapter has provided an overview of the complex ways in which LGBT people's identities are constructed. It has examined the complexities within the term LGBT, and the ways in which LGBT identities are crosscut by a variety of other social characteristics.

Summary

- There are differences between the groups within the LGBT acronym, including prejudice amongst some people towards other (for example gay men being misogynist, gays and lesbians being biphobic or transphobic). There are also alliances across the groups.
- LGBT people do of course exercise agency in the ways they manage intersectional disadvantage, as well as advantage.
- The structuring effects of race, ethnicity and nationality; these are extremely important in terms of understanding the contextualized nature

of LGBT people's lives and the impact that other, possibly overriding structural, inequalities may have.

- Faith: this overlaps with race, ethnicity and nationality in many ways, but is worth addressing specifically both because of the importance of faith-based prejudice in impeding LGBT equalities and because of the myriad ways in which LGBT people of faith are exercising agency in their interpretations of faith and religion.
- Socio-economic class dynamics play out in varied ways across different countries. In the UK class forms a major (possibly overarching in many cases) structuring factor, and hence LGBT people of less privileged classes have different choices and life chances compared to those of wealthier and better-resourced classes.
- Age: life expectancy varies considerably both across and within countries, forming a major structuring force affecting LGBT people. The chapter looks at some of the challenges and opportunities associated with younger and older LGBT people in a number of countries.
- Ability: Recent years have seen the development of social models of LGBT ability and disability, the emergence of crip theory, and a robust critique of normative assumptions concerning disability and sexuality.
- Space: There has been a substantial amount of scholarship in countries such as the UK and the US concerning LGBT identities and space, including rural/urban divides. Clearly discussions about space overlap with other discussions about race and ethnicity, nationalism and class.

In the following chapter we consider a key aspect of recent struggles for LGBT rights, the 'turn to citizenship'.

Sexuality and Citizenship

3

This chapter examines the relationship between sexuality and citizenship. The term citizenship can be used in a variety of ways that have different implications for how we understand in/equality. This is the focus of the first section of the chapter, which looks at different ways of thinking about citizenship, highlighting how, in addition to being informed by ideas about gender, race and class, understandings of citizenship are grounded in normative assumptions about sexuality. Typically, heterosexuality is constructed as a necessary if not sufficient basis for full citizenship. In this sense one can think about citizenship as a sexualized concept, as others have analysed how citizenship is both gendered and racialized. The next section addresses the development of a specific notion of sexual or intimate citizenship, and goes on to consider the limits to its conceptual and political utility. Finally, the last section looks at the processes by which LGBT people are constructed as 'ordinary citizens' and considers some of the broader implications of lesbian and gay 'normalization'.

This chapter focuses on lesbian and gay citizenship, although it does include some discussion of bisexuality and transgender citizenship in the section on sexuality, citizenship and diversity. The issues facing bisexual and trans people are somewhat different compared to those facing lesbians and gay men, which make it difficult to address LGBT citizenships comprehensively in one chapter. Moreover, little theoretical attention has been given to bisexuality and its relationship to citizenship (Evans 1993), although notions of trans citizenship have been developed more recently (see, for example, Monro and Warren 2004; Monro 2005, 2011; Hines 2007, 2009). The chapter uses the acronym LGBT here as elsewhere in the book, but it is recognized that there are substantial gaps regarding discussion about trans and bi citizenship.

The discussion is situated in the context of social and legislative changes that have taken place within western democracies over the last decade or so, and have extended citizenship rights to LGBT people. These are, however, global issues and debates and in recognizing this illustrative case studies from the global south are included, which have to date been marginalized in the literature. In terms of its broader relevance it is also important to point out that although the focus of the chapter is on sexuality and citizenship, it addresses themes that cut across citizenship studies more broadly, including understandings of the public and the private, universalism and differentiation, processes of normalization and the disciplinary requirements of citizenship.

Understanding citizenship

What is citizenship? Citizenship, like sexuality, is a contested concept, which means that it can be understood in a variety of different ways. Traditionally, within liberalism, the term citizenship has been understood in relation to the rights and responsibilities of citizens within a given nation-state. In the classic liberal model, citizenship is constituted in universalistic terms. The other traditional model of citizenship has been characterized as the 'town hall' model, which emphasizes the participation of citizens in civil society, and is linked to communitarianism (which emphasizes the responsibility of the individual to the political community) and republicanism (where, in a 'republic', the head of state is not a monarch). In contrast to the traditional liberal conception of citizens as autonomous individuals who make choices, advocates of civic republicanism see citizenship as communal, where citizens are people whose lives are interlinked through shared traditions and understandings that form the basis for the pursuit of the 'common good' (Delanty 2000).

Historically, the work of T.H. Marshall (1950), a British sociologist, has been very important in the developments of understandings of citizenship. Marshall defined citizenship in terms of three stages of sets of rights: civil or legal rights, political rights and social rights. Civil or legal rights are institutionalized through the law and include things such as the right to own property; freedom of speech, thought and faith; liberty of the person and the right to justice. Political rights are institutionalized in parliamentary political systems and councils of local government and include the right to vote and participate in the exercise of political power. Social rights include the right to a certain level of economic welfare and security as well as rights that are institutionalized in the welfare state, for example unemployment benefits, and provision for health and education.

Since the 1990s debates over the inadequacies of these two traditional models have led to the development of new ideas about citizenship. These include broader considerations of belonging and associated practices of citizenship, that go beyond rights-based understandings. Definitions of citizenship as national identity, for instance, have increasingly been brought into question in the face of social and political changes that have challenged traditional boundaries of nation-states on a global scale (Turner 1993; O'Byrne 2003). This has prompted debate about the need to think about citizenship developing within the context of larger forms of social membership than nation-states.

There are already shifts towards 'rights being linked to the status of human beings (human rights), rather than citizens of the state' (Pakulski 1997: 84; McLaughlin et al. 2011). Associated with these developments is the emergence of new scales of citizenship, such as the concept of cosmopolitan and global citizenship (Dower 2003).

This broadening out of understandings of citizenship is also seen in the development of new areas of citizenship. As well as the traditional contexts of law, politics and welfare, it has been suggested that a cultural dimension to citizenship should be included. These debates about cultural citizenship examine the idea of cultural rights and obligations as a new set of citizenship practices, in particular within the context of the globalization of the cultural industries and new forms of mass communication and information technology (Stevenson 2001, 2003; Miller 2007). This notion of cultural citizenship is distinct from that developed by Renato Rosaldo (1994), who defined it in terms of the demands and claims of immigrant or minority groups for full citizenship in spite of their cultural difference from mainstream society. Finally, there has also been a move in recent years towards defining citizenship in terms of consumerism, where the focus is on the rights of citizens as consumers of goods, commodities and services (Evans 1993; Daunton and Hilton 2001; Soper and Trentmann 2007). Here one might think about the presumed economic worth of different social groups in relation to citizenship.

In addition to the expansion of the idea of citizenship evidenced in the diversity of arenas in which citizenship is being claimed and contested, new understandings have also developed out of critiques of the concept of citizenship itself. That is, rather than merely contesting the range and locus of citizenship, some argue for a much more fundamental revisioning of the very construction of citizenship. In particular, highlighting how it is encoded with meanings that produce exclusions which can reinforce and sustain inequalities. For example, the Marshallian view of citizenship has been critiqued for being too simplistic both in its focus on class, to the detriment of considering other forms of inequality, and in terms of a chronological determinacy in seeing rights evolve in a particular set order (Walby 1997; Plummer 2003). Feminist writers among others have addressed these concerns pointing out that access to citizenship is a highly gendered process and that, despite claims to universality, a particular version of the normal citizen/subject is encoded in dominant discourses of citizenship. Historically, citizenship has been constructed in the 'male image' (Pateman 1988; Lister 2003). Traditional accounts of citizenship have also been much criticized, again often by feminist writers, for neglecting to consider how ideas of citizenship are connected to race and ethnicity, as well as gender (Yuval-Davis 1997; Glenn 2002; Fredrickson 2003). Within schemes of racial difference, 'whiteness' has been the symbol of 'ideal legal and moral citizenship' (Ong 1996: 742). A further aspect of this process of re-thinking citizenship is the question of how notions of citizenship are grounded in normative assumptions about sexuality.

Sexuality and citizenship

Chapter 1 highlighted how the language of citizenship has in recent years become the dominantspeak of lesbian and gay activism and political claims for 'equal rights' on a global level. These developments, alongside the wider attention given to the concept of citizenship more generally within social and political theory, have prompted a new literature, emerging in the 1990s, linking 'citizenship discourse and "sexualities" discourse' (Wilson 2009: 74). The relationship between sexuality and citizenship, and the construction of concepts of sexual and intimate citizenship, has subsequently become an important theme across a number of disciplines (see, for example, Evans 1993; Cooper 1995; Berlant 1997; Weeks 1998; Bell and Binnie 2000; Phelan 2001; Plummer 2003; Carver and Mottier 1998 (2005); Cossman 2007). Within this body of work it is possible to identify a number of strands that draw on different epistemological concerns. Some, for instance, have focused on the question of what is meant by sexual rights and responsibilities, including research on the welfare of lesbian and gay citizens (Kaplan 1997; Richardson 2000b; Wilson 2007). One of the main strands running through this literature, however, is how claims to citizenship are constituted through specific sexual norms and practices. Specifically, it has been argued by a number of writers that hegemonic forms of heterosexuality underpin the construction of the 'normal citizen' and that, related to this, heterosexuality is a necessary if not sufficient basis for full citizenship (Phelan 1995; Richardson 1998; Bell and Binnie 2000; Cossman 2007). Moreover, it is important to recognize that this is a dynamic process: such constructions of citizenship both reflect *and* reproduce the privileging of heterosexuality (Richardson 2000c).

In response some writers have contested this link between heterosexuality and citizenship. Bryan Turner, for example, has emphasized parenthood rather than heterosexuality as the defining characteristic of the 'normal citizen' and as the basis for social entitlement, raising the question of whether it is more useful to think about *reproductive* citizenship than sexual or intimate citizenship (Turner 1999, 2008; E.H. Richardson and Turner 2001).

Is Turner right? Consider, for example, the extent of social resistance to lesbian and gay marriages and, more especially, of lesbian and gay parenting. What does this tell us? In some countries where domestic partnerships between lesbians or between gay men have been legally recognized one of the limits to gaining access to such forms of citizenship status has been a restriction on parenting rights. In Scandinavia, for example, registration of partnership legislation at first denied same-sex couples the right to adopt children. We also need to consider gender and it relation to reproductive citizenship. Traditionally, women's citizenship has been linked to motherhood in the context of heterosexual marriage (Lister 2003). Lesbians therefore occupy a complicated relationship to citizenship, one that reveals the intersections between gender, sexuality and citizenship in ways that are different from those for gay men (Ryan-Flood 2009). Nor was it clear in our research on LGBT equalities in the UK that parenting was key to the 'making' of lesbians and gay men as 'normal citizens'. Despite the passing in 2002 of the Adoption and Fostering Act, giving lesbians and gay men the right to legally adopt and foster, this was seen as one of the most contentious areas of LGBT equalities work. One Equality and Diversity Officer in the South of England talked about this as one of the 'aspects that people find more extreme and people aren't ready for', in contrast to what they saw as 'a middle ground that a lot of people would buy into and fully support'. They went on to say:

> Our leaders, and this is going back a few years, made statements that we weren't going to allow lesbian and gay people to be foster carers or adopters, and that had to be retracted … and I know that for a lot of people it is a really difficult issue, isn't it. It's been highlighted recently by this case where the grandparents were looking after their grandchildren and the daughter died and now the children are not going to stay with their grandparents, they are going to be placed with a gay couple.
>
> (Manager, Southern England)

Where grandparents are increasingly taking a significant role in informal childcare in the context of the rolling back of welfare and economic austerity measures we could read this as part of a wider debate about rights in relation to child care and institutional claims for grandparent citizenship. However, in one or two cases it was difficult to interpret the views expressed as anything other than discriminatory towards gay parenting. For instance, a councillor with responsibility for equalities work had this to say:

> Being a grandparent and knowing exactly what I think of my grandchildren and how I would love and care for them, to have them taken away and then, you know much worse in my view, to hear of them in the care of a gay couple, is really sad. I don't think that can be condoned.
>
> (Councillor, Southern England)

As more countries extend parenting rights to lesbians and gay men it will be possible to address in more detail the relationship *between* parenthood and heterosexuality, and the significance of this for understanding the construction of citizenship. The question is whether individuals become 'good citizens' simply by fulfilling their obligations to society in being (re)productive and shouldering the burden of raising children, or whether this is influenced by how they become parents and in what relational contexts? In other words, it is important to analytically separate parenthood from a married or marital style relationship, *and* a specifically heterosexual context, as the norm for 'good reproductive citizenship'.

Transforming citizenship?

One of us, Richardson (1998, 2000a), has detailed how the (hetero)sexualization of citizenship can be evidenced across different notions of citizenship: as a set of civil, political and social rights, as social membership of a nation-state and also belonging conceptualized more broadly, as cultural rights and in terms of consumerism. Demonstrating, in each case, how lesbians and gay men are only partial citizens in so far as they are excluded from certain aspects of these forms of citizenship. More than a decade later do the same arguments still apply? Certainly, given recent and increasingly global lesbian and gay human rights recognition, we are now at a point where the argument that the normal citizen has largely been constituted as heterosexual would appear to be queried. This is prompted not only by social changes that have led to new forms of citizenship status for (some) lesbians and gay men, but also by the emergence of a new citizenship discourse that asserts the 'normality' of being lesbian and gay (Seidman 2002). Indeed, as outlined in Chapter 1, it is primarily through such claims to normalcy that social integration is justified.

Jeffrey Weeks argues that this 'moment of citizenship' is also a 'moment of transformation', where 'to claim full citizenship for dissident sexual minorities is to argue for the transformation of the concept' (Weeks 2000: 191). But is it? What is and is not transformed or reformulated in the extension of certain rights of citizenship to lesbians and gay men? Can this moment of citizenship happen without contesting the norms and conventions of 'good citizenship'? One might agree with those who argue that there has been some loosening of the compulsory status of heterosexuality (if not heteronormative practices) as a condition of institutional belonging (see, for example, Seidman 2009). This is evidenced through a move towards cultural normalization and social integration of lesbians and gay men in the UK and elsewhere in Europe, Canada, Australia and the US. However, although the heterosexual requirement for certain rights may have been displaced, heterosexuality has not been displaced as the reference point for 'equality' and 'normality'. In other words, while certain forms of citizenship status may have been extended to lesbian and gay people, citizenship is still largely constituted in terms of particular forms of (hetero)sexual relations as the yardstick for recognition.

At the same time it is important to recognize that the consequences of lesbian and gay 'normalization' may be uneven, and we should be careful to collapse analysis into a simple dichotomy of assimilation versus contestation across all sites and locations of citizenship, or even within one particular rights issue (Richardson 2004: 522). In our study on the implementation of sexualities and trans equalities policies the primary focus was on legislative and policy changes: civic inclusion and civil rights. There was, however, recognition on the part of those who took part of increased cultural visibility and recognition of LGBT issues and people, greater access to cultural citizenship in other words, which was seen by many as a driver of LGBT equalities more broadly. As one person commented:

Yeah, I think it's probably, to a degree it has been, erm, and I wonder maybe that's why there's not been the sort of resistance that I've been aware of to, you know, the LBGT issues, in that we had things...we'd had those basics already in policy, and of course you see it's far more mundane, it's far more everyday to see portrayals of different sexualities on the television.

(Local Authority Officer, Wales)

Jan Pakulski (1997) has analysed cultural citizenship in terms of full inclusion in culture. Cultural rights, he argues, represent a new set of claims including the right to symbolic presence and visibility (versus marginalization); the right to dignifying representation (versus stigmatization); and the right to propagation of identity and maintenance of lifestyles (versus assimilation). It is this last point in particular that prompts questions over the limits to these wider cultural changes in everyday life. Whilst lesbians and gay men (and to a lesser extent bisexual and trans people) are more culturally visible and in less stigmatized ways, following Pakulski's argument heterosexual privilege may still be at work in access to cultural citizenship if the forms of representation tend to be assimilationist rather than portraying sexual and gender diversity. This is the critical distinction between toleration or acceptance of difference and an appreciation and valuing of difference.

Finally, in terms of political citizenship although LGBT people are a part of the electorate, their ability to influence political space has in the past been delimited (Riggle and Tadlock 1999). For example, being 'out' as lesbian or gay has historically been seen as a disadvantage or even a disqualifier for political office (Rayside 1998). This is an under-researched area, however a recent research report on barriers to participation in public life for LGBT people in the UK found that a key issue was the complex feelings, attitudes and experiences associated with being 'visible', including fears for safety (Ryrie et al. 2010) (see also the Equality and Human Rights Commission report on *Pathways to Politics* by Durose et al. 2011). In addition, as previous studies have found (Cooper 2004; Monro 2006b), political parties have typically distanced themselves from advocacy for LGBT equality. This is also manifest in political leadership as Lewis (2005), for example, demonstrates in his analysis of the issue of same-sex marriage in the context of the 2004 presidential election in the US (see Chapter 4 for further discussion).

Although there appears to be a lessening of the view that problem of LGBT equalities is politically damaging, it was still apparent in our research findings. One councillor remarked: 'We're not going to go there because it could have serious repercussions when it comes to seeking election next time (laughs)'. A more benign view, perhaps, is that even if LGBT equality is not perceived as a 'vote loser' it is unlikely to be seen as a 'vote winner'. This too can close down political space. For instance, the following contributor, who was himself an elected member, touches on this when he states that it is rare for people to raise LGBT issues during political canvassing:

I can't ever remember in the years of politicking that people feel that there are issues around sexual orientation within the LGBT community which are important enough for people to raise on the doorstep, and we don't particularly feel that we need to raise them. We just feel that if there is acceptance, then that's the grounds for moving opinion on to the next stage.

(Councillor, North East England)

To go back then to the original question: Do the same arguments about the (hetero)sexualization of citizenship still apply after a decade of social and legislative change in advancing LGBT equalities? For the reasons outlined, it is clear that in many parts of the world there has been some loosening of the compulsory status of heterosexuality in terms of cultural citizenship, as well as in the classic Marshallian rights-based model. However, what is also clear is that this 'loosening' is uneven across different areas of citizenship and rights demands. Despite the successes claimed inequalities remain and the 'heterosexual assumption' continues to underpin key areas of citizenship, especially aspects of cultural and political citizenship.

Sexual and intimate citizenship

The second main strand that runs through the literature on sexuality and citizenship is the articulation of a notion of 'sexual citizenship' or, as some prefer, 'intimate citizenship'. The public/private distinction has been central to how sexuality and citizenship have been defined as belonging to the private and the public spheres, respectively. There might therefore appear to be a certain conceptual tension in bringing together sexuality and citizenship. However, the division between what are understood as the public and the private spheres has been the focus of a great deal of debate, much of it pointing to how it is a socially produced binary and, in many ways, a false distinction. Our 'private' and 'intimate' lives may often be talked about as if they were outwith the public, the social and the political, but in fact they are deeply connected to and regulated by public discourses and social institutions. Nor can we speak about citizenship only by reference to public spheres. It is claimed that a shift is taking place in the locus of citizenship, as increasingly people's everyday 'private' practices are becoming the bases for discussing citizenship (Richardson 2000c). This is one aspect of what some have referred to as the *personalization* (Brown 2006) and *privatization* of citizenship (Phelan 2001; Phillips 2006). This can be seen, for example, in debates over 'healthier citizenship', where in addition to smoking and patterns of eating and drinking, 'private' and intimate (safer) sexual practices are also part of how healthy citizenship is constituted. In recognizing that the 'personal and the public cannot be so readily split up' (Plummer 2003: 69), it is possible to open up conceptual space to think about sexual and intimate citizenship.

One of the first to engage in debates about sexual citizenship was David Evans (1993). In his book of that name, Evans conceives sexual citizenship as materially constructed through the dynamics of capitalism; particularly through consumerism and the growing commodification of sexualities. This is a concept of sexual citizenship understood as involving 'partial, private and primarily leisure and lifestyle membership' (Evans 1993: 64). The sexual citizen here is the consumer citizen, where sexual citizenship rights are expressed primarily through 'participation in commercial "private" territories' (Evans 1993: 64). This has prompted debate over whom such sexual citizenship includes and, importantly, does not include (Bell and Binnie 2000; Badgett 2001), especially in the context of classed assumptions about lesbians but more especially gay men as having plenty of pink pounds at their disposal. Here, it is a person's economic worth that demonstrates their potential as good (consumer) citizens.

This construction of lesbians and gay men as relatively 'well off' was one that was voiced by several contributors in our study (see also the previous chapter for a discussion of class and material inequalities). As can be seen from the following quotes, one of the concerns this raises is how such assumptions may work to shape views about rights to citizenship in a much broader sense than those of the consumer-citizen.

> We know that people are discriminated against because of the colour of their skin, 'Look we can see this, this, this and this', we know people can be discriminated against because of having, you know, because of having different abilities, 'Look they can't access this building, they can't participate in this meeting because the BSL [British Sign Language] is their first language, not English', but do they see people as being discriminated against in the same way because of their sexual orientation, I don't know whether they do . . . And when you have, as well, media images which show a lot of, you know, certainly gay and bisexual people as being affluent, money-earning, successful . . .
>
> (Local Authority Officer, Wales)

As noted earlier, some writers have chosen to use the term intimate rather than sexual citizenship. Applied to intimacies, the term citizenship allows consideration of a broader array of arenas of personal life than merely what are designated as 'sexual' rights and obligations, for example, in terms of patterns of care, forms of violence, reproductive practices and different kinds of intimate relationships. One of the first to elaborate an idea of intimate citizenship was Plummer. In his work, Plummer examines the transformations taking place in the realm of our intimate lives and considers the implications this has for understanding what it is to be a citizen through the idea of 'intimate citizenship'. This he defines loosely as a cluster of emerging concerns over the rights to choose what we do with our bodies, our feelings, our identities, our relationships, our genders, our eroticisms and our representations (Plummer 1995: 17). Intimate citizenship, he argues, looks at:

... the decisions people have to make over *the control (or not) over* one's body, feelings, relationships, *access (or not) to* representations, relationships, public spaces, etc.; and *socially grounded choices (or not) about* identities, gender experiences, erotic experiences. It does not imply one model, one pattern or one way.

(Plummer 2003: 14, original emphasis)

In this sense intimate citizenship can be understood as both political and social status and as constituted through everyday practices (see, for example, Olesky (2009) documenting ways of' 'practicing' intimate citizenship).

Sexuality, citizenship and diversity

Differentiated forms of sexual citizenship?

Paralleling debates in citizenship studies more generally is the focus on the question of whether to theorize sexual citizenship in terms of a universalistic notion of 'the sexual citizen' or through a differentiated or particularist model which would allow for a specific notion of, say, lesbian citizenship, gay citizenship, bisexual citizenship and so on. So far, this chapter has taken a somewhat particularist approach in its focus on lesbian and gay citizenship, but particularist approaches could include, for instance, discussion of trans citizenship, highlighting how gender is (re)constructed through practices of citizenship and addressing the rights claims of trans people. Other particularist approaches have looked at how citizenship norms are constructed through specific forms of gendered embodiment through a focus on intersex citizenship (Grabham 2007).

One argument for a differentiated approach is that key issues of trans people are different from those of LGB people, although as was discussed in Chapter 1, there has been a broad shift towards placing them together in the acronym LGBT (or LGBTQI). There is broad consensus amongst members of the trans community and elsewhere that trans concerns gender rather than sexuality, although fetishistic cross-dressing is an exception to this (Monro 2005). Of course some members of the trans community identify as LGB, but others identify as heterosexual. Early authors working in the field of sexual citizenship, particularly Evans (1993) and Plummer (1995), addressed some forms of trans, and their work was used by subsequent authors looking specifically at developing trans citizenship (Monro and Warren 2004; Monro 2005, 2011; Aizura 2006; Hines 2007, 2009). Other authors such as Whittle (2002), Currah et al. (2006) and Whittle et al. (2007) have also provided important contributions, which focus on the legal and social discrimination experienced by trans people and means of gaining citizenship rights.

There is little discussion within the literature of bisexual citizenship (for a notable exception, see Evans 1993), although it is worth noting the overlap between LG and B citizenships where, for example, bisexual people are in long-term same-sex relationships and will both support and access relevant rights. Monro (2005) began to lay the foundations for developing a western notion of bisexual citizenship, arguing that:

> Bisexual citizenship can be seen to be unique because bisexual identities are different from lesbian, gay, and heterosexual identities in a number of ways. Bisexuality typically includes the experience of fluid and multiple desires. Some bisexual people are attracted to people on the basis of characteristics other than sex, others desire men, women and others simultaneously, others shift in cycles between desire for women and men. Bisexuality is subjectively different from monosexuality [same-sex or opposite-sex desire, which is the norm for lesbians, gay men and heterosexuals].
>
> (Monro 2005: 155–6)

Western models of bisexual citizenship come with the caveat that in countries – or localized communities – where homosexuality is illegal or heavily sanctioned, people's methods of managing their sexualities are likely to be very different. Rather than seeking recognition for their sexual identities via citizenship claims, bisexuals (and indeed lesbians and gay men) may opt for staying in the closet and surviving, placing their sexualities firmly in the private sphere.

Bisexual citizenship revolves around the following issues:

■ Recognition of a bisexual identity.
■ Support for full equality for people in same-sex relationships (a goal which is of course shared with lesbians and gay men).
■ Acceptance that desire can be fluid, which entails support for lesbian and gay rights but also an understanding that sexuality can be changeable and that people with more fluid or complex identities also require citizenship rights.
■ Recognition of the identity challenges that bisexual people face (given dominant binary sexuality/gender systems of the west).
■ Statutory and other change to support social recognition of polyamorous arrangements.

A differentiated universalism?

As was discussed in Chapter 1, the framing of LGBT politics that is increasingly dominant in numerous national settings is in terms of human rights discourse (Kollman and Waites 2009), grounded in the liberal democratic tradition with its universalist rhetoric (Brown 2006; Phillips 2006), as opposed to the kind of particularist stances described above where specific identities are used as a basis for rights claims. Drawing on such discourses would imply the adoption of a universalistic rather than a differentiated model of sexual citizenship, as is illustrated by both the adoption of the umbrella term LGBT and the emphasis in LGBT claims for equality on being 'ordinary citizens' the same as anyone else.

A sexuality-neutral (echoes here of the discussion on diversity neutral) rather than sexually-differentiated model of sexual citizenship is also evident within the literature. For example, Weeks (1998) refers to 'the sexual citizen' in his discussion of shifting understandings and social 'transformations' in intimate life. According to Weeks (1998: 35) the sexual citizen:

> ... could be male or female, young or old, black or white, rich or poor, straight or gay: could be anyone, in fact, but for one characteristic. The sexual citizen exists – or, perhaps better, wants to come into being – because of the new primacy given to sexual subjectivity in the contemporary world.

However, despite his very inclusive definition of 'the sexual citizen', Weeks is alert to issues of diversity. He argues for a 'differentiated universalism', rather than any simple binary characterization of the universal versus the particular, echoing much of the feminist literature on the relationship between gender and concepts of citizenship (Lister 2003). For example, Monro's (2007a) discussion of trans citizenship and feminism addresses the univeralist-differentiated debate in some depth, arguing that a combination of both approaches is necessary.

In these debates we see once again the issue raised in Chapter 1 of an apparent tension in the policy of 'Equality and Diversity': of arguing simultaneously for a neoliberal concept of universal equality *and* the recognition of difference. Thus, for example, Weeks talks about the importance of 'balancing the claims of different communities with constructing new common purposes' and of 'learning to live with diversity at the same time as building our common humanity' (Weeks 1998: 49). This idea of a 'common humanity' that binds us together beyond the kinds of particularisms grounded in, for instance, sexuality, gender, religion or race is often linked to cosmopolitanism (Fine 2007; Held 2010). Although it was not articulated in these terms, the idea of an interconnectedness of citizens was apparent in the research findings. For instance, a number of participants referred to recent legislative and policy developments in relation to sexual orientation and gender assignment in terms suggestive of a notion of the 'common good'.

> This is a message for us folks and getting to understand that homophobia isn't, you know, addressing it and correcting it isn't an issue for the gay community, it's an issue for the others, you know, for once you're the others, and it is an issue for everybody really, it's about what kind of world you want to be in, you know.
>
> (Manager, Wales)

And if people are being harmed, within the whole community that affects everybody, even if people aren't aware of it.

(LGBT Community Representative, Southern England)

As the literature on sexuality and citizenship continues to grow, with varying readings of the relationships between these terms, it is perhaps unsurprising that a number of critiques have emerged over the conceptual meaning and utility of the terms sexual and intimate citizenship. The following section considers some of these.

Limits to sexual citizenship

What are the limits to, and limitations of, sexual citizenship? One can think about this question in a number of different ways, and at different levels and scales. This section will focus on three distinct albeit connected levels: conceptual, political and, briefly, in terms of the implementation of LGBT equalities.

Some conceptual issues

One aspect of critiques over the conceptual meaning and use of the term sexual citizenship is a contestation of the locus of sexual citizenship. For some, as was discussed in the previous section, this has led to a broadening out of the concept through notions of 'the intimate' rather than only 'the sexual'. Others, however, are concerned that whether articulated as intimate or sexual citizenship the emphasis remains on personal life which, although arguably it need not be so, risks leading to a (re)privatization of sexual citizenship. Following this argument over the construction of sexual citizenship as located in 'the private', various writers have focused on the meaning of sexual citizenship in *public* spheres which, for some, also incorporates a concern to give greater consideration to sexual practices (see, for example, Bell and Binnie 2000; Hubbard 2001).

A growing number of writers have raised concerns not only over the use of specific meanings, but also over the conceptual utility of sexual citizenship. This includes asking questions about whom it includes (and excludes), which can be read as both a limit to and a conceptual limitation of, sexual citizenship. This has already been mentioned in relation to class and material inequalities within LGBT communities (though we can also consider this in relation to other intersecting social divisions). Indeed, the concept of sexual citizenship as currently imagined may have less purchase in looking at lower income societies and groups, especially where basic legal, political and/or welfare rights have not yet been attained. We might, then, ask: Is sexual citizenship a distinctly western concept? However, we need to recognize that 'the West' is itself a problematic term, especially when used in relation to rights claims in relation to sexual orientation. Plummer rightly recognizes this point, drawing attention to how ideas of sexual and intimate citizenship with their predominant emphasis on the *right to choose* – your partner; whether to marry or not; to have gender reassignment surgery; have a child or not; your sexual activities – need to be situated as emerging from debates within particular socio-economic and geo-political contexts. For many people, women in particular, in many parts of the world these are unintelligible as 'choices'. Indeed, in many countries the injustices carried out against sexual and gender minorities are seen as 'morally justified' rather than as forms of inequality. As he states in his own words:

> Once low income societies and the poor of rich societies are brought into the picture the concept of intimate citizenship starts to demand further clarification. Looking at issues of abject poverty, forced marriages, sexual slavery, the commodification of bodies etc, intimate citizenship takes on wider meanings. For here are people who often have little control over their bodies, feelings, relationships; little access to representations, relationships, public spaces etc; and few socially grounded choices about identities, gender experiences, erotic experiences.
>
> (Plummer 2005: 25)

This does not necessarily mean abandoning the notion of sexual or intimate citizenship as a 'luxury' concept. What it does mean, however, is that there is a need to develop conceptual understandings beyond what has so far been an emphasis upon a 'politics of choice', detailing what both enables and constrains how people experience intimate lives across different societies and different groups within these.

Research in Nepal on the livelihood opportunities for women post trafficking, examining how these are shaped by cultural norms around gender and sexuality and the models of citizenship operating, brings this into sharp relief (see Box 3.1). Similar issues are also highlighted in a consideration of the case of LGBT citizenship in South Africa (see Box 4.1).

Box 3.1   Sexual and gendered citizenship: Focus on Nepal

After a decade of civil war Nepal is undergoing political transformation by restructuring the nation and re-drafting the constitution through a Constituent Assembly process. Associated with this is a re-definition of citizenship rights, where it is hoped that an established gender bias in accessing citizenship will be overturned (Laurie et al. 2011). Nepalis must apply for a citizenship certificate when they reach 16 years of age. However, historically the right to citizenship was passed through the paternal line, and is linked to particular forms of kinship. Since 1963, women have been unable to apply for citizenship without the support of a male relative, typically a woman's father or husband. Once she has married a woman has been 'given away' and it is only through the endorsement of her husband or male relatives in his family that she can obtain citizenship. This has huge implications for women who are perceived as a 'shame' to their family and are rejected by them, or who are married to husbands who are unwilling to support them. Not having a citizenship card severely limits women's livelihood options. They and any children they have may have difficulty accessing government services, health and education, skills training and waged employment.

The interim Constitution of 2007 proposes two models of citizenship: by descent and naturalized. In both cases there is evidence of gender discrimination in the conditions for gaining citizenship. To obtain citizenship by descent the Constitution recommends that any person whose father and mother is a citizen of Nepal shall be a citizen of Nepal. This may seem like progress in the sense that not only fathers but mothers will be able to endorse the right of citizenship to their children. However, this recommendation will still deprive citizenship to a person born to a Nepali mother who is a citizen but where the identity of the father is unknown or he is absent, highlighting the continued importance of fatherhood in conferring the right to citizenship. Also, this is a model of citizenship that continues to be based on forms of kinship, as distinct to the state conferring citizenship on the basis of a person being born in Nepal (One of the problems of implementing a state-sanctioned model if it were to become law would be the question of 'proof', given that many people lack birth certificates and relevant documentation to establish the country of their birth.)

Gendered models of citizenship are further evident in the proposed conditions for naturalized citizenship. For example, if a foreign (male) national marries a Nepali woman and renounces the citizenship of his country, he is eligible to be a naturalized citizen but only after living in Nepal for 15 years. However, a foreign woman married to a Nepali man can acquire naturalized citizenship immediately providing she renounces the citizenship of her country of origin. These decisions have been criticized for discriminating against women and for creating a situation of statelessness for many Nepali women who remain 'non-citizens' in their own country (Pant and Standing 2011).

Normative assumptions about acceptable and appropriate sexuality, constituted through marriage and motherhood, intersect with these gendered models of citizenship. For some women such as trafficked women, widows, single and childless women, and lesbians, sexual stigma can make becoming a citizen difficult. For returnee trafficked women in particular the stigma and rejection they experience from their families and villages means they frequently lack the support of a father or husband and therefore are unable to obtain formal citizenship status. However, while representing one of the most stigmatized, excluded and vulnerable groups in Nepal, returnee trafficked women are beginning to organize around rights to sustainable livelihoods, where citizenship is seen as the key mechanism for establishing new forms of belonging (Richardson et al. 2009). Some anti-trafficking organizations, such as Shakti Samuha an organization formed and run by returnee women themselves, have also campaigned for citizenship to be granted based on being born in Nepal, without parental endorsement being required.

LGBT citizenship in Nepal, as shown in Box 3.1, can be usefully compared with LGBT citizenship in South Africa, outlined in Box 3.2, given that both have implemented new constitutions that bear on the making of new forms of citizenship (adopted by the Constitutional Assembly in South Africa in 1996 and more recently in Nepal in 2011).

Box 3.2   LGBT citizenship: Focus on South Africa

Gender and sexuality were rigidly demarcated in apartheid-era South Africa, and some 'homosexual' acts were criminalized. However, during the run-up to the transition to democracy in 1994 there was a concerted and effective anti-sexist movement, which succeeded in embedding gender equality within the new South African Constitution and the state machinery (see Goetz and Hassim 2003; Hassim 2006). As was mentioned in Chapter 1, there was also activism regarding gay and lesbian rights, and the new Constitution made South Africa the first country in the world to constitutionally guarantee non-discrimination on the grounds of sexual orientation (Gunkel 2010). As Vasu Reddy says, 'the context of post-apartheid South Africa demonstrates a radical departure from criminalization of sex acts to recognition of identities' (2009: 342). This recognition of lesbian and gay identities has come about not just through the Constitution, but through a range of subsequent developments in case law which decriminalize same-sex sexualities and which support lesbian and gay people's rights. These include the landmark judgment in the case of *Fourie v Minister of Home Affairs* by the Supreme Court of appeal in November 2004 (Reddy 2009: 342–3), which means in practice that same-sex marriages can now be legally recognized. This shift includes redress of discrimination against gays and lesbians in the military, bringing lesbian and gay citizenship into line with the broader, seismic, citizenship-related shifts concerning South African national identity. South African authors such as Reddy (2009) have analysed lesbian and gay citizenship in a similar way to some western authors, unpicking the links between the institution of marriage and patriarchy, analysing the arguments against same-sex marriage, and pointing to the way in which marriage rights help to normalize lesbian and gay identities within broader society. It is noticeable that 'gay' and 'lesbian' rights are emphasized in such discussions, with little mention of bisexual or trans people's citizenships. However, the broader LGBT movements and scenes in South Africa, which (as in western countries and elsewhere) are focused in urban areas, are more inclusive (see Spruill 2004).

To summarize, South African LGBT people have gained substantial citizenship rights. However, there are serious problems with homophobic hate crime in South Africa, which sit in stark contrast to the progressive legislation and case law. Intersectionality concerning race and sexuality is also important in understanding LGBT citizenship in South Africa, because of the intertwined nature of gender, sexuality and ethnicity (Swarr 2004). The legacy of apartheid also provokes intersectional analysis; authors such as Gunkel (2010) document the racial segregation of gay cultures in South Africa. Partial racial segregation was noticeable to one of us (Monro) when attending Pride in Cape Town in 2008 and engaging in informal research concerning the LGBT 'scene' in South Africa. Such systems of segregation reflect broader inequalities (in South Africa and elsewhere), underlining the need for intersectional analysis to be brought to sexual and trans citizenship studies.

Some political issues

Of course the conceptual limitations of, and limits to, sexual citizenship are at the one and the same time political issues. Theoretical frameworks shape the ways in which issues of equality and citizenship rights are addressed (or not as the case may be), as was discussed in Chapter 1 in relation to understandings of what 'makes' someone gay and 'strategic essentialism'. Equally, as Wilson (2009) observes, political activism can drive forward social and political theory, in this case commentary prompted by the deployment of human rights and citizenship discourses within LGBT politics. In this respect, Wilson urges caution in what she sees as conceptual developments arising out of the 'fashionable' use of citizenship and 'human rights' in the field of sexual politics, especially uses of the term sexual citizenship that fail to recognize power dynamics involved in articulating specific claims for rights and the conferring of citizenship by the state. This goes to the heart of a number of questions about the theorizing of LGBT politics. It may be 'in the name of equality' that rights claims are being made and new forms of citizenship status – to a certain extent and for some more than others – have been 'won' (Weeks 2008a). However, just because such approaches 'play well politically' and have moved LGBT claims into the mainstream does not mean that we do not need to consider the political utility of developing a conceptual (and political) language of sexual citizenship. We do. Otherwise there is a real danger of framing the political successes that have ensued as somehow 'the end game'. We need to ask: What are the limits of this 'turn to citizenship' in LGBT politics? What are the restrictions and exclusions of contemporary forms and practices of citizenship? Is this equality? Is it a valuing of diversity? Is it enough? And is it, in any case, sexual citizenship?

The answers to these questions are complex and may play out differently in different societies. In asking 'Is this equality' it is clear that there are continuing inequalities. A good illustration of this is where laws have been implemented that legitimize same-sex couples through civil unions or 'registered partnerships', but the institution of marriage continues to be defined as a specifically heterosexual privilege as it does, at the time of writing, in the UK and in most of the US. In Europe, only in the Netherlands is same-sex marriage fully recognized. The sanctioning of a two-tier system is significant not only in terms of civil rights, in relation to whether or not LGBT people have 'formal equality' with heterosexuals, but also in terms of cultural citizenship, specifically the limitations to recognition arising from cultural norms that privilege heterosexuality and reinforce discriminatory practices and beliefs towards sexual and gender minorities. For example, as Stevi Jackson and Sue Scott (2010: 74) point out, the granting of citizenship to sexual minorities and greater public recognition of sexual diversity exists 'alongside continued homophobic harassment, bullying and violence in schools, workplaces and on the streets'. A recent report entitled *Beyond Tolerance* from the EHRC (2009) echoes this, highlighting how despite the progress made over the last 40 years LGB people still experience entrenched discrimination. This was also apparent in the findings from our study, where various participants made the point that although sexual orientation and transgender were now included as equality strands, there were still important limits to citizenship in terms of delivering equality. For instance, as one participant remarked:

> LGBT equality is becoming more accepted and understood, but at the same time there are still quite a lot of people who don't understand why we're doing it or have the attitude of 'It's OK, so long as you don't kiss in front of me, or shove it in my face', who don't see equality as actual equality.
>
> (Stakeholder, Wales)

We can also consider the question 'Is it equality?' in terms of broader policy trends towards LGBT inclusion, by thinking about how such developments might be productive of new exclusions as well as belongings. That is, how new forms of lesbian and gay citizenship status are associated with 'citizenship requirements', which can serve as a means for establishing new boundaries in relation to sexuality, ones which are constitutive of 'other' sexualities that can be figured as problematic and in need of control (Seidman 2002). This is one aspect of what might be referred to as the 'costs of recognition' (McLaughlin et al. 2011), where assumptions about what constitutes 'good citizenship' are part and parcel of the disciplinary requirements of citizenship. For instance, according to some, this new 'othering' might include women and men who form intimate associations and family relationships that are not based on traditional gender and familial norms (Smith 1994; Phelan 2001; Richardson 2004). As well as 'gay marriage' and civil partnerships, some have suggested that access to parenting rights may divide lesbians and gay men as 'respectable' normative LGBT citizens (Lewin 1993; Barker 2006). A view that would appear to be sympathetic to the arguments, discussed earlier, regarding the centrality of parenthood in defining citizenship status rather than heterosexuality *per se*.

What this discussion highlights is that practices of citizenship are associated with both inclusion *and* exclusion, and that the costs of recognition as well as the benefits may be uneven across diverse groupings. Taylor, for instance, considers the significance of class as well as gender to these new forms of sexual citizenship that have been rendered possible through state recognition (Taylor 2009, 2011; see also Browne 2011). In a similar vein, Priya Kandaswamy (2008), in a US context, draws attention to the differential benefits of rights enabled through same-sex marriage within a welfare state that is racially stratified. It is, then, important to acknowledge how discourses of equality may not only conceal continuing inequalities, but also produce new ones.

Secondly, and connected to this last point, one might ask: Is it enough? The answer to this question, of course, is that it depends on what you wanted in the first place. Where the emphasis in political rhetoric is less about the pursuit of 'formal equality' and rights of citizenship and more about transforming the heteropatriarchal organization of society, the answer is surely a resounding no. This applies to the sexual politics of earlier gay liberation and lesbian/feminist movements in the 1960s and 70s, discussed in Chapter 1. But it is an answer that also rings true for some contemporary critiques, in particular by feminist and queer writers who have problematized the 'turn to citizenship' in LGBT politics as a narrowing of political space that fails to adequately address wider issues of social justice. They ask, can the concept of citizenship encompass the transformations that feminist and queer politics seek (Lustiger-Thaler et al. 2011). At the same time, it is important to acknowledge the need to be careful in talking about going 'beyond citizenship' given that in parts of the world many people, women in particular, are still 'non-citizens', and basic legal, political and/or welfare rights have not yet been attained (Laurie et al. 2011).

Finally, is it sexual citizenship? The relationship between sexual citizenship and the 'desexing' of lesbian and gay equality described in Chapter 1 is an interesting one. In one sense, surveying the kind of legislative and policy developments that have occurred on a global scale over the past two decades, it clearly *is* about sexuality. This is evident in terms of both the distinct areas of concern and resistance to rights claims that frequently arise (see Chapter 6), and in so far as it is primarily through assumed *sexual* coupledom that a normalized lesbian/gay citizenship status is achieved. But in other respects you might well be forgiven for asking, is it about sexuality? As was discussed in Chapter 1, the dominant framing of extending equal rights to LGBT people is as human rights rather than sexual or trans rights: rights conferred as individuals rather than collective rights as lesbian, gay, bisexual or trans. In conjunction with the emphasis on 'sameness' with heterosexuals and the (re)privatizing of sexuality that Warner (1999) claims is part and parcel of state recognition of lesbian and gay rights, this works to decrease the association of sexuality and citizenship and delimit the sexual in sexual politics. Indeed, as Davina Cooper has similarly argued:

> ... the project of lesbian and gay inclusivity forged an equivocal relationship to sex. In seeking to treat sexual orientation as analogous to gender and race, the specific relationship to sex came to be both denied and disavowed. Who one had sex with might determine one's sexual orientation, and hence one's needs and vulnerability but, once determined, sex had no further part or place.
>
> (Cooper 2006: 940–1)

Some implementation issues

The distinction between having certain rights of citizenship and being able to realize these is an important one to make. A person may have rights but whether or not they are able to access such rights is a different matter. This was clear in our findings. There was a clear sense from the research that as a result of the legal drivers and associated monitoring by performance assessments within local government, there has been significant progress in building the importance and language of LGBT equalities. However, the sexual cultures of the local authorities researched varied widely, from authorities where the words lesbian and gay were 'taboo' and bisexuality (and to some extent trans also) was completely 'off the radar', to those where more LGBT positive contexts were being established. This goes back to some of the issues raised in the previous section. There may be a variety of limits on materializing citizenship: both material and subjective. For instance, the following quote highlights how processes of social exclusion can operate even where rights of citizenship have been established.

> Because, there is the whole political thing about 'We don't want gay people to be given importance, because then they're real people', almost ... So if we can't build trust with gay people, if we can't inform gay people that they are citizens, if they don't feel as if they are citizens, they won't become citizens.
>
> (LGBT Community Representative, Southern England)

Issues of implementation are considered in more detail in Chapters 5 and 6, and they look at organizational change and resistance to change, respectively. The following section goes on to examine what this quote also draws attention to: citizenship as a process of identity-making and the formation of new subjectivities. That is citizenship as determined by both the state and its subjects; citizenship as a process of self-making and being made as citizens. Highlighting, in other words, how extending citizenship not only involves the 'making' of LGBT rights, but also the 'making' of LGBT people as 'ordinary' citizens.

Desiring 'ordinariness': Constituting LGBT citizenship

As was discussed in Chapter 1, the history of sexuality reveals the many and various ways in which 'homosexuality' was defined as inferior, abnormal, unequal and subordinate to heterosexuality. It is perhaps then understandable why lesbians and gay men might come to desire 'ordinariness', or at least desire to be understood as 'normal', in claiming equality with heterosexuals. Being ordinary in this sense is about wanting to belong to a wider imagined community of citizens. This is supported by recent studies that demonstrate a desire among some lesbians and gay men to name themselves and their relationships as ordinary (Taylor 2009; Coleman-Fountain 2011). However, in addition to seeing this as a rejection of 'outsider status', there may be other reasons why people might desire ordinariness. For instance, Weeks sees the appeal of ordinariness as a desire for validation not absorption, and a demonstration of a commitment to the 'ordinary virtues of care, love, mutual responsibility' (Weeks 2008a). Indeed he states that 'We should never underestimate the importance of being ordinary. It has helped transform the LGBT and the wider world' (Weeks 2008b: 792). The desire to be seen as an 'ordinary' person can also be understood in terms of a claim for individuality. Previously LGBT people were typically viewed as one-dimensional, their sexual and gender difference constituting them: to be 'a homosexual' was to be nothing but 'a homosexual'. Ordinariness in this sense can be seen as a desire for 'difference' to be incidental, one aspect of a person's life and identity, allowing LGBT people to be seen in terms of individualized personhood (Coleman-Fountain 2011).

The process of constructing normative understandings of LGBT rights and LGBT citizens raises issues about the conditionality of citizenship alluded to earlier. As Janice McLaughlin et al. (2011: 1) point out:

> ... the mechanisms and institutional responses to recognition appear to be producing new or altered forms of 'conditionality' within rights and citizenship. By that we mean that groups and individuals need to 'prove' that they should be recognised by the state in certain ways in order to claim resources and legitimacy.

This process of 'proof making' is an important aspect of what is meant by 'normalization'. Within traditional models of normalization this process is explained in terms of reducing or eradicating forms of 'difference' that are ascribed to people which render them devalued citizens. Discussing immigration, some have argued that in the first stage of citizenship the immigrant does not become, for example, British or American, rather they cease to be a 'foreigner' (see Ong 1996). One can think about this in relation to sexual citizenship also, in terms of LGBT people becoming less 'foreign' or what Phelan (2001) refers to as 'sexual strangers'. For instance, a common stereotype of 'the homosexual' in the past was as the 'enemy within', threatening social stability and traditional moral values (Blasius and Phelan 1997; Epstein 1999; Weeks 2009). One way this has been resisted, as discussed in Chapter 1, is to contest the meaning of lesbian and gay as political identities critical of and opposed to mainstream society, emphasizing instead similarity and commonality with heterosexuals and with mainstream cultural norms and values. A further site of contestation is the historical construction of homosexuality, but more especially male homosexuality, as an intensely sexualized category. In contrast to the conduct-based rights claims of earlier political campaigns, which focused primarily on the rights of same sex (male) consenting adults to engage in sex in 'private', since the 1990s there has been a gradual move towards focusing on identity and relationship based rights claims (Richardson 2000b). Warner (1999) claims that this represents a process of 'purification' or 'gentrification' via a decoupling of homosexuality and sex, which he sees as central to the process of gay normalization. If this is the case, then it would suggest that what is occurring is a re-evaluation of the meanings attached to 'being gay', as this is increasingly constructed as a social rather than a sexual identity.

The process of becoming intelligible as 'ordinary' is not only about eradicating 'differences', it is also about 'proving' ordinariness through claims to sameness. What are the cultural values and norms through which rights claims through 'sameness' are asserted and the attribution of being normal 'ordinary' citizens may be achieved? What are the markers of 'ordinariness'? What practices are cultural signifiers of 'normality'? In addition to participation in the market (Chasin 2000; Bell and Binnie 2002), a key site for the operation of these normalizing processes is same-sex marriage and/or civil partnership recognition (Seidman 2002). The normal lesbian/gay citizen, it is argued, is in the process of being materialized primarily through an adherence to dominant intimate norms coded as heterosexual and monogamous. It is 'the couple', within a particular domesticated setting, that has become the rights-bearing subject of lesbian and gay claims to citizenship. It is important to note, however, that there is a residual tension in establishing ordinariness and normality in this way, as it is primarily through (presumed) *sexual* coupledom that a normalized lesbian/gay status is achieved. It is, then, a certain kind of citizen subject that is both mobilized as politically legible through specific forms of intimate practices and relationships and, some would argue, is *brought into being* by these politics. What is highlighted here is the relationship between subjectivity and politics. One could argue that identities are not created through political activism rather they are its basis, which are then consolidated by struggles for recognition. A different view, one that Moya Lloyd (2005), for example, advances, is that subjectivities are an effect of politics rather than simply the source. What this suggests is that these recent claims to citizenship are productive, as well as reflective, of lesbian and gay subjects. In other words through constituting lesbian and gay citizenship we are also constituting what it means to be lesbian and gay. This is what is meant by citizenship as subjectivity, where in addition to change at the level of social institutions and cultural practices we can also think about change at the level of notions of self.

Duggan (2002), in her analysis, terms this the 'new homonormativity' which '.... does not contest dominant heteronormative assumptions and institutions but upholds and sustains them, while promising the possibility of a demobilised gay constituency and a privatised, depoliticised gay culture anchored in domesticity and consumption' (Duggan 2002: 50). This notion has been very influential in the literature; however, it deserves more critical analysis. For example, it would seem important to distinguish a lack of political critique from positively desiring and enacting forms of 'homonormative' practices. In other words, one might ask does it necessarily follow that by not contesting certain assumptions and institutions one is upholding those same assumptions and institutions simply by omission of critiques of them? Or, does upholding require certain practices of identification with certain assumptions and institutions? This seems an important distinction to make, in particular in relation to ongoing debates over the effects of LGBT normalization and the relative extent of the diffusion of neoliberal governance into LGBT lives.

Duggan, in her analysis, argues we need to understand what she identifies as (homo) normative processes through an analysis of the relationship between various forms of neoliberal governance and the politics of sexuality. The dominance in much of the world of neoliberal models of governmentality places emphasis upon individual freedom and rights, and the importance of self-surveillance and regulation over direct state control and intervention. Central to neoliberal modes of governance is normalization, the means by which norms of behaviour are identified, encouraged and (re)produced within populations.

This is the process of establishing the normative standards of 'good citizenship', in particular through shared family and market values. The primary goal is to establish the self-regulating citizen, who has internalized the norms and goals of government to decrease the burden on society and claims on the state through self-reliance and self-discipline (Lupton 1999; Rose 2001). This neoliberal model of citizenship seeks to enable people to make responsible choices in their lives in terms of how they think and behave, in ways that are considered normal and desirable for society and 'the common good'. This is what is meant by the term 'responsibilised citizens' (Rose 1999).

Arguably, lesbian and gay politics in prioritizing civil recognition of domestic partnerships and a desire for recognition by the state are drawing on what the state also desires in the form of state-sanctioned and regulated desires. This is the self-regulating homosexual subject who chooses stable co-habiting relationships. This aspect of the contemporary sexual citizenship agenda has been subject to considerable critical debate (Hull 2006; Meeks and Stein 2012; Rimmerman and Wilcox 2007; Weeks 2008a; Badgett 2010). However, what is of relevance to the discussion here is that there would appear to be a new partnership at work between activists and policymakers, in sharing common goals and political language. Indeed, in the context of a neoliberalism's policy agenda for 'rolling back' the state it is possible to see how governments might well be motivated to introduce civil recognition of lesbian and gay relationships insofar as these are seen as a form of private welfare, providing economic interdependency and support. In this respect, one might argue that there is a convergence occurring between contemporary lesbian and gay politics and neoliberal state practices (Cooper 2002; Richardson 2005; Smith 2005).

Having said this, it is important to recognize that under the rubric of 'normalization' there are a range of approaches and viewpoints which may reflect different levels of engagement with neoliberal agendas. For some, a shared language may be strategic – a means to a political end; whereas for others, there is a shared commitment to a politics of normalization. What is significant in the adoption of such measures is the way in which they are presented by neoliberal governments as supportive of the choosing responsibilized lesbian/gay subject, who is demanding the right to make lifestyle choices that are approved of as 'low risk' to society (Nussbaum 1999). Through such neoliberal techniques of governance, the promotion of lesbian and gay rights can appear to be necessary and benign. Another way of interpreting such policy shifts, however, is that they represent a new form of social regulation as well as recognition of lesbian and gay subjectivities by neoliberal nation-states that aim to 'domesticate' and defuse any *presumed* threat to social order (Phelan 2001). Or, to put it a different way, seeking equal recognition as citizens is also about governance. Governance on two different levels: governance of the self and governance of sexual relationships by the state.

In considering the consequences of lesbian/gay 'normalization' it is important not to collapse analysis into a dichotomy between the 'old' homosexual (especially male) subject as in need of external regulation and control, and the newly emergent self-regulated neoliberal lesbian/gay subject who has internalized new norms of responsibilized sexual identity and practice. Arguably, it is a condition of their social oppression that lesbians and gay men have long been self-reflexive, self-regulating subjects. The realities of living lives in 'the closet', a 'life shaping' social pattern that involves episodes of passing and coming out (Seidman 2002), both necessitate and shape a self-monitoring self. However, what is significant is that there may be a shift from a 'policing of the self' because of fears of violence and shame, to a desire for normativity and respectability. Lesbians and gay men were previously constrained by representations of themselves as mad, bad or sad; it would seem that now they are being shaped through normative constructions of responsible and respectable sexual citizenship.

Summary

- Citizenship is a contested concept; it has a number of different meanings.
- Historically the 'normal' citizen has been constructed as male and heterosexual.
- There has been a considerable amount of work concerning lesbian and gay citizenship and much less about bi and trans citizenship.
- Practices of citizenship are associated with both inclusion and exclusion. This means that policy trends towards – in this case – LGBT inclusion might also lead to new exclusions as well as new forms of belonging.
- In addition to producing new forms of exclusion, certain discourses of equality may conceal continuing inequalities, for example framing LGBT people as having all the same interests in relation to citizenship erases the specificities of bisexual identities and the key concerns that trans people have with gender issues.
- In recent years a new concept of sexual or intimate citizenship has emerged.
- There are debates over universalist versus differentiated models of sexual citizenship.
- Critiques of sexual citizenship focus on its political and conceptual limitations.
- Citizenship is not only about rights but also about the formation of new subjectivities.
- The 'making' of lesbians and gay men as 'ordinary citizens' is an example of this, and it takes place through processes of normalization.

Democracy

'Equality', 'democracy' and 'human rights' are concepts that are tied together in western popular consciousness. The concept of equality underpins democracy; 'its basic premise is the idea of equal human worth or dignity, and its core value is that of human self-determination or autonomy' (Beetham 1999: 7). Movements supporting the equality of LGBT people have emerged in a wide range of countries, but they have their origins in the liberal democracies of the west, notably the US and western European countries such as the UK. The development of scholarship about LGBT equalities and politics (including electoral politics, state machinery (organizations and structures), and the interface between pressure groups and the state) has varied internationally. There have been a number of important contributions, particularly from political scientists in the US and Canada (for example Phelan 1989, Blasius 2001, Currah et al. 2006, M. Smith 2008) and to a lesser extent in Europe (Bristow and Wilson 1993, Carver and Mottier 1998). Sociological approaches, for instance Mohmin Rahman's (2000) contribution, have been more evident in the UK, where mainstream and feminist political scientists have largely overlooked LGBT issues. There have been a number of studies of LGBT social movements and democracy across the world, including for example Steven Brown's (2002) work on the LGBT movement in Argentina. As Brown states, there are now formal lesbian and gay, or LGBT, activist organizations in many developing countries as well as in the US and western Europe. Sonia Correa and her colleagues (2008), building on earlier work by Rosalind Petchesky (2000), discuss the way in which sexuality is 'the new kid on the block' with regard to human rights debates internationally; the same could be said to be true overall regarding LGBT issues and debates concerning democracy. Bisexual and to an extent transgender people are barely visible within the literature that exists on democracy and sexual/gender minorities (with exceptions such as Whittle's (2002) and Currah et al.'s (2006) rights-focused work on transgender). This raises concerns that these literatures could be discursively reinforcing the erasure or marginalization of these groups, and that bisexual and trans issues are being overlooked.

This chapter will focus on LGBT people and democracy, including democratic systems as a whole and also in some cases their component institutions.

Democratic states have different structures which all involve the separation of state powers to ensure that no one part of the state has overall control. Typically, there is an executive (the branch of government with responsibility for implementing state powers), legislature (deliberative assembly, for example Congress or Parliament, where legislation is debated) and judiciary (the courts and related institutions, where legislation is tested and enforced). The chapter will address the executive, the legislature and related institutions, and the processes by which LGBT citizens (and their allies and opponents) influence the democratic process. It will look at both democratic processes (such as elections) and outcomes (such as same-sex couples having the same rights as heterosexual couples) (see Riggle and Tadlock 1999). Whilst not focusing on feminist analysis of democracy *per se*, we would like to acknowledge here the contribution of feminists such as Nancy Fraser, whose work has been important in understanding the way in which LGBT claims for social recognition plays out against the egalitarian liberal emphasis on redistribution (see Fraser 2003, Chapter 2). In addition, women organizing via democratic processes at a national and international level have had a significant impact on democratic agendas (Gould 2004; Lloyd 2005).

The chapter begins by providing an overview and discussion of LGBT issues and democracy in an international context, including case vignettes from South Africa and the US. The chapter will then move on to a more in-depth case study of LGBT equalities and democracy in the UK, drawing on empirical material about LGBT equalities in local government. This latter section will focus on two important forms of democracy, as these were particularly evident in the research findings: *participative democracy,* which involves people getting engaged in political and policy processes (for example campaigning or neighbourhood forums) and influencing society this way, and *representative democracy* (this is sometimes know as *electoral democracy*, although electoral and representative forms of democracy do have some differences) in which the emphasis is on voting for politicians who are supposed to represent peoples' interests. It is worth noting that there are various forms of democracy, and authors have developed their own approaches, for example associative democracy (Hirst 1993), deliberative democracy (Miller 1993) and strong democracy (Barber 1984). There are many definitions of the term 'democracy', here we shall follow Amartya Sen (2009) in defining democracy as 'government by discussion':

> Democracy must [also] be seen more generally in terms of the capacity to enrich reasoned argument through enhancing informational availability and the feasibility of interactive discussions. Democracy has to be judged not just by the institutions that formally exist but by the extent to which different voices from diverse sections of the population can actually be heard.
>
> (Sen 2009: xiii)

Before the discussion of democracy, it is important to point out that both democracy and the notion of human rights that underpins it are social constructs (see Plummer 2006). This means that democracy and human rights are not something that exist outside of the realm of the social, and their emergence takes place through struggle and conflict. As has been documented earlier in this book, there have been claims to rights by various LGBT pressure groups, some going back for many years; these claims have been opposed by counterclaims by religious organizations and also by transnational organizations such as the United Nations (Plummer 2006). It is not that democracy and human rights approaches are fundamentally flawed, but rather that the struggle for LGBT rights takes place within a context of competing interests.

The next section of the chapter discusses LGBT issues and democracy in an international context, including a brief overview of some of the transnational organizations that are relevant. It addresses the ways in which globalized capitalism shapes the world in which struggles for LGBT equality take place, and flags up the debates about democracy as a political form that originated in the west but that is now used, and adapted to context, in many countries across the world.

An international overview

Why is it important to place discussions about LGBT equalities and democracy in a global context? We live in an increasingly globalized world, one that has changed profoundly with the advent of greater possibilities of travel and migration, and enhanced global communications systems. This section of the chapter aims to outline some key themes regarding globalization and democracy in relation to LGBT equalities. It does not provide a review of the situation regarding democracy and LGBT issues internationally, or look at the importance of powerful undemocratic countries such as China to LGBT equalities internationally; the chapter will rather tease out some of the current and emerging issues.

International LGBT rights and democracy

Our world is shaped by the activities of global infrastructure organizations such as the International Monetary Fund (IMF) and the World Trade Organization (WTO), as well as (to a lesser degree) trans-national interest groups attempting to implement environmental and social standards. Following arguments by Fraser (2008) we cannot assume that the modern nation-state is the unit that is being analysed, because of the critiques of trans-border injustices stemming from feminists, human rights activists and anti-globalization activists. Overall, there has been a shift towards globalized organizing: both organizing against LGBT equalities (as in the case of the United Nations and some religious organizations, as mentioned above (Plummer 2006)) and organizing to support LGBT equalities. The Yogyakarta Principles which were developed in 2006 provide an international, universal guide to rights for LGBT people, aimed at supporting the compliance of all nation-states with these rights (http://www.yogyakartaprinciples.org accessed 1 February 2011). There are also a number of transnational organizations concerned with LGBT rights and equality, for instance the International Lesbian and Gay Association (ILGA) and the International Lesbian and Gay Law Association (Elliott 2005; see also Chapter 1). In addition, policy harmonization across the European Union has helped to catalyse a shift towards LGBT equality across Europe (see Paternotte and Kollman 2010). However, the broader institutionalization of human rights internationally has largely overlooked LGBT people (see Koenig and de Guchteniere 2007, Correa et al. 2008). This oversight reverberates internationally, for example:

- In cases where LGBT people who are being victimized in their countries of origin seek asylum elsewhere.
- In immigrant communities internationally.
- In the ways in which international networks and organizations over-look, or are complicit in, human rights abuses against LGBT people. For example, concerns have recently been raised in the UK press about the Commonwealth abandoning its commitment to defending human rights; since 2008 the Secretary General has ignored calls to at least express concern about member state abuses, including the Gambian president threatening to behead homosexuals (2008) and a Malawi court giving a gay couple a jail sentence for being gay (Borger 2010).

There are, therefore, issues to consider in relation to LGBT democracy that go beyond the fight for equality and justice within individual countries. How can LGBT people and their representatives engage democratically at an international and regional level, and how can the international structures that support democracy be broadened to include LGBT people?

Globalization and democracy

The issue of globalized LGBT equality (or lack of it) and democracy sits within a much bigger discussion which we need to have about democracy and globalization. As Chantal Mouffe (2005) argues, the universalization of liberal democracy across the globe is not necessarily a positive development, because of the way in which conflicting interests are represented via the democratic process. Globalization currently favours the wealthier nation states and powerful economic interests, at the expense of the poor (Gould 2004, Sandbrook et al. 2007). This fact is relevant to our understanding of LGBT equality, because it affects the experiences of LGBT people in the different countries that make up our world. It is also important because processes of democracy are increasingly shaped by global processes, in particular processes by which individual nation-states are surrendering power to globalized networks (see Sandbrook et al. 2007). These issues are perhaps even more pertinent since the international financial crisis of the late noughties, and the recent onslaught of climate-change-related environmental disasters, which have overwhelmingly impacted on poorer countries. Issues concerning environmental fragility and access to basic resources such as food affect LGBT and other sex/gender diverse people, arguably more so than heterosexuals overall because LGBT people already face social marginalization. In other words, LGBT people are at risk of being cut off from the kinship and community networks that may provide sustenance in poorer countries, and at the same time the structures required to support human rights and equality are thinner in poorer countries.

Why is democracy important internationally? As we have shown, notions of democracy have their roots in the western world. However, there has been a global movement towards democracy over the past century, and hence now the majority of countries worldwide are democratic at least to a degree. There are of course difficulties associated with the development of democracy, including in some cases the legacy of colonialism and authoritarian rule in post colonial countries, and increasing levels of social inequality (Sandbrook et al. 2007).

The shift towards democracy internationally has been accompanied by a critique of the ethnocentrism of western democratic theory. For example, Sen (2009) criticizes the 'parochialism' of western political theory, drawing on ancient Indian political philosophy in his discussion of political science, describing a shift in understandings of democracy by a number of thinkers, beyond electoral democracy. There are other, broader, critiques of western democracy. In particular, Daniel Bell notes:

> the rather huge gap between liberal democratic ideals and the reality at home, and the repeated history of misadventures abroad due to (at least partly) an ignorance of local conditions (Guatemala, Iran, Vietnam, Iraq) [in relation to the US] (2006: 85).

Other authors also point to the broad failings in global governance that are associated with neoliberalism, including a decline in international security, and a widening gulf between the rich and the poor internationally and within many countries (Wilkinson and Hughes 2002). These failings have been widely criticized by grassroots movements against globalized capitalism, and this is reflected in the work of scholars such as Marianne Maeckelbergh (2009), who argue for alternative, grassroots-based forms of democracy.

LGBT equalities and democracy

Does the problematic nature of democracy render it fundamentally flawed as a means for the creation of the conditions of equality for LGBT people internationally? No, because there has been a growth in the number of democracies worldwide and concurrent development of LGBT activism in many countries in the global south and east as well as the west and north; activism which appeals to democratic notions such as rights and justice. There has also been a substantial recent shift regarding state recognition of LGBT equality internationally, at least in Europe, where 22 European countries have implemented national laws which recognize same-sex partnerships (Paternotte and Kollman 2010).

However, democracy, especially the thinner version which consists only of open elections, is not necessarily tied to an LGBT equalities agenda. Hate crime against LGBT people, and state-sponsored discrimination, takes place in some European counties and some US states. There are also plenty of examples of democratic deficit regarding LGBT people in democratic countries, for example Ian MacGillivray (2000) discussed the lack of equal representation and social justice that gay, lesbian, bisexual, transgender and queer students experience in US schools. There are a number of southern countries which claim to be democratic, in which state-sponsored human rights abuses of LGBT people are (or have been) common, including for instance Egypt, where Scott Long (2005) reported torture and beatings of gay men by the police, and Sri Lanka, where Andrea Nichols (2010) describes police engaging in the verbal, physical and sexual abuse of trans sex workers. With respect to the countries that we have chosen for our comparative work, there is a substantial amount of literature available on both South Africa and the US, which we present here in snapshot form. It is important to note that the literatures in both countries overlook and erase bisexuality; we have followed their conventions but note that this is very problematic and that there is a large gap in the literature regarding bisexuality and democracy.

The situation for LGBT people and democracy in South Africa, as discussed in Box 4.1, can be usefully compared with that of the US, outlined in Box 4.2, as both have LGBT communities which have engaged in various ways with democratic processes and state machineries.

Box 4.1 LGBT and democracy: Focus on South Africa

Historically, the apartheid state of South Africa (a pseudo-electoral democracy which excluded people of colour) entrenched narrow gender-binaried, heteronormative and violently masculinized identities via its core state institutions, and stigmatized people who were black, gay or transsexual. During the 1970s, people who were suspected of being homosexual [sic] were pathologized and subject to electro-shock therapy, and a substantial number of sex change operations were performed as a 'cure' for being gay, with a high rate of casualties (Vincent and Camminga 2009). As noted in Chapter 2 pressure from the South African lesbian and gay movement was key to placing LGB rights on the agenda of the ANC, which became the ruling party in South Africa after the transition to democracy in 1994 (Croucher 2002). South Africa's constitution was the 'first in the world to expressly protect the rights of gays and lesbians' (Croucher 2002: 315) and there have been substantial gains subsequently (Goldblatt 2006). Trans people's rights have been less supported by the South African state, and:

> ... a certain enthusiasm on the part of the patriarchal apartheid state for surgical reconstruction of the body to produce a fit between sexual desire and a hetero-sexual framework of assumptions reflects this ... the state, even the postapartheid

state, has proven itself less able to adapt to transsexualism clothed in the language of choice, of self ascription and social, legal, and political support for the self interpretation of the individual.

(Vincent and Camminga 2009: 696)

Overall, there has been a struggle since 1994 to re-define the South African state in a way which acknowledges the apartheid atrocities and rebuilds democratic structures at the same time. In this context, the dismantling of the apartheid state structures has enabled the development of increased gay and lesbian rights (Spurlin 2006). As Sheila Croucher (2002) argues, the democratic transition provided a political opportunity structure that enabled mobilization regarding lesbian and gay equality claims; this helped support both democratic processes and democratic outcomes for LGB people. In essence, there was a window of opportunity during the transition to democracy, when government was relatively open and accessible, there were somewhat unstable political alignments and the capacity for building effective alliances with other groups, and there was a dominant pro-equalities discourse which LGB activists were able to tap into. In South Africa, the openness of government in the mid-1990s went beyond free and fair elections, for example the drafting of the constitution involved substantial consultation, with public meetings and workshops which included gay and lesbian groups (see Croucher 2002). Therefore both representative and participative forms of democracy were operating with respect to LGB equalities.

As noted earlier, there remains a disjuncture between the progressive South African constitution and the high levels of homophobic (and biphobic and transphobic) discrimination and violence in South African society (see Reddy 2009). After the transition to democracy, quotas of female electoral candidates were introduced and state machinery was developed to support the equality of women (for example gender equality units) (see Hassim 2006). These measures were not adopted regarding sexuality equalities or transgender, and a few years later even discursive commitment to LGBT equalities was weak or absent. For example, an examination of Hansard reports of parliamentary debates in the 2000s (conducted by Monro) provides ample evidence of a rhetorical commitment to some forms of equality, but an erasure of LGBT people. A typical excerpt is as follows:

As with all our other development programmes, the Black Economic Empowerment process will focus on the challenge of the empowerment of women, people with disabilities, and the youth. [Applause.]

(Proceedings at the Joint Sitting of Parliament, President Thabo Mbeki, 21 May 2004: 21)

However, the democratic process regarding LGBT equalities continues to develop in South Africa as the gay and lesbian movement has now developed into a pressure group which engages with the state across political parties.

Box 4.2   LGBT and democracy: Focus on the United States

The US also has a specific history of criminalization of homosexual [sic] behaviour, and prior to the US Supreme Court's 2003 decision in *Lawrence*, sodomy laws prohibited various private sexual practices by both straight and non-straight people, usually including oral and anal sex (Smith 2008). Other areas of statute were more progressive, and were influenced by the LGBT rights movement, so that as far back as the 1970s the US gay rights movement began to focus on fighting for access to political structures, and subsequently much LGBT rights activism and adversary activism has taken place within state institutions (see Werum and Winders 2001). Arguably:

> Gays and lesbians (and, in recent times, many would add bisexuals and transgendered persons) have transitioned from outsiders to insiders in the political process, from the liberationists of the sixties and seventies to the lobbyists of the nineties.
>
> (Riggle and Tadlock 1999: 2)

Like other constitutional democracies, the US separates state power into the legislative, executive and judiciary. This horizontal fragmentation is complemented in the US by vertical fragmentation, and hence there are different state arenas at local, state and national levels, each allowing different points of potential influence by those seeking to achieve or oppose LGBT equalities. Substantial amounts of literature are available about lesbian and gay equalities strategies, gains and impediments in each of these arenas. Miriam Smith (2008), for instance, examines the crucial role of courts in effecting policy changes regarding lesbian and gay issues in the US and the way in which popular reactions to court rulings have acted to reassert marriage as a heterosexual institution. The importance of the courts is also evident in the literature about transgender rights: 'transgender advocates have successfully fought for inclusion in non-discrimination and hate crime laws in several states and dozens of municipalities' (Currah et al. 2006: xiii). At a state level, research includes Barth and Parry's (2009) survey of Arkansas voters that showed that the majority of Arkansans are uncomfortable with homosexuality [sic] but that they are reluctant to support state-sanctioned discrimination. Crosscutting themes are apparent with respect to electoral behaviour and legislative developments; Ellen Riggle and Barry Tadlock noted in 1999 that a number of openly gay and lesbian political candidates had run for election and that there were at that time over 200 openly gay or lesbian public officials. However, there are also major blocks to achieving LGBT equality in the US, that are linked to US democratic processes and structures. For example, Riggle et al. (2009) demonstrate that 'As of December 2008, 46 states (and the US Federal Government) had excluded or prohibited the recognition of same-sex couples by statute, judicial ruling, or amendment to their state constitutions' (2009: 80). Smith (2008) (citing Barry Adams) describes the 'glacial' pace of legislation to achieve full citizenship rights for gay and lesbian [sic] Americans. Smith traces the way in which the federal structure and the limited power of the courts, as well as the legacy of previous policies, cause obstacles to policy change for the lesbian and gay movement in the US, in comparison to other countries such as Canada where the core political institutions are different and rapid movements towards equality have been possible. There is a US liberal democratic assumption that the rights of the majority should be protected from the tyranny of the minority and that the state has an important role in arbitrating conflicts (see Riggle and Tadlock 1999). However, democracy in the US has manifested in only partial protection of LGBT peoples' rights, and so the movement for LGBT equalities continues.

This chapter has provided an overview of globalization and democracy with regard to LGBT equality, and has highlighted some of the international issues associated with democracy and LGBT equalities. It has provided some insight into the situation in two contrasting democracies, South Africa and the US. This section of the chapter finishes by flagging up some issues to consider regarding democracy and LGBT equalities at an international level:

- There are some links between the development of democracy worldwide and LGBT equalities but these are not clear-cut because of the antagonistic nature of democracy – a minority of people can be oppressed within the democratic framework. Majoritarian homophobia, biphobia and transphobia can be magnified or at least reinscribed via electoral democracy if this is not counterbalanced by a strong human rights agenda.
- The basic requirements for democratic engagement apply to LGBT people as well as others; these include not only free and fair elections, but also the capacity to engage in elections, which means having access to basic resources such as food and transport to polling stations, as well as freedom from violence and intimidation.
- The capacity of people worldwide to engage in democracy is affected by global inequalities, climate change and the economic expansion of the more powerful countries. Almost all democratic states are structured by capitalism, which embodies forces that can work against democracy because an interest in profit easily overrides human rights concerns.
- There are ongoing difficulties with the imperialist ways in which countries such as the UK and US have used the notion of 'democracy' to justify wars on foreign soil, often in countries with very poor human rights records regarding LGBT people. There is a danger that backlashes against 'western style' imposed democracy can be linked with a reassertion of hatred against LGBT people and the view that LGBT equalities is a 'western disease'.
- The difficulties associated with the imperialist imposition of 'western style' democracy on other countries and associated backlashes also concerns women's rights, an issue which is particularly important for bisexual, lesbian and trans women.
- Although it has fallen outside of the remit of the discussion, there are LGBT or related organizations in non-democratic countries, sometimes underground or 'below the radar'.

This section of the chapter has provided a sketch of some of the key issues and dynamics associated with democracy and LGBT equalities on an international level. There has been a substantial shift towards democracy internationally (including the 2011 developments), as well as an increase in the influence of transnational organizations. The notion of democracy has a chequered history, being tied to postcolonial and neoliberal structures of domination and inequality, and this inevitably frames the ways in which LGBT equalities related movements develop. Democracy in its broadest sense (open elections, rights to the basics necessary for life) clearly supports the equality of LGBT people as well as everyone else (although of course totalitarian systems can also provide the basics necessary for life at least for some people). However, as has been outlined, there are a number of challenges concerning democracy and LGBT equality worldwide.

LGBT equalities and democracy in the UK

So far, this chapter has reviewed the literature about LGBT people and democracy, and discussed key issues concerning democracy and sexual and gender minorities at the international level. This section of the chapter examines the UK situation. The UK is a democracy with the central legislature based at Westminster, but some devolved decision-making powers to Northern Ireland, Wales and Scotland. As a European Union member, the UK also has elected politicians sitting in European Parliament, and it is subject to EU law. UK politicians are elected at local levels (where they are called 'councillors') and national levels (where they are called Members of Parliament (MPs)), as opposed to the federal system present in countries such as the US. Representative and participative forms of democracy are both important in the UK and the focus of this chapter is on LGBT issues and these two forms of democracy, drawing on journalistic coverage and empirical material from the study of LGBT equalities in local government. This will provide an opportunity to interrogate the ways in which these forms of democracy do – or do not – support LGBT equalities.

David Held (1995) discusses liberal or representative democracy and participative democracy, as distinct forms of democracy:

- *Liberal or representative democracy* is a means of government in which elected members 'represent' the interests of citizens, whilst also maintaining the rule of law (Held 1995). All liberal democratic states embody principles such as equality before the law and equal political and civil rights for everyone to some degree (Parekh 1994). As Anne Phillips (1991) suggests, liberalism rests on:

  - The notion of individualism (that is, individual citizens vote for politicians and political parties that they think will represent their interests).
  - A separation of public and private realms because certain things, such as statutory sector service provision, are seen as belonging in the 'public sphere' and therefore open to public debate, whereas other things (for example gender roles within families, sexuality, gender changes) are seen as (at least partially) beyond the remit of the public sphere.
  - In neoliberal democracies, the role of the state being restricted because too much state interference would supposedly stop the economy working in a 'fair' way (unless of course the state interference is to bolster the banking system using taxpayers money, as happened in 2008 in a number of western countries).

■ For neoliberals, the role of the state includes the protection of individual's rights, although as discussed above there is a tension between this and the structures of democracy.

■ *Participatory models of democracy* differ in their approaches, usually re-defining the parameters and rules of engagement, so that democracy is seen as going beyond a concern with elections and political representation to include mechanisms for citizens to 'make a difference' in other ways such as by taking part in policy consultations, or partnership work between the voluntary and statutory sectors.

Following previous work (Monro 2005), liberal democracy is important for LGBT politics, in the sense that LGBT-friendly politicians have a key role to play in representing the interests of LGBT people, the ways in which liberal democracy includes the concept of self-determination that is so crucial for LGBT equalities and the liberal democratic state's potential to introduce various legislative and other protections that can support the equality of LGBT individuals. 'Representation of sexual and gender minorities [in party politics] is particularly important because of the small numbers of individuals involved, and current levels of exclusion, although representation by other people may also be successful in supporting their causes' (Monro 2005: 179).

However, there are also issues and difficulties associated with liberal representative democracy and LGBT equalities. They take a number of forms, some of which were already discussed above in other national contexts:

■ The dangers of homophobic, biphobic and transphobic majoritarianism.
■ The individualism of liberal theory, which overlooks the nature of the LGBT communities and the constraints that shape individual LGBT people's choices.
■ A failure to recognize the systematic way in which power relationships regarding sexuality and gender play out in society and at the individual level.
■ The liberal reliance on unified notions of the (LGBT) self – a self that is socially constructed – and the ways that ongoing use of the socially constructed categories of LGBT and heterosexual serves to reinforce social divisions (see Rahman 2000).
■ Difficulties where individuals have fluid or multiple identities that are incomprehensible to those operating within the liberal democratic model, for example gender transient or multiply gendered (Monro 2005).
■ Other difficulties such as the issue of 'free riders' – people benefiting from living in a liberal democracy without contributing anything (Cunningham 2002).

This section focuses on one particular difficulty with liberalism and LGBT equality: the majority/minority issue, or, in other words, the challenges that LGBT people have, as marginalized minorities, in achieving political clout via a system where the majority opinion is what counts. This issue, which relates to the democratic paradox and *agonistic democracy* (democracy as inherently conflictual) (Mouffe 2005), has been a theme throughout the chapter. This section will also touch briefly on the problems associated with liberal individualism.

The dangers of majoritarian rule were identified by the earliest theorists of democracy, such as John Stuart Mill in the 1870s. Mill argued that there was a need to limit people's power and protect key liberties, as a majority and mass culture could oppress a minority. These key liberties included 'The freedoms of conscience, thought and feeling, holding and expressing opinions, pursuing one's life plans, and combining with others for any (nonmalicious) purpose' (see Cunningham 2002: 28). As discussed above (see Riggle and Tadlock 1999), the state should in theory act to protect the interests of minorities against those of the majority. However, as far back as 1989 Phelan argued that some of the issues raised by groups affiliated on the basis of race, gender or sexuality could be addressed via a liberal democratic framework, whilst others could not, partly because of the individualism which permeates liberal politics, and partly because of the implicit public–private divide, which the interests of groups such as lesbians straddle.

The need to limit majoritarian rule, in political, economic and social spheres, is of clear relevance to LGBT people as a minority population. This is not to say that LGBT people are a homogenous group, who are pitted against a larger homogenous group of cisgendered and heterosexual people. As was outlined in the chapter on intersectionality, there are many different social characteristics that cut across gender identity and sexual orientation. Moreover, it can be argued that countries such as the UK are increasingly pluralist. However, thinner forms of democracy, in which only representative and electoral forms are in place, are of little use to LGBT people, unless the public mood supports LGBT equality. In the UK there has been a big shift in public consciousness in recent years. A recent British Social Attitude Survey showed that 75 per cent of the population thought that homosexuality was 'always or mostly wrong' in 1987, this had lowered to 32 per cent by 2008 (Ward and Carvel 2008) and this shift is mirrored in the party political realm. For example, journalistic coverage documents how out Conservative party MP Nick Herbert gave a speech about 'how the [right wing] Tories have come a helluva long way' at London Pride 2010, and the Tory Mayor of London led Pride in 2008, wearing a pink Stetson (Pidd 2010). All of the main political parties in the UK now pay at least lip-service to LGBT rights, and it appears that a certain type of gay identity – homonormative – has been somewhat appropriated as a trope (symbol) for cosmopolitanism by a right wing party attempting to project a contemporary image. This shift stands in stark contrast to Thatcher's Tory party, which infamously introduced the homophobic legislation Section 28 on the back of a virulent right wing backlash in the late 1980s. Section 28 was in place between 1988 and 2003 in England and, as was pointed out in Chapter 1, it sought to prevent local authorities from 'promoting' homosexuality.

It is important to note that the LGBT equalities battle has not been won in the UK; there is still a substantial amount of homophobia, biphobia and transphobia within the public realm. Politicians and other public figures unsurprisingly feel constrained by this and may stay closeted, which interferes with the processes of representative democracy but is understandable given the devastating consequences that being out in public can provoke (witness, for example, the fate of Justin Fashanu, the first out gay professional English footballer, who suffered homophobic abuse that was so severe that he killed himself in 1998). Whilst levels of homophobia vary across different sections of UK society, homophobia, biphobia and transphobia still impact substantially on politicians. For example, journalists documented the way in which Liberal Democrat David Laws had to resign following a scandal in which he claimed expenses for accommodation owned by his male partner, allegedly in order to stay closeted (see Saner 2010). Political scandals concerning sexuality are structured in a particular way in the UK, with bisexuality usually being erased. This erasure was noticeable in the 2010 debacle involving the Conservative MP William Hague and a supposedly same-sex sexual relationship. The scandal was quickly squashed on the basis that Hague was married and trying for a baby (see Rayner 2010); commentators assumed that because he was married he was monogamous, and could not possibly be bisexual.

Issues around majoritarian rule and LGBT equalities are noticeable at the level of local government in the UK. Party political support for the LGBT equalities agenda is important, and this was evident in earlier research (see Monro 2006b), and there has been a shift towards greater cross-party support for the equalities agenda. In effect LGBT equalities have become less of a minority issue, and representative democratic politics is arguably working better for LGBT people. Our research also indicated that in England and Wales there may be a lessening of the view that LGBT equalities is an electoral liability due to homophobic views amongst the general population, something that was very evident in previous eras (see Cooper 2004; Monro 2006a, see further discussion in Chapter 6).

Despite these advances, the research demonstrated difficulties with representative forms of democracy and LGBT equalities, which related to issues of majoritarianism. This is partly because of the structure of the electoral system, in which numbers and visibility count. For instance, a Council Deputy Leader in North East England remarked that:

> It would be difficult in my ward [electoral district] if I said that I wanted to have a particular ward-based engagement with the LGBT community [because of low visibility/numbers]. I wouldn't really know who to go to or how I'd go about it. I'd probably go back to contacts and ask for their advice.

A substantial number of research participants across the UK also referred to the negative impact of councillors who are predominantly from majority communities (white, male, heterosexual), especially those in rural areas; these are potentially, though not inevitably, unsympathetic to minority community issues. This is partially because LGBT equality is not seen as a vote winner in most localities (this is also discussed in Chapter 6.) In Northern Ireland, one of the councillors we interviewed discussed the way in which local political resistance to the centrally imposed LGBT equalities legislation was seen as a matter of pride by some local authority councillors (the Northern Ireland case is dealt with in more depth in Chapter 7). Overall, there was evidence of councillors being deliberately obstructive, and unwittingly homophobic or heterosexist, across the different countries. In order to illustrate the difficulties with local representative democracy regarding LGBT equality, we have taken three snippets out of one of the interviews with an older, white, male councillor in a senior position within the council, with responsibility for all Equalities work. This councillor was not representative of all elected politicians, and it needs to be emphasized that this material is illustrative of the type of heterosexism that can be found in local politics (see Box 4.3).

Box 4.3   Case study: LGBT equality in UK local government

Interviewer: . . . As well as the portfolio responsibility can you say a little bit about how you as a councillor representing your constituency, see your role, including representing people within the community who are lesbian, gay, bisexual transgender.

Interviewee: As far as I'm concerned all my residents are, are equal erm therefore I haven't made any special effort to represent gays or lesbians, erm neither do I think I should . . .

Interviewer: What terminology would the [local] authority use, would they use 'LGBT' as a cluster or 'sexual orientation' in general documentation?

Interviewee: . . . erm how do we refer to this group? Erm [pause] I don't know, I've never, I don't think I have seen er a collective noun [laugh] for them I mean its erm . . . . right, if I saw that I wouldn't know what it meant, I will now [laugh] . . .

Interviewer: Can you think of any major changes over the period of 20 years since you've been a councillor in relation to work that acknowledges LGBT communities?

Interviewee: . . . work within the council? No, I can't, obviously public perception has changed enormously erm I was talking to someone about this the other day erm and erm I was saying are things so different today than they were say 30 years ago . . . I mean I'm thinking about the erm [pause] the child that was taken no the mother erm did the mother die or what happened? But there was a single parent family and the grandparents were looking after the child and the local authority social services came along took the child away and, and put the child in the care of a gay couple. *Personally I think that is wrong and I think 90 or 95% of the country would think the same way* [our emphasis].

In these quotes we can see that the politician in question – who is supposed to be leading on the political representation of LGBT people within an entire district in the UK – demonstrates a universalist heterosexist position with no consideration for sexuality/trans specific issues, a lack of knowledge about the most basic aspects of LGBT equalities and overt homophobia about adoption.

A further issue concerning democracy and majoritarianism is the individualism on which representative democracy is based. This individualism, in which people are seen as rational actors with bounded identities, is particularly problematic for some LGBT people. In other words, some people have fluid, complex gender and sexual identities which means that they cannot identify as, for example, a lesbian all the time because some of the time they may identify as lesbian, and at other times as a trans man. The problems with individual bounded identities is also relevant because the countercultures associated with some LGBT scenes (particularly those groups who are more embattled because they exist in hostile regimes) form a *group* culture, where people are – at least to a degree – interdependent. For instance, Sally Hines (2007) discusses the caring networks found in the trans communities in the UK, whilst Monro (2005) documents the ways in which polyamorous bisexual communities in the UK foster a sense of group identity and complex familial structures that do not lend themselves well to the individualism associated with liberal democracy. In intersectional terms, those LGBT people who are also disabled, poor, have caring responsibilities or belong to minority ethnic groups may feel particular affiliations with groups other than the LGBT community – and may be particularly reliant on mutually supportive social networks on a day–to–day basis – rendering liberal individualism even more problematic.

Overall, whilst liberal representative democracy provides an important means of effecting social change, its usefulness for LGBT people is hampered by the minority status of LGBT people. This minority status is arguably reinforced by the lack of LGBT equality internationally; if LGBT people were completely equal, more people would probably come out (especially bisexuals, because when bisexuals are embattled they are probably more likely to pass as heterosexual than to try and live as bisexual) and then representative democracy would become more relevant. It is clear from the case study material from the UK that there are difficulties with liberal representative democracy and LGBT equalities, in terms of the representation of LGBT people amongst elected politicians, and in terms of the high levels of heterosexism amongst some elected politicians. The next section will explore participative democracy, as an alternative, or complement, to representative democracy.

Participative democracy and LGBT equalities

How is participative democracy relevant to the equality of LGBT people? Participative democracy was mentioned earlier in the chapter as going beyond a concern with representation. It involves ordinary people becoming involved in the public sphere and decisions with political implications, and some blurring of the public–private divide being implied because of this. Participative democracy initially stemmed from notions of direct democracy, in which citizens are directly involved in decision making about public affairs (Held 1995). In practice, LGBT participative democracy can involve activities such as activism in order to increase the public discussion of LGBT issues (Kirsch 2000), consultation exercises, and partnership working between statutory and community sector actors. Participative democracy therefore bypasses, or complements, representative democracy because it uses structures which are different from those associated with electoral democracy. It is possible to demarcate a continuum of participation generally, ranging from tokenistic involvement in citizen participation, through consultation by public bodies, to shared or delegated power, in which ordinary LGBT people are involved in decision making regarding policy issues that affect them and service planning and provision (see Leach and Wingfield 1999).

How useful are participatory models of democracy for LGBT people in general? Participatory models of democracy regarding LGBT rights and equalities are in use in some local councils in different European countries. For instance, Barcelona municipal authority has undertaken an extensive participative democratic exercise with its LGBT population, including providing forums for themed debates, a widely publicized online questionnaire, and supporting LGBT partnership work. This has resulted in plans for a range of actions, including the establishment of an LGBT resource centre and involvement of LGBT activists in the International Cities of Refuge Network (which supports people facing persecution in their countries of origin) (Ajutament de Barcelona 2010). In this section of the chapter, however, the focus is on the UK.

During the 1980s and 1990s, structures were established in some local authorities to support the participatory democratic engagement of LGBT people at a local level, although these were decimated in a subsequent right wing backlash (see Cooper 1994). There was a significant movement towards participative democracy in the UK generally after the 1997 election of a Labour government, which included attempts to increase citizen participation in local government (see Leach and Wingfield 1999). There was an expansion of participative partnership and community engagement mechanisms generally, including engagement mechanisms which supported LGBT equalities work over the 2000–2010 period. These included the involvement of LGBT people via local partnerships, service-specific partnership boards and networks, engagement in citizen's panels, and consultation with LGBT groups and individuals. LGBT staff groups and local LGBT community members influenced the work of local authorities in various ways, directly in terms of the work of local councils, but also by exerting pressure on central government to produce policies which were implemented at a local level.

There are a number of difficulties with participative models of democracy, as will be outlined and discussed here with reference to data from the LGBT equalities in local government project and Monro's (2005) previous work on bisexuality and trans. These include:

- The capacity of the LGBT community sector and structural barriers to participation.
- Difficulties with increasing levels of participation whilst also ensuring that people have equal say (Phillips 1991): the problem of the 'loudest voices'.
- Participative mechanisms also include the views of homophobic, biphobic, transphobic and heterosexist people.
- LGBT people who construct their identities in opposition to mainstream society (including separatist feminist, queer-identified and anarchist LGBT people) and are unlikely to want to do business with statutory organizations, thereby lacking representation via participatory democratic mechanisms.
- Some LGBT people may remain outside of public processes either because they wish to keep their identities private (for example LGBT people who are also fetishists, LGBT practitioners of Bondage, Domination, Submission and Masochism (BDSM) and/or because their sexual practices are illegal or heavily stigmatized (especially in countries where LGBT people are persecuted)).
- Difficulties with the participative representative process itself, including government use of participatory mechanisms such as consultation to reduce and contain the impact of activism.

In this section a number of these issues are addressed, beginning with capacity, resourcing and barriers, followed by the challenge of the loudest voices, and the issue of people taking oppositional positions to the mainstream.

Capacity and resourcing

The difficulties associated with LGBT people finding the time, energy and resources to take part in participative democratic activities are long-standing (see, for example, Monro 2006a). The research about LGBT equalities initiatives in local government in the UK indicated that the trans and bisexual communities are particularly under-resourced in terms of funding being made available to them from statutory sources, which means that activism and engagement activities tend to fall on a few active people, who risk getting burnt out. There are difficulties with certain groups falling off the agendas of the organizations associated with participatory democracy (such as the local partnership boards that are supposed to represent their local communities), and people may not develop the skills and knowledge (capacity) that are necessary to effect social change through the mechanisms of participatory democracy. There are other barriers associated with capacity, which are associated with intersectional disadvantage, for instance young LGBT people having insufficient funds to travel to consultation events, especially if they live in rural areas. A contributor to the research said for example:

it feels really quite problematic trying to get funds, simply from the fact that the funds in [region of] Wales are all focused very much on one little area, and you can't really run a group, apart from the problems that [interviewee's partner] mentioned, because we are quite a small minority, you probably wouldn't get more than sort of, I mean we've got sixty registered members, we occasionally get others who come and drop in, erm, but as I say if you split that up in about six, you've got about ten members per area [laughs].

(Trans Community Members (B), Wales)

In the UK, there has historically been funding made available to support community engagement, and the research shows that there have been tensions around who gets this money – both within the LGBT communities and more broadly. This issue leads into discussion of the next area of difficulty – the problem of the 'loudest voices'.

The problem of the 'loudest voices'

What happens to power dynamics and hierarchies when 'ordinary' LGBT people become involved in the structures and processes of participative democracy? The 'loudest voices' issue operates in a number of ways:

- Within the broader equalities context, other 'equalities' strands such as race and disability being more visible than the LGBT strand.
- Some groups within the LGBT acronym tending to assert themselves more powerfully – or simply being more evident – than others.
- Individuals within the LGBT communities dominating the agenda.
- Different groups associated with the equalities agenda (in countries where there is an agenda of this sort) having different levels of visibility, capacity and recognition. For example, the following quote illustrates the way in which a bisexual community group (which was actively engaged with its local authority) did not include the voices of all bisexual people:

We [the bisexual community] are unrepresentative of bisexual people, for example rural bisexual or small town bisexuals. Our community groups are incredibly valuable but they generally happen once a month in cities... there are elements – mental health issues, social skills issues, that don't fit the bisexual model... there are certainly issues of 'coolness' in [a particular group].

(John, cited in Monro 2005: 183)

The 'loudest voices' issue was very apparent in the research about LGBT equalities in local government, in terms of some groups that are part of the equalities agenda in the UK (specifically minority ethnic groups and disability groups) being seen as more important, worthy and credible than LGBT groups (see Monro and Richardson 2010), and also in terms of differences within the

LGBT communities. These differences can revolve around personality differences and networks, class capital or education, and intersectional patterns of privilege and disadvantage, as well as levels of 'outness'. For example, one contributor said:

> How do we make our services and our information sensitive to people who don't say they are gay, straight, bisexual, lesbian, whose sexuality is something private, but which also needs to be respected and acknowledged and given status in our work. It's a really complicated area.
>
> (Local Authority Officer, Northern Ireland)

The difficulties of LGBT activists representing others were acknowledged in the research, with contributors mostly agreeing that there was a need for people included within the LGBT acronym to act together, because of the minority status of the groups, but that less visible subsections of the community also need to be heard.

Oppositional politics

The issue of whether LGBT people should take political positions which oppose mainstream society and the heterosexist structures that go with it (such as the institution of marriage), or attempt to assimilate and change society from within, is a long-standing source of tension which has been discussed widely in the literature (for example Phelan 1989, see also Chapter 1). Some authors, such as Weeks (1995, 2008a), suggest that both oppositional and assimilationist politics are necessary and that in fact they can work in tandem. The issue of people who position themselves in opposition to the mainstream democratic process is important for understanding LGBT democracy. For a start, in societies where LGBT identities were, or are, illegal, the oppositional stance (whether this is overt or covert) is the only form of activism available to LGBT people – and it is from the oppositional position that more mainstream LGBT political engagement has historically developed in countries such as the UK and the US. But also, when thinking about participatory democracy, we have to consider the way in which sections of the LGBT communities in the UK are actively critical of mainstream political processes and the attendant assimilationist policy developments, such as the Gender Recognition Act (2004) and the Civil Partnerships Act (2004). The people whose identities conflict most with the positions supported in recent legislation (which to a degree entrench homonormative and gender normative identities) include the following:

- People with fluid, multiple or non-male/female gender identities.
- People involved in polyamorous arrangements, because these are not acknowledged by the Civil Partnerships Act, which arguably acts to reinscribe monogamous partnership norms (see, for instance, Klesse 2007).

■ Bisexuals generally, because the specifics of bisexual experience such as understandings of fluid sexual desire, and social difficulties with negotiating the straight and gay scenes, are unrecognized in mainstream policy developments.

■ LGBT people who reject participation in the mainstream on political grounds – including some feminist, queer and anarchist LGBT people, but also others who develop alternative lifestyles, such as women in lesbian separatist eco communities (Sandilands 2002).

Arguably, the structures supporting participative democracy should be broadened to make participation more accessible to all sections of the LGBT communities, and then disenfranchised communities could usefully engage more with the state. There are some arguments for this type of engagement coming from within some of the communities above, for example Noel (2006) suggests that polyamorists must build political coalitions and develop norms of inclusivity. A more serious engagement with the fringes of the LGBT communities would potentially alter the make-up of the mainstream because issues such as identity fluidity would have to be more fully acknowledged. However, it could be imagined that this would involve the antagonist democratic processes discussed by Mouffe. In other words, conflicting agendas would be apparent, and there would be a need for the formation of a "vibrant agnostic" public sphere of contestation where different hegemonic political projects can be confronted (Mouffe 2005: 3).

This section has explored the ways in which participative democracy can act as a complement to electoral democracy, given the difficulties associated with the latter, particularly those associated with LGBT people and majoritarianism. It has also identified a number of difficulties associated with participative democracy in the UK context, including community capacity, the problem of the 'loudest voices', the lack of participation of groups that are oppositional to the mainstream, and the ways in which participative mechanisms can channel prejudice, as well as pro-equality standpoints. The issue with actors who have homophobic, biphobic and transphobic agendas joining the participative process and potentially overriding the generally fairly 'quiet voices' of LGBT people is a serious one in UK politics and internationally. This dynamic mirrors tensions regarding majoritarianism and liberal representative democracy, and the democratic paradox, as discussed above. In particular, the crunchy interface between faith communities and the LGBT communities is very evident in recent UK and international debates, although of course, as was explained in the chapter on intersectionality, some LGBT people belong to faith communities, and there are wide variations in approaches to LGBT equalities within some faith groupings.

Conflict between interest groups is one of the staples of democratic thinking. The classical pluralist approaches developed in the 1960s viewed conflict between interest groups as central to democratic society. Critics of classical pluralism point to the lack of a level playing field: some groups have more power than others (Cunningham 2002), and as noted above, Mouffe's agonistic democracy emphasizes conflict as an inherent part of the democratic process. Power inequalities play out when considering whose voices get heard within the forum of representative and participative democracy. The moderating force of the 'liberal' part of liberal democracy is extremely important in preventing human rights abuses against LGBT people that would otherwise be perpetuated due to majoritarianism, because liberalism is meant to protect the basic rights of individuals. This means that structures such as local government are supposed to channel different views but also support the rights of the population to live in a safe environment, free of homophobic, biphobic, transphobic and other forms of abuse.

This dynamic of contestation can be related to debates about the paradox of democracy that Mouffe (2000, 2005) has developed. Mouffe discusses the way in which there has been a recent shift, in socio-democratic politics, towards a consensual politics of the centre left, in a number of countries. This was exemplified in the UK by New Labour's 'Third Way' (a period in which a raft of legislative and other advances were made regarding LGBT equalities). However, according to Mouffe, there are serious difficulties associated with the consensus model of democracy. Mouffe discusses the way in which there are two aspects to modern democracies; democracy as a form of rule (that is, the actual processes of election and representatives of the population ruling them) and as a symbolic framework within which democratic rule is exercised (that is, the idea that power should be exercised by the people *within the framework of liberalism, which is based on notions of individual rights).* This framework is in itself hegemonic – it forms a power structure. What this means is that certain people (those who break the rules of democratic engagement) are excluded from the very process that is meant to represent everyone. This process of exclusion relates very neatly to the discussion in the previous chapter about normative notions of citizenship, where certain lesbians and gay men are seen as 'good citizens' and others are not. The paradox described by Mouffe also means that there is a risk that some decisions made through democratic processes can undermine certain rights. This is because of the tension between liberalism (which emphasizes individual human rights) and democracy (which involves everyone having a say in political and social processes).

In the UK, the democratic structures that can support LGBT equality are highly likely to be negatively affected by broader global economic processes. For instance, the right wing cuts to the statutory sector in the UK during the ConDem coalition administration that was formed in 2010 will undermine participatory democracy because the structures (such as consultative mechanisms) will be limited or destroyed, and because LGBT people will overall be poorer and may be less able to engage in democratic activities. The discussion therefore returns us to the beginning of this chapter, and the discussion of the structuring role of globalized capital in LGBT democracy. Ultimately, it is this structuring role that frames both representative and participatory forms of

LGBT democratic activity, at least in countries where the neoliberal economic model of democracy predominates.

Summary

- The notion of democracy is both socially constructed and historically and culturally contingent, with difficulties relating to the imperialist history of western democracies.

- Globalization acts to frame and structure the activities of individual states, including moves to embed – or indeed resist – LGBT equalities. There are a number of important transnational networks and organizations which can support, but may also impede, progress towards LGBT equalities. There is a tendency for international human rights organizations to overlook LGBT people.

- There is a substantial, if somewhat piecemeal, literature regarding LGBT people and democracy internationally, much of it relating to activism and rights, but some of it addressing democratic institutional processes concerning LGBT equalities.

- There are many different ways of thinking about LGBT democracy and areas of potential focus. For example, one could focus on LGBT representation in political parties, dynamics in the legislature, court cases and the judiciary, the executive and state machinery, or the participation of LGBT pressure groups in state processes and structures.

- Existing research and scholarship about sexual minorities and democracy almost universally excludes or overlooks bisexuals, and where work has been done about trans and democracy, this mostly focuses on rights.

- Democracy does not automatically mean LGBT equalities or the protection of LGBT people's human rights. In some supposedly democratic states, human rights abuses against LGBT people are common, even though LGBT people are of course part of the electorate.

- Democratic states are supposed to offset damaging majoritarianism (for example homophobic, transphobic and biphobic tendencies amongst the general population), but majority prejudice can be channelled through electoral processes and participative structures, or can manifest as homophobic, biphobic or transphobic lobbying by pressure groups.

- Within the countries focused on in this chapter (South Africa, the US and the UK), democracy for LGBT people can be described as 'work in progress'. There have been substantial gains in each country, but there are also forces impeding the equality and rights of LGBT people, which manifest in a range of ways.

Organizational Change

5

Why have a chapter on organizational change in a book about LGBT equality? Organizations are a ubiquitous feature of our lives at every level, from the private sector organizations that produce our food to the statutory sector organizations that regulate, and in some cases provide, basic services such as healthcare and education. National organizations operate within an international context, with many companies and networks spanning the globe. Sexuality is rarely overtly addressed within organizations, with the exception of organizations involved in the sex trade or related activities such as fashion and cosmetic surgery. However, sexuality – and heterosexuality in particular – can be seen to pervade organizations.

Organizational studies has, until recently, overlooked sexuality, but there has been a mushrooming of interest in organizational sexualities, including some work about LGBT issues and heterosexuality in organizations. The 'queer' end of organizational sexuality studies has largely remained divorced from mainstream organizational studies, and one of the objectives of this chapter is to place LGBT organizational sexuality studies in relation to organizational studies more broadly. A further aim is to bring trans into the organizational studies picture. The overall aim in this chapter is however to focus on processes of organizational change, as these are of particular importance to achieving LGBT equalities. Although the focus is on organizational studies, it is important to realize that there are other bodies of related and overlapping literature which also yield useful insights, including sociological institutionalism (Monro 2007b; Mackay et al. 2009) and poststructuralism (Monro 2005).

The chapter begins with an overview of the development of organizational studies, which provides an important context for LGBT organizational analysis. It then moves on to outline developments in diversity studies, and organizational gender and sexuality studies to date. The chapter then provides an analysis of organizational change regarding LGBT equalities in UK local government and partner organizations, as a means of exploring the conceptual issues and making them 'live', by looking at organizational change at different levels:

■ Society
■ Institutions
■ Individuals

Finally, the chapter applies specific strands of organizational change theory.

The history of organizational change theories

Where does organizational theory come from? Organizational studies can be traced back to antiquity, but the approaches that developed in the west after the industrial revolution began with the Classical school. The Classical school (which includes key theorists such as Frederick Taylor and Max Weber) takes a number of forms, all of which share the view that people are *rational actors* who will behave in a way that maximizes their own economic well-being, and that an emphasis on rules and procedures (bureaucracy) is important. The Human Relations school developed from the 1920s onwards in response to the rationalist approaches taken by Classical theorists. Human Relations approaches and others that developed from them, such as the Behavioural school and Systems theory, drew on social psychology in order to look at *emotional, cognitive and social aspects* of organizational behaviour (see Bowditch et al. 2007). Human Relations approaches suggest that:

> Organisations are composed of informal structures and as such, the operation of organisations owes more to group norms and values than it does to structures and procedures as in Taylorism [the Classical School].
>
> (Collins 1998: 17)

Contemporary management and organizational theory takes a pluralist approach, drawing on the many strands of organizational theory, so that people are seen as complex beings with a range of motivations. Organizations are also seen as complex, and there is acknowledgement of the ways in which organizations are (in many cases) affected by wider social factors such as systems of regulation (including legislation) and the shift to post-industrial society (Bowditch et al. 2007, see also Hatch 1997).

This chapter will draw on the organizational literature generally, especially one particular strand of it: Organizational change. This is because we are interested in the ways that organizations can change in order to support LGBT equalities. Most of the literature that looks at organizational change does so from a management perspective: organizations are there to be 'fixed', and managers want 'solutions'. These 'solutions' are provided partly by the strand of organizational studies known as Organizational Development which stemmed from the Human Relations school. Organizational Development seeks to improve various aspects of organizations (Yu and Ming 2008). It locates change primarily in the individual: change happens by a process of individuals (and groups) 'unfreezing', 'moving' and 'refreezing'. In other words, during the process of change, people's core beliefs are disrupted (this is likely to be uncomfortable and provoke resistance), they then go through a process of cognitive restructuring and the replacement of old mindsets with new ones that are then consolidated, or 'refrozen' (Carnevale 2003).

David Collins (1998) rightly argues that most of the organizational change literature focuses on practical issues, hiding the complex theoretical issues that lurk underneath the surface. The different approaches are each problematic in their own way, for example the texts by management 'gurus' serve to consolidate the elite social positions of managers, whilst more critical Marxist approaches are arguably impractical. There is, however, a growing sense of disillusion with mainstream approaches to organizational studies (Grant et al. 2005). The alternatives that have developed include the work of authors writing within Critical Management Studies, which draws on poststructuralism and critical thinking in order to address issues of power, politics and identity formation (Voronov 2009). Mainstream approaches to organizational studies take pluralist approaches, drawing on the idea that society is made up of different competing interest groups, and that this competition is healthy. However, mainstream organizational studies do not include the more radically critical stances that interpret inequalities as group-based (for example class, postcolonial, race, ability, sexuality and gender). Arguably, this is because the goal of mainstream approaches is to make organizations work, so that capitalism can function, and support for sexual and gender diversity is part of this.

This chapter will not attempt to grapple with all of the theoretical issues that the organizational change literature throws up; rather it will address organizational change in relation to sexual and gender diversity, drawing on the literature. We take a critical approach, whilst recognizing that the approaches that are found within mainstream organizational practice may actually be helpful in driving forward certain critically informed agendas. Specific issues that are drawn from the literature that will be helpful in framing the discussion include the following:

- The way in which change operates at formal and informal levels (see Carnevale 2003).
- The way in which power works via organizational change approaches; organizational change can be used to suppress rebellious workers, so we cannot adopt them in an uncritical way.
- The gulf between critical academic approaches such as Critical Management Studies and 'the world out there' where organizational studies focus on making organizations 'work' (see Voronov 2009).

Diversity, gender and sexuality in organizations

How does LGBT equalities play out within the context of organizations? How does the literature deal with LGBT equalities? This section of the chapter looks at gender and sexuality in the literature on organizational diversity;

organizational diversity has emerged as a substrand of organizational studies. Diversity studies developed as a specific strand in the 1990s within the context of neoliberalism, overtaking earlier equal opportunities approaches that took group-based (and often critical) approaches to industrial relations. It developed into two camps: the employers and consultants who embraced diversity with the aim of increasing efficiency and productivity (see, for example, Bowditch et al. 2007), and more critical approaches developed by scholars and trade unionists. These critical approaches look at the way that the concept of diversity individualizes difference, obscures power relations, and fails to tackle structural inequalities such as racism and sexism (see Ozgilbin and Tatli 2008). Critical diversity studies share:

> a non-positivist, non-essentialist understanding of diversity – as well as the socio-demographic identities subsumed under this term – as socially (re)produced in on-going, context-specific processes. Crucially, they underline how such processes both reflect existing unequal power relations within a given context and contribute to maintaining, resisting and/or transforming them.
>
> (Zanoni et al. 2010: 10)

The shift towards diversity rather than equality approaches means that arguments for equalities initiatives for LGBT people are sometimes framed in terms of the 'business case' (which is linked with diversity approaches) rather than more critical approaches such as the 'social justice case', which challenges fundamental inequalities within organizations and wider society. Diversity approaches can be seen to fit neatly onto the Organizational Development approaches examined earlier in this chapter, because both share an emphasis on individuals and on organizational process rather than structural inequalities.

It is important to point out the way that gender and sexuality are intertwined within organizational processes, so that certain gender/sexual configurations are rendered challenging to (heterosexist) organizational norms. For instance, Hassard et al. writing in 2000 described an out lesbian experiencing her male colleagues being at a loss as to how to relate to her as a woman with a lack of sexual interest in them. What this suggests, claim Hassard et al. (2000: 11), is that organizational interactions are 'implicitly structured by sexual preference routinely ascribed to gender identity'. This interrelationship between gender and sexuality is one of the reasons why discussions of LGB equality in organizations need to include some mention of gender. The other reasons are of course that LGB people are affected by intersectional issues concerning gender, whilst for trans people, gender forms a fundamentally structuring social force (see Chapter 2 for a discussion of intersectionality).

How is gender dealt with in organizational studies generally? Gender was overlooked in mainstream approaches to organizations, including the Classical and Human Relations schools (Burrell and Hearn 1989), but a brief perusal of mainstream organizational texts shows that gender is now often discussed, as part of diversity within organizations. Mainstream organizational studies have a disconcerting tendency to define gender wholly in terms of either male or female, and then to assert that various organizational traits are linked to these two genders in an essentializing fashion. Trans and gender variance are usually completely erased in both mainstream and feminist organizational literatures (see, for example, Barrett and Davidson 2006).

Gender is less evident in the organizational change literature, according to Stephen Linstead et al. (2005), who review this literature and some of the barriers that women face in the workplace. Work by authors such as these is useful in addressing the very real inequalities that women face and the masculinist and sexist informal (and in some cases formal) structures that operate in organizations. However, the literature also reveals a difficulty with work that focuses on social categories (here, female and male), which can end up reinforcing them in the process, as is now recognized within feminist and critical literature (see, for example, McCall 2005's work on intersectionality). There is now an alternative body of literature concerning gender and organizations, stemming from the work of feminists and now moving into approaches that draw on poststructuralism (Pullen and Knights 2007).

How is sexuality addressed in the organizational literature? There is some literature concerning sexuality and organizations (for example Hearn and Parkin 1995, 2001) but this frequently uses a broad definition of sexuality. For example, sexuality is seen as concerning bodily desire, flirting, appearance, sexual behaviour, sexual harassment and so on. As James Ward (2008: 1) states, 'sexuality is arguably the most under-researched of all diversity areas in work organizations, with minority sexuality being one of the most difficult areas to research.' Historically, there has been a lack of attention to sexuality in organizations in comparison to the increasing interest in gender (Burrell and Hearn 1989; Hearn and Parkin 2001). Fiona Wilson suggests that: 'Perhaps this is because sexuality is the antithesis of what organization is about. Organization is about control, instrumental rationality and the suppression of instinct as emotion' (Wilson 2003: 193). The erasure of sexuality can, therefore, be seen to stem from the impact of rationalist thinking on organizational studies, and limited engagement with issues of sexuality amongst Human Resource approaches and those that followed them. Organizational studies has been sanitized, with emotions and sexuality being supposedly relegated to the private sphere, although of course really sexuality and emotions are an ubiquitous aspect of organizational life (see Burrell and Hearn 1989).

How about LGB sexualities in organizations? It seems that 'Most writing on sexuality in organisations tends to assume heterosexuality as a given' (Wilson 2003: 196), although some of the diversity literature includes sexual orientation (see Zanoni et al. 2010; Wright 2011). A small body of literature has developed concerning the ways in which LGB people are discriminated against in the workplace (including Levine 1979; Humphrey 1999; Ward 2008; Bowring and Brewis 2009). This literature includes research in specific contexts, such as trade unions in the UK (Humphrey 2002), and in the UK transport and construction industries (Wright 2011).

There has been a fairly recent flurry of interest in organizational sexualities, including some critical queer scholarship (Cooper and Monro 2003; Bendl and Fleischmann 2008), which addresses the ways in which organizations reproduce heteronormativity, as well as studies that explore LGB sexualities and the operation of heterosexism in organizations and organizational studies (see Brunni 2006; Rumens 2007). There are also approaches that examine strategies for attaining LGB equalities in organizations, including Monro's (2006b, 2007b) and Fiona Colgan et al.'s (2007, 2009) work. Lastly, there is work concerning particular aspects of LGBT organizational studies, such as research about US non-profit organizations as queer spaces in the US (Andrucki 2007) and work on organizational cultural impacts on sexual minorities (Ward and Winstanley 2006).

This section of the chapter has examined the way in which diversity studies has developed, and in particular the trajectories of organizational studies approaches to gender and to sexuality. In doing so it has provided a base for developing analysis of gender and sexuality in organizations, focusing on LGBT equalities and on heteronormativity. In the next two sections we will return to the organizational change literature, applying different aspects of it to the case study on LGBT equalities work in UK local government. By doing this the aim is to extend LGBT organizational studies, and provide the means with which to critically examine different aspects of the organizational literature.

Case study of organizational change: UK local government LGBT equalities initiatives

How does organizational change concerning sexuality take place in practice? This section of the chapter explores LGBT equalities work in the public sector (particularly local government) in the UK. Organizational change concerning LGBT equalities can be seen to take place at three levels: the wider society of which organizations form a part, organizations themselves (and the different levels within them) and individuals (see Collins 1998). Before investigating organizational change at these different levels, it is necessary to first contextualize the case study, briefly looking at organizational change in the public sector.

US-based David Carnevale (2003) discusses the way in which organizational change objectives, such as improved organizational performance, are shared across the public and private sectors. This is particularly the case since the introduction of neoliberal New Public Management, and Managerialism to public sector organizations. New Public Management, and Managerialism, have involved the transfer of organizational change techniques from the private sector to statutory sector organizations, in other words a change of management style. New Public Management, and Managerialism draw on management methods developed by the Classical school (specifically neo-Taylorism). There are various different approaches to New Public Management, and Managerialism, but they share a rationalist, performance-, cost-, and efficiency-oriented focus (Farnham and Horton 1996; see also Pollitt et al. 1998). In the UK, the introduction of New Public Management, and Managerialism has taken place in conjunction with the decentralization and fragmentation of public sector organizations, and a blurring of the public/private divide. This means that there has been a shift from public sector organizations that are centrally managed, with strong steer from local and central government to a public sector that contracts out parts of its work to private companies.

There are various key differences between private and public sector organizations, including the way in which public sector organizations are created by government or related bodies, so are inherently political, and the extensive regulation and scrutiny that public sector organizations experience (see Farnham and Horton 1996; Carnevale 2003; Andrews et al. 2008). In the UK, the public sector has changed enormously as a result of New Public Management, with a shift towards greater regulation but also the above-mentioned fragmentation and contracting-out. These changes raise concerns about the impact of New Public Management on equalities, but perhaps also provide opportunities for equalities work in the public sector (Colgan and Wright 2011).

Change in public organizations is arguably difficult:

> The operational domains of public institutions are structured so that change demands the involvement of multiple actors. Politics, not economics, run the show ... the public OD [organisational development] agent requires superior political skills.
>
> (Carnevale 2003: 24)

However, historically, public sector organizations have provided a relatively fertile territory for the development of LGBT equalities initiatives, and have been seen as preferred employers for LGBT people (see, for example, Cooper 1994; Carabine and Monro 2004; Monro 2006b, 2007b; Colgan et al. 2007). This is largely because of the political structures and processes associated with the public sector and the impact of the business case for equality and diversity, as well as the value systems (of public service and a commitment to justice) that – to a degree – underpin work in the statutory sector.

Context is extremely important in understanding the issues around LGBT equalities, and the UK public sector does provide a specific context for LGBT equalities, although many of the broader issues and processes will be familiar in other countries and types of organization. The wider social forces and changes associated with LGBT equalities play out in statutory organizations, and it is to these that the chapter now turns. The chapter will then address general changes within local government and related institutions, and organizational change processes at the level of the individual.

Wider society

There are indications that public attitudes towards LGBT people in the UK have changed (Ward and Carvel 2008). These changes were reflected in our research across the UK; with contributors saying for example:

> ...the biggest help has been education, and particularly the amount of trans people that have got exposure in the media, and one of [contributor's] favourite quotes is, 'It's who's telling the story now, and it's us now', rather than people telling us who we are and what we can or can't do [laughs].
>
> (Trans Community Member (B), Wales)

> ...an older [gay] couple were receiving a lot of harassment in the [local] area, a story appeared in the paper and you had twenty to thirty neighbours calling over to see if you were OK, the local taxi firm started stopping at the house now and again just to say 'Is everything OK folks?', wow that's a big difference, do you know what I mean that's a major difference and maybe sure some of those drivers twenty years ago would have been the people shouting 'fag' at us as we were organising our first gay disco up in the college so you know. So no, we are seeing positive social change here in a way that does give us encouragement.
>
> (LGBT Community Sector Worker, Northern Ireland)

In the context of the broader shift towards a society that supports LGBT equalities, it is important to realize that being LGBT is not necessarily linked to inequality, at least in some social spheres (see Miles 2008). However, for some lesbians and gay men the fight for equality has not been won. Firstly, public attitudes vary across region and country, for example a 2008 survey found that homophobia and biphobia were increasing in Northern Ireland overall (Equality Commission for Northern Ireland (ECNI) 2008a, see also Breitenbach 2004), even though there is some positive change. Trans and bisexual people also face ongoing discrimination, although there appears to have been a shift in social attitudes concerning trans. Stephen Whittle et al. (2007) demonstrated that UK trans people experience high levels of inequality, primarily in employment, access to healthcare, leisure, education and social relations. In England, research demonstrates a lack of awareness in the workplace generally concerning bisexuality, with a tendency for prejudice concerning bisexuality to extend into the workplace (Chamberlain 2009).

The general UK shift towards a more equal society for LGBT people impacts on local authority LGBT equalities work in a number of ways, including:

- Changes to the attitudes and behaviours of people working for local authorities.
- Changes in the expectations and behaviours of the service users (the public).

■ Shifts relating to public accountability and democracy, including pressures exerted on local authorities to provide equal services, and the effects of elected member's (politicians) views and actions.

■ Changes in legislation and frameworks of legitimacy, including the rise of the business case.

Institutional

Overall, the research findings indicated that LGBT equalities work has become a normalized aspect of the local authority service provision remit in the UK to a degree, alongside other strands of equalities (race, gender, disability, age, faith and Welsh language in Wales). This has taken place partially as a result of the legislative drivers that have been imposed on local authorities from outside. In a substantial number of local authorities and other statutory sector (and private sector) organizations, there is now competition to achieve good practice regarding equalities – including LGBT equalities. This has been substantially influenced by the efforts of the LGB national organization Stonewall, who have developed programmes for organizational change for both public and private organizations including its Diversity Champions scheme (see Box 5.1) (see www.stonewall.org.uk accessed 4 February 2011).

Box 5.1 Organizational change: Case study on diversity schemes

A national LGB organization representative discussed the Stonewall Diversity Champions scheme and similar programmes as follows:

Interviewer: Sure. OK. I'm just wondering what role, what you think the impact of the Diversity Champions scheme has had?

Interviewee: Oh huge. I mean it's the biggest, fastest growing employment forum. It works, people love it. It's good value for money, it's not extortionately expensive. People like it, they like using our logo, you see it on all their adverts. They advertise, they follow our recommendations and they really like it. Yeah, it's great and local authorities do quite well. I mean there's quite a few local authorities in the top 100.

Interviewer: Yes, yes and you were talking earlier on about you know the fact it's got the targets. I mean is that what people like, the fact, you can sort of splice it into your impact assessments, your targeting.

Interviewee: Well there are two bits. There's the Diversity Champions Programme and there's the Workplace Equality Index, which are two different things. So the Diversity Champions Programme is the program they joined to become part of our family if you like; and when they're part of our family they get a client lead who looks after them. We listen to them, we talk to them, if someone calls us and says there is something going on. We phone them up and go 'Do you know that your housing department is riddled with this that and the other'; and we're their friends and we take care of them, and we run a seminar programme.

They have access to our research, they can come along to our conferences. Our leadership programme goes down very well with local authorities, because the leadership programme is classic, positive action stuff and works very, very well; and enables them to kind of promote their gay staff and things like that.

This interview in Box 5.1 demonstrates a substantial shift from earlier eras, when lesbian and gay equalities work was either done only in a few left-wing councils (in the 1980s), completely in abeyance (later 1980s and early 1990s) or very piecemeal and dependent on political goodwill (later 1990s). It has taken place as a result of effective partnership work between a professionalized voluntary and community sector organization (Stonewall) and organizations such as local authorities, police and fire services. There has also, over the past few years, been a development of complex partnership and consultation arrangements, enabling greater cross-fertilization between different organizations and the sharing of ideas and support. However, it is important to point out that this kind of professionalization does not necessarily include bisexuals and trans people, and that there are ongoing issues about inclusion/marginalization, and limited bisexual and trans community capacity to effect organizational change concerning equalities (see the Intersectionality chapter).

Organizational culture is another important factor affecting organizational change at an institutional level. Organizational culture refers to 'the *shared pattern* of beliefs, assumptions, and expectations held by organisational members' (Bowditch et al. 2007: 320). Our research demonstrated that the sexual cultures of the local authorities, and their statutory partner organizations varied very widely, from organizations where the words 'lesbian and gay' were seen as taboo and bisexuality was completely 'off the radar' to those where rich, LGBT-positive cultures were established. This contrast is demonstrated in this quote (from a statutory sector partner organization) and the following section of an interview with a councillor from Southern England:

I find that what goes on in front of me tends to be generally OK. I know that there is stuff going on and I do know that one of my colleagues who is gay, there is some tension and I do think that things aren't perfect. I think that where he is, he is probably reasonably happy, but I don't get to hear or see what's actually happening. I just have a gut feeling that there probably are homophobic jokes going on and sort of innuendo and stuff like that, same as around women, sexism, same as around race...I don't tend to hear it, because they don't do it in front of me...I've sometimes sat down on the mess-deck at one of the tables and it goes pretty quiet and the conversation becomes very sort of stunted and I think it's either what they were talking about (laughs) or they're frightened to say anything. I do get that sometimes. I do think people are on their best behaviour and actually somebody told me yesterday that people are on their best behaviour around me.

(Fire Service Diversity Representative, Southern England)

Interviewer: Yeah, I mean I suppose I'm talking at the moment particularly about the kind of, the culture within the council, you know, not looking specifically or actual practice at the moment, but you know, in terms of the things that are said, the things that are seen as acceptable to say, erm, you know, people being able to talk about same-sex partners in the council, or a kind of sense that, you know, 'Yes of course we'll do something for LGBT equalities alongside race and gender' or, do you see what I'm saying? How much has it kind of become sort of part of the sort of norm or scheme of things?

Interviewee: Oh, I think it is part, in [Council] it is part of the normal scheme of things, I mean, erm, I suppose to give you an example of that, erm, as an openly gay councillor I'm talking about, erm, an ex-councillor from a different political group, erm, when she passed away, erm, I was the person that did the, one of the people that made speeches at the council meeting.

Interviewer: Yep.

Interviewee: Erm, about her passing, and it was about, erm one of the things that I remembered and I said was about me and my [same-sex] partner drinking with her in a gay pub, erm, and those were the sorts of, and to be able to say that about someone as they had passed away, acknowledging all of that within the council, I think that that is a step, I would say you know, no-one passed comment on it at all, they were probably saying it was a nice thing to say.

(Councillor, England)

Whilst cultures clearly varied across different local authorities and their statutory partners, there was also considerable variation across different sections and levels of the local authorities and their partner agencies. There is an ongoing cultural issue with the low profile that equalities work – and LGBT equalities work in particular – has in some organizations; it may be there in higher level policy documents but erased via the day–to–day practices of the organization.

Overall, where change is taking place in local authorities regarding LGBT equalities, the research findings suggested that this is due to a range of factors including:

- Strong leadership
- Efficient structures and practices (so that the organization and its partners can respond effectively to policy drivers)
- Committed individuals
- Visible LGBT people
- An engaged and resourced LGBT community sector
- A relative absence of impeding factors such as faith-related homophobia and biphobia in the local community
- Adequate resourcing

Action Learning Sets (ALS) were used in the research, and by doing this we helped to facilitate processes of organizational change. ALS are a key aspect of Organizational Development (Carnevale 2003), and provide an interesting opportunity to look at the types of action regarding change that can take place within organizations regarding LGBT equalities. Each ALS met four times in each of the four localities in which the research was conducted (Northern Ireland, Northern and Southern England, and Wales) and the ALS aimed to provide a forum for each group of participants to move agendas forward in their organizations. The ALS attracted officers from a variety of levels within the local authorities as well as some members of partner agencies such as health authorities, and in one of the ALS LGB community representatives were also involved. Participants were asked to identify issues and barriers to change that they worked on as a group, providing each other with information and support. They also identified actions that they wished to take forwards within their organizations. An example, provided by one of the participants in the Northern Ireland Action Learning Set, is shown in Box 5.2:

Box 5.2   Case study: Identifying barriers to change – Action Learning Sets

Action Learning Set Session 2
Action 1: Speak to Human Resources and ask re LGBT employee monitoring – how does it happen and has it identified LGBT staff?
Action 2: Make contact with local LGBT group.

Spoke to Human Resources about monitoring and they provided a monitoring form, and advised that there is one identified LGBT employee. Telephoned (local group) who were enthusiastic about meeting. The group forwarded information leaflets which were put in the civic centre reception area (only one left). Need to meet up with group representative.
Constraints are: a degree of suspicion, and knowing what to do with information
   Further actions identified:

- Have already made contact and got the names of people to meet, so next step is to meet and continue to build a relationship
- Internal general equality training – get councillors/senior staff on board

Action Learning Set session 3
Action 1: Find out about LGBT training locally. Next step was to work with local project to pull together training for council staff.
Feedback: Design of training has started, and it will incorporate awareness-raising. Plan is to use personal stories from people's work and personal lives as a powerful way of encouraging attitudinal change. As well as personal stories, legal issues re-employment will be included, to inform staff of their responsibilities to colleagues and people who use services. An example was shared of homophobic behaviour in one service area in the council. There was discussion of the potential of inviting the team where this happened to take part in training (but not only involving them).

Action 2: Find out about communication mechanisms used by groups. Next steps are:

■ Finalize training with local project and Human Resources department (arrange programme for September to October 2009) and include information about gender recognition legislation
■ Draw up a code of conduct
■ See what work is being done in schools

Change within institutions is by its nature an ongoing process, and it does not necessarily follow the progressive steps envisaged in modernist approaches. However, we found that the ALS provided space for participants to address issues regarding sexuality and trans, in some cases catalysing progressive change concerning equalities, as indicated above.

Individual

The processes of organizational change regarding LGBT equalities will be discussed in more depth below, in relation to key aspects of the organizational literature such as control-type change and leadership (as associated with New Public Management), and emotions and affectivity. First, however, individual aspects of change are considered. Needless to say, many things affect employee commitment to change, including for example the fit between the change and the person's vision, job motivation and employee–manager relationship (Parish et al. 2008).

The research indicated that whilst there has been a general shift towards the normalization of LGBT equalities in the UK, this has impacted in particular ways at the level of the individual. Firstly, individual champions of LGBT (historically, usually lesbian and gay equalities) have for many years been key to effecting change regarding sexuality in local authorities (Cooper 1994; Humphrey 1999). Secondly, discrimination or inappropriate attitudes are sometimes tackled directly, which can be uncomfortable for the individuals involved, for instance:

> ...some fire fighters, they came back in a fire engine and decided to go past a gay cruising site, and there was some shining of torches and stuff like that, and there was somebody from the Terence Higgins Trust there, who then made a complaint that that was personal intrusion...I think the fire fighters got off reasonably lightly...one of them was demoted I think for a period of time...they really did feel like they'd been hard-done-by, when they couldn't actually see what they'd done wrong.
> (Fire Service Diversity Representative, Southern England)

Thirdly, LGBT equalities work in the UK is centrally concerned with achieving a pro-equality professionalism amongst each local authority employee, so that people are inclusive of sexual and gender diversity whilst at work, regardless of their private views. This is done in a number of ways, drawing on classical techniques associated with Organizational Development such as staff trainings, but also through the consultation exercises that are now part of the New Public Management 'package'. A number of contributors to our research discussed pro-equalities professional practice, for example:

> Adult Social Services are doing some good stuff really, because what we, about twelve months ago, we looked at what we look at in care plans, when we're writing a care plan for somebody, and we've put race and ethnicity in there, and we put sexual orientation, you know, because if you're delivering personal care to somebody, you know, who sees you naked, who sees you on the toilet, who's going to be wiping your bottom, and really, we need to be very sensitive about that, and erm, understand the need for that sensitivity and the need to recognise serious relationships, you know, going into the home and not just assuming the man there is the person's brother or the girl there is a friend, or, and equally not making any assumptions the other way round.

(Manager, Wales)

The research also showed that identity management concerning LGBT equalities work is complex, and hence individuals might support change towards equalities but in the process distance themselves from certain forms of ideological baggage in a strategic way. For example, a Welsh lesbian housing officer who directly challenged discrimination regarding sexual orientation in her department then said that 'I'm not a you know red-flag waving unionist, but I tend to sort of say, "Right, this is what's happening, you're out of order" or whatever', whilst an ALS member from Southern England discussed the way in which she tackled difficulties with impact assessments: 'I . . . talk about local and national evidence about different equality groups. If I can give people more of the evidence, then they almost begin to do one [impact assessment] straight away'. In the first quote, the officer was discursively demonstrating her distance from left-wing politics (UK lesbian and gay equalities work was associated with the left in the 1980s), and in the second, the contributor distances themself from the LGBT equalities agenda by using standard professional mechanisms.

Overall, it can be seen that change regarding LGBT equalities takes place at a number of levels. Organizational change cannot be separated from the wider social context in which organizations operate, so some attention must be paid to this. Organizations themselves form the main focus of LGBT organizational studies, but the role of the individuals within these organizations is crucial. The chapter now moves on to apply and extend some of the concepts drawn from the organizational change literature.

Aspects of change regarding LGBT equalities in UK local government

There are a number of key aspects to organizational change regarding LGBT equalities in UK local government, including the 'control and leadership' aspects that were initially associated with the Classical school and then subsequently with New Public Management, and affectivity (emotions) and normative aspects, which lend themselves to change using techniques drawn from Organizational Development and Human Resources Management. These aspects of organizational change are explored, whilst acknowledging that changes in these areas are set in the context of broader social shifts, as outlined above.

Control, bureaucracy and leadership

As mentioned in the introduction to the chapter, Classical school approaches to organizational change and the New Public Management approaches which drew on the Classical school (along with other approaches) see people as rational actors who make choices that they think will be best for them. Structures, control, rules and leadership also form important aspects of these approaches. This section will consider the ways in which, since the mid-late 1990s, LGBT equalities work in the UK has been driven using New Public Management. Whilst the primary impetus for change towards LGBT equalities in local government has come from outside of local authorities (initially, pressure from the LGBT communities, more recently the legislative and cultural changes that have taken place in the UK), it can be argued that New Public Management, managerialism, and the associated Local Government Modernization Agenda are successfully being used to bring about progressive change concerning sexuality. In order to demonstrate this, the mechanisms for achieving change, including structures, leadership and impact assessments will be examined. There are other mechanisms for effecting change that fall within the Classical and New Public Management approaches, including the Equalities Standard, monitoring and performance management.

Local authorities in the UK have complex, bureaucratic structures. Equalities work within local authorities is often based in the chief executive's office or similar, sometimes in a designated Equalities unit, sometimes elsewhere such as within a Social Inclusion Unit. In the more proactive authorities, there are equalities leads within each directorate or department, charged with implementing equalities within the department, including front line service delivery, for example Kirklees Council's strategy *Equality and Diversity: An Enabling Framework for treating everyone fairly and valuing diversity*[1]. (This council was not one of the case study localities, however there was a wish to sample local authority strategies more widely). The strategy outlines the structure for the six strands of equality work in that authority, with Cabinet and Director Leads on equality and diversity, plus champions on the specific themes. There is representation on the Local Strategic Partnership from the local LGB Network. Work is driven down through the local authority via the *Equality and Diversity Strategy Action Plan 2007–2010*,[2] a 49-page document which outlines actions across the range of local authority services and employment and training, delineating which equalities strands the actions pertain to as well as who will take responsibility for implementing each action. Actions relating to sexuality include an Equality Impact Assessment of the Educational Psychology service in schools, and raising the issue of safety on public transport. Overall, the strategy demonstrates leadership, structures and control in relation to the equalities agenda.

The literature indicates that 'Most organisational theorists agree that the quality of leadership is a powerful contributor to organisational success' (Chemers and Murphy 1995: 157) and the research findings substantiated this. A range of contributors confirmed the value of leadership at senior management level, for instance:

> I have reported a couple of staff in the past for derogatory [in relation to LGBT] comments and they have been dealt with. I have to say I've got very good support from my management team. All of my managers are very supportive of anything anti-discriminatory, not just LGBT, anything, and they stamp it out.
>
> (Local Authority Officer, Southern England)

> . . . senior member of staff who made a stray comment about gays, and I just said 'Look, that's just not on', and he said 'Oh I hold my hand up, I shouldn't have done it', and it never happened again.
>
> (Senior Manager, Southern England)

LGBT equalities work is conducted most effectively when the views of key players are confluent with those evident in the central government initiatives and the legislation. The importance of supportive local politicians (elected members/councillors) was a strong theme to emerge from the research, and there were examples of positive leadership and action by elected members (see the chapter on democracy). This leadership was apparent where local politicians were supportive of the LGBT equalities agenda for value-driven reasons, but also where the agenda has become politically advantageous. For instance the North East England Action Learning Set members discussed competition between different councils to improve their Equalities Standard rating and how in one particular authority, the Leader of the Opposition was an openly gay man 'so therefore the ruling party have to demonstrate that they are reaching the gay community, and doing things for the gay community, otherwise they're going to lose that vote'. In addition to the importance of positive leaders, the key role played by proactive and committed staff throughout the organization was underlined in the research. These staff were often lesbian or gay (and/or were perceived to be lesbian or gay); bisexual and transgender staff were less visible within the organizations. It is worth pointing out however that an organizational reliance on LGBT people to promote the LGBT equalities agenda incurs a number of problems, including a lack of continuity (when staff leave) and the possibility of individual burnout. Also, a reliance of this sort acts to section off LGBT equalities so that rather than being mainstreamed, LGBT equalities can be seen as the responsibility of a few LGBT staff.

Impact assessments currently provide a means by which local authorities mainstream and implement equalities throughout their services. They involve vetting service provision in two stages, in order to assess the ways in which specific services or initiatives impact on the range of equalities groupings, firstly in terms of who the authority might need to consult and then adjusting policies in response to consultation. A Welsh officer described the way in which his authority has a programme of impact assessments:

> ... we monitor how many impact assessments have been done in accordance with that programme. I see every single impact assessment, we've just written our new programme now for the next three years and there's nearly 300 impact assessments there, we've looked at all our functions and policies, a policy might be Registration Services, the registration of births, deaths and marriages, so we've looked at all those functions and how they might be related to sexual orientation.

Impact assessments were viewed positively by a number of contributors. For example, an officer from North East England described the equalities impact assessments that are done whenever services are significantly changed as 'really good work because the old process kind of relied on people knowing the issues so if they didn't know about them, they wouldn't go out and consult with the community, so they'd say "Oh there's no equalities impact" '. In some cases impact assessments were also being used to directly challenge homophobia. For instance, one of the Welsh Action Learning Set members discussed a petition presented to a local authority asking for it to support the notion that heterosexual marriage was the 'only safe environment to bring up a child' (sic):

> The moment this was received it was sent to the equalities department for an equality impact assessment to prove by a proper audit, going through the proper equality impact procedures, that this was in its nature offensive to LGB people. But instead of just saying 'Oh this is offensive on sexual orientation grounds' they actually went through the whole process and that was publicised.

Structures, leadership and mechanisms such as impact assessments are all important for the implementation of LGBT equalities work in local government. These management methods, which are drawn from the New Public Management, are alive and kicking in UK local authorities. However, they are combined with techniques taken from Organizational Development, and it is to Organizational Development related approaches that the chapter now turns.

Organizational development and affective change

Earlier in the chapter we outlined the way in which Organizational Development, which evolved from the Human Relations school, focuses on effecting organizational change by getting organizational members to revise their mindsets: change happens by a process of individuals (and groups) 'unfreezing' and then 'refreezing'. In this section of the chapter the importance of Organizational Development style approaches to achieving LGBT equalities is discussed, using the case study of local government in the UK. Organizational Development approaches are particularly important in tackling entrenched inequalities because heteronormativity and prejudice against LGBT people have no rational basis – they are located in the realm of attitudes and feelings (affect). The research findings indicate that sexualities equalities work is particularly subject to affective issues such as nervousness and embarrassment, as well as normative judgements around notions of worthiness and legitimacy (this is discussed in more detail in the following chapter). The affective issues associated with tackling entrenched heterosexism can take place at any point in the work of local authorities or associated activities. For instance, one Action Learning Set member talked about the way in which they felt uncomfortable about being seen coming out of the LGBT group's community base, and this person explained (to the Action Learning Set) that this followed people disclosing personal experiences during the meeting:

> They highlighted to me people's perceptions of them. I thought 'Gosh, I never thought of all this', but as I said at our Action Learning Set, I was self-conscious when I was coming out of the door. I thought 'I wonder what people will think of me when I come out of this building, because my personal circumstances are that I'm (age) and never been married?', so I was thinking in my own head 'Will people associate the fact that I decided never to marry with my sexual orientation?'
>
> (Local Authority Officer, Northern Ireland)

Training provides one example of the influence of Organizational Development on organizational sexualities in local government in the UK. Organizational Development approaches were strongly evident in the local authorities that were proactive about LGBT equality, particularly with regard to training. Well-designed and inclusive equalities training programmes for officers and councillors were identified as crucial in order to develop organizational understanding and capacity in dealing with LGBT issues, given the ignorance that appears common within local authorities concerning the LGBT equalities agenda, as well as tackling embarrassment and fear. A common theme was the need for training that equips practitioners to challenge discriminatory and disrespectful behaviour by service users and colleagues. Emotional safety was also mentioned:

> People are terrified here about being labeled racist, so you'd rather not say anything. And I think it's the same thing that if you say something that is perceived to be offensive about sexuality, you're going to get the big stick. So people just don't say anything and I think that's a real pity. We need to open up the debate so that people can say: 'I'd never thought about that

particular aspect' or 'I didn't realise' or 'You know, I still feel uncomfortable about that but I do understand now where that's coming from.' And until you have a safe environment to have those discussions people are just going to bottle down any prejudices and, you know, they will come out when they are angry, or threatened, or drunk.

(Manager, Southern England)

It is clear that organizational change regarding heterosexism and LGBT equalities in UK local authorities is taking place in a way that draws on both New Public Management and those strands of management thinking that focus on the affective, normative aspects of change, specifically Organizational Development. There are also other drivers of change, including legislation, wider social attitudes and the role of committed individuals and groups within and outside of the local authorities.

The literature on LGBT-related processes in organizations is emerging rather than well-established; within this literature, there is a paucity of work concerning bisexuality or transgender. The chapter showed that the two broad schools within organizational studies (those relating to the New Public Management, and Human Resource Management style approaches, including Organizational Development) were both strongly evident in the case study of LGBT equalities work in UK local government. The strength of these all-pervasive management styles in pushing forward the LGBT equalities agenda provides an intriguing take on critical approaches that frame such approaches as working only to reinforce group-based inequalities. In other words, inequalities concerning sexuality and gender can clearly be addressed at an organizational level using mainstream management techniques, which do not have – in themselves – a particularly pro-equality agenda. Importantly, mainstream organizational change techniques do not seek to change underlying social inequalities concerning the distribution of resources, although they may – as part of a wider diversities package – seek to support greater recognition for groups such as LGBT people (see Fraser 2003). It is impossible to argue – from a critical stance – that mainstream organizational change methods cannot support progressive social change regarding LGBT people, even though these methods may have their limitations. Overall, therefore, the situation concerning organizational studies and LGBT equalities is a complex one.

It is possible to argue that organizational studies contribute both to the sedimentation of inequalities (specifically those concerning resource distribution) and to organizational transformation. This paradoxical process can be drawn on to develop understandings of LGBT organizational change. On the one hand, the management processes found in UK local government and partner organizations form a mechanism for challenging heterosexism, homophobia, biphobia and transphobia, or, at least, tackling overt discrimination against LGBT people. On the other, they consolidate notions of worthy citizens who contribute labour, and consumers who will be welcomed into the neoliberal fold because their money fuels the capitalist system, irrespective of sexuality and gender, at the expense of those people who do not conform to the model of 'good consumer and good citizen'. Discussions about LGBT organizational change need to show conversance with this paradox, which is mirrored elsewhere in this book, for example discussions about the shifting boundaries of citizenship, where 'good gay citizens' are becoming part of mainstream society. The organizational studies picture is further complicated with respect to statutory sector organizations because many service users will not necessarily be 'good consumers', and political and value-driven interests intersect with business interests at the organizational level.

This chapter has explored organizational change regarding sexuality and gender, focusing on heterosexism and LGBT identities. The chapter presented a snapshot of sexualities organizational studies and it then provided a case study of organizational change concerning LGBT equality work in the UK statutory sector (primarily local government), addressing change at three levels (society, institutions and individual) before looking at change in more depth using the organizational change literature.

Summary

- Sexualities organizational studies have begun to develop recently. LG and queer organizational studies are the 'new kids on the block', and bisexual and trans organizational studies are very underdeveloped.

- The range of approaches to organizational change are all relevant to LGBT equalities, in varied ways. The more traditional approaches, which focus on factors such as leadership and control, are important in providing structure, direction and implementation mechanisms.

- The approaches associated with a focus on attitudinal change are particularly important in relation to tackling affective blocks to LGBT equalities such as embarrassment and nervousness as well as overt prejudice.

- Organizational change takes place at different levels: wider society, institutions, and individuals; and change concerning LGBT equalities was apparent at each of these levels.

- The more critical and poststructuralist approaches to organizational change, whilst potentially useful, were not very evident in the organizational strategies and processes associated with statutory sector LGBT equalities work in the UK.

Having explored organizational change, the next chapter goes on to look at organizational resistance to change.

Resisting Change

Introduction

As the previous chapter highlighted, change in organizational cultures can be difficult and in the case of taking forward the LGBT equalities agenda there may be a range of factors operating at various levels that accentuate this. This chapter examines some of these in more detail, drawing on the literature on organizational change. The first part examines *Barriers and forms of resistance to change*, including cultural knowledge, attitudes and norms about sexuality and gender, organizational cultures and the visibility of LGBT people and sexualities and trans inequalities. The following section, *Areas of resistance*, considers where resistance occurs, including spatial dimensions of resisting change. Finally, the last part of the chapter on *Agents of resistance* looks at resistance at the level of the individual actor, through an exploration of constructions of the resisting subject, who may draw on narratives of resistance to block change.

One could think about taking a proactive approach to change and resisting change as two distinct and opposing positions. However, it is rarely if ever that simple. In recognizing the complexity of these processes it may be more helpful to think about a continuum of *narratives of change and resistance*, ranging from those approaches that emphasize the importance of organizations taking a positive proactive stance through to those which demonstrate various forms of direct and indirect resistance towards change. This way one can think about organizations and individuals being more or less proactive or more or less resistant in relation to specific issues (for example housing, violence, adoption) and certain contexts (for example geographical, political, religious). This allows for a more nuanced view of processes of resistance across different issues and contexts. In addition, as was demonstrated in the previous chapter, we also need to consider these variations at different intersecting levels. That is:

- *Societal*, in terms of shifts in public understanding and attitudes.
- *Institutional*, both formally in terms of legislative and policy changes affecting citizenship status and management practices and informally in terms of workplace cultures.

■ *Individual*, in terms of everyday social interactions and individual identities and subjectivities

In the following discussion different narratives of resistance are examined,
drawing on the findings from the research into LGBT equalities initiatives
in local authorities in the UK as a case study of why and how change may
be resisted within organizations. In this chapter there is a greater focus on
England and Wales as the situation in Northern Ireland is explored in depth
in Chapter 7. While the themes raised are of broad significance, the discussion is obviously more relevant to countries where there is a public mandate to
support LGBT rights.

Barriers and forms of resistance to change

Previous research in the UK has tended to focus on local authorities where
a substantial amount of work concerning sexualities equalities has occurred,
including councils with a long history of work in this area that predates
recent shifts in the policy landscape: for instance in Brighton, London and
Manchester (Cooper 1994, 1997; Cooper and Monro 2003; Browne 2007;
Lim and Browne 2009). Yet historically the majority of authorities have been
inactive or minimally active in this respect. In the research reported on here, a
key objective therefore was to include authorities that were relatively inactive
or resistant to conducting work in this field in order to understand both drivers
of social change in relation to sexualities and trans equalities work, and forms
of resistance. In particular, how change *and* resistance is legitimated, both in
terms of organizational cultures and at the individual level.

A continuum of approaches to responding to the LGBT equalities agenda
was evident in the study. We have broadly characterized five main approaches
along this continuum representing differing degrees of support, ambivalence or
resistance to LGBT equalities:

■ **Proactive** – This is something we positively support and champion.
■ **Compliance** – You do it because you have to.
■ **Omission** – We would if we could.
■ **Erasure** – Is there a need?
■ **Active Resistance** – We don't really want to know, we oppose LGBT
equalities.

In line with the notion of a continuum mentioned earlier, we do not regard
these as 'fixed points' in relation to each other. These characterizations are
better understood as discursive resources representing particular narratives
that organizations and individuals working within them may draw on to
implement or resist change. The previous chapter looked at drivers of organizational change in relation to promoting and supporting equality for lesbian,

gay, bisexual and transgender people. In this chapter the various forms that resistance to progressive constitutional and legislative frameworks concerning sexualities and transgender can take are examined, beginning with compliance.

Compliance: You do it because you have to . . .

Although legislative and policy changes, as well as local government modernization, were identified as the main drivers of change, what the findings also clearly demonstrated in line with other studies was that there is an 'implementation gap' between policy and practice on sexual orientation and trans issues (see, for example, Colgan et al. 2007), which often manifests as the inclusion of LGBT equalities in high-level policy documents with little being done 'on the ground'. The most common articulation of this was through the frequent reference in the interviews and the ALS to a 'tick-box approach' to LGBT equalities work. Although some could see certain benefits even with a 'tick-box approach' in getting the issues on the agenda at least, the overarching view was that this was compliance for its own sake. That is, where local authorities and other statutory agencies tick the LGBT equalities box because 'they want to be seen to be doing the right thing' without actively supporting or achieving change. This form of institutional resistance might be described as tokenism, doing the bare minimum to comply with equality law. As one person said: 'You know, we'll do what we have to, we'll tick a box if we have to.' One could see this as a form of passive resistance. However, several participants reflected on how compliance was not necessarily benign and could mask forms of discriminatory practice. For instance, one manager describing compliance within educational settings commented:

> And so what they do is they'll comply, but they simply can't go beyond that and, you know, compliance is just the beginning of it. In fact, you can be very effective in complying with something and do quite negative practice.
>
> (Manager, Southern England)

This is something that Sara Ahmed (2007) draws attention to in her analysis of the 'politics of documentation', which takes equality and diversity as measures of institutional performance. Focusing on the promotion of race equality, Ahmed discusses how compliance can mean that you end up 'doing the document, rather than doing the doing' (Ahmed 2007: 599). She highlights the introduction of performance indicators as key to this. In so far as they can be read as signs of good institutional performance, an organization can be *imagined* as having a commitment to equality despite adopting a minimalist approach. Performance management can be a lever to mainstream equalities, as was the case in our study, but what Ahmed is pointing to here is that it is also part of the problem of resistance. Compliance, like active resistance, might sustain forms of inequality by failing to fulfil the requirements of equality law, allowing institutions to block action and recognition of the work there is to do, at the same time as being seen to be doing this.

Omission: We would if we could . . .

In addition to a minimalist 'going along with it because you have to' approach, participants also gave examples of barriers to taking forward the LGBT equalities agenda which might mean that 'you want to, but you can't'. Many participants across the UK highlighted lack of resources as a key factor given the cultural value of equality and diversity work, and the low status of LGBT equalities initiatives in particular. This takes on particular significance in a climate of economic austerity, and in areas with high deprivation levels and poor quality of life indicators. As one of the South of England Action Learning Set member commented, in practice this often means that 'It's a "might do" after everything else'. Lack of capacity can lead to people feeling overstretched in their organizational roles. Several participants talked about the risk of people becoming exhausted and 'burnt out' by the struggle to effect change across the equality strands. For instance:

> I think what makes it difficult is there are still limited resources to do the work . . . we're still a very small number of people in terms of workers who are kind of consistently involved so you always feel like you're over-stretched in all you do, and that's quite hard. You know you're very motivated, but also very tired.
>
> (Local Authority Officer, North East England)

In considering forms of resistance to equalities initiatives, it is important, therefore, to consider the constraints on individuals taking on such roles and carrying out such work. Colgan et al. (2009), for instance, in exploring factors encouraging good practice in 'sexual orientation' equality work, highlight how such work continues to be perceived as a 'sensitive' area, in ways that did not appear to characterize other areas of equalities work, posing a significant challenge to getting organizational as well as individual commitment to sexualities equalities initiatives. Similarly Julian Randall and Stephen Proctor (2008), in their study of senior managers' responses to imposed organizational change, found that although individual staff may welcome change they may find its implementation 'uncongenial' in practice. They discuss this in terms of the concept of ambivalence, which they suggest involves differences across the cognitive, emotional and intentional dimensions of change. For example, it may be that a person accepts the principles and values involved and is intellectually on board, while at the same time feeling emotionally challenged by the implications of what this will mean in practice in their day to day working lives and relations with colleagues.

In our study there were a number of aspects that appeared to make sexualities and transgender equalities different from other forms of equalities work, including affective and moral issues, which could result in ambivalence towards taking the LGBT equalities agenda forward. In particular, cultural norms about sexuality – and LGBT issues in particular – being 'personal' and belonging in the 'private sphere' appeared to be particularly salient barriers to sexualities and trans equalities work. Echoing this public/private division between sexuality and the workplace, in much of the literature in mainstream organization studies 'organizations are considered formally desexualized spheres' (Fleming 2007: 239). This is despite studies which show that sexuality is clearly a significant feature of organizational cultures and workplace spaces (Hearn and Parkin 1995, 2001; Williams and Dellinger 2010).

Shona Hunter in her analysis of equality and diversity policies highlights how there are complex sets of emotional dynamics which complicate what is an already contested terrain of social policy making (Hunter 2011). Characterizing this as 'impossible governance', Hunter's focus is on how cultures of whiteness are sustained. However, her argument about the importance of affective factors in structuring diversity and equality policy making and practice is one that is also highly relevant to LGBT equalities work. In both the interviews and the ALS such issues of 'appropriateness' and being 'out of place' were seen as leading to people being generally much less comfortable talking about LGBT equality. Levels of personal discomfort were frequently described in terms of feelings of nervousness and embarrassment.

> **Interviewee:** Erm, I mean that again was, you could see people squirming in their seats, you know it was something that I've, you know, 'Do we really need?' [laughs], 'Do we really need to discuss this?' sort of thing [laughs], without saying it, but you could tell (–)
> **Interviewer:** Yeah.
> **Interviewee:** You could see, you could hear people sort of starting to shuffle in their seats, and you know, suddenly their eyes are sort of on the floor [laughs]. (Local Authority Officer, Wales)

A further barrier to this area of equalities work, also influenced by cultural norms about sexuality, is the stigma that is sometimes attached to it. Combined with the fact that sexual and transgender identities may be relatively 'hidden', this can lead to fears amongst some staff in being associated with supporting LGBT equalities initiatives, in particular that their sexuality might be under question. As one person stated, 'I don't do this because I am gay'. Participants also expressed fears that engaging in equality and diversity work might hamper career opportunities linked, in part, to its low status: indeed one person went so far as to say that this would represent 'career suicide'. As was highlighted in Chapter 3, there were also perceived political as well as personal risks of reputational 'damage' associated with fears about public reactions and not getting re-elected, as other studies have similarly found (Cooper 2004; Colgan et al. 2006; Monro 2006b). For instance, the following quote describes resistance among local politicians in an authority in the South of England toward attending a transgender consultation event.

> I think equally it would have been totally against their [councillors] principles, and then there would have been the consideration of 'If I am seen there and if I have my picture taken there, or are known to be there, then how is this going to play out in the press?', and all that sort of thing. So there is a bit around how they would perceive their reputation or any sort of reputational damage.
>
> (Senior Manager, Southern England)

There were also fears of a different nature. A significant number of respondents talked about fears about 'not knowing' about LGBT issues and the risk of being ignorant in working with LGBT people, talking almost as if they were 'a race apart', which seemed in stark contrast to the equality in sameness model of citizenship underpinning contemporary equalities work and LGBT politics. For instance:

> I think it is this fear of, fear of not getting it right, 'cause people do want to do a good job here, that's something that I think is fantastic about [this locality] really, how dedicated people are in difficult situations really, but people do want to do a good job but I think they're worried if they don't know enough.
>
> (Local Authority Officer, Wales)

Such fears could lead to inaction despite good intentions or, less generously, provide a 'good excuse'. A senior figure in one authority in the North East of England commented: 'People sometimes feel that they need to have a problem that they can understand and grasp, before they can start to find solutions or ways in which they can deal with it.'

Non-implementation through omission may then result from LGBT equalities 'falling off the agenda' as a consequence of organizational capacity issues, political concerns and the cultural valuing of equality and diversity as low priority work. It may also be a consequence of individual avoidance because, for the sorts of reasons that have been outlined, it seems too hard or too challenging. Acknowledging such factors, several participants ventured that doing sexualities and transgender equalities work 'takes a lot of guts', demanding bravery and courage.

Erasure: Is there a need?

Another way in which LGBT equalities initiatives were seen as different from other equality strands was in terms of visibility (though this may, for instance, be relevant to forms of disability, religious affiliation and ethnicity). For example, one of the members of the North East of England Action Learning Set said that staff often expressed the view that LGB people do not exist in their locality. This was a view which she saw as affecting the level and quality of service provision LGB people receive. Similarly one of the Welsh interviewees reported sitting in meetings with councillors who would say, 'We haven't got any gay employees'. These kind of attitudes, which were more apparent in rural contexts and can be interpreted at best as a barrier in the form of benign naiveté or, more negatively, as resistance through active denial of the existence of LGBT populations, illustrate the process of erasure. A process that is manifested in the wider culture of LGBT erasure that still prevails despite the greater visibility of lesbians and gay men (less so bisexual and trans), for instance within the media and through the public recognition of civil partnerships.

This lack of visibility of LGBT people can lead to the assumption of a lack of the need to address LGBT equalities. A situation that is further compounded by the barriers to LGBT people coming out, which may mean that they do not necessarily engage as 'customers' of local authority services and remain a 'hidden population'. This can also be used as an excuse for inaction, on the grounds that because 'we don't hear about it' or 'we don't get any complaints' discrimination doesn't exist or at least can be presumed to be the case. Other studies lend support to this argument. For example, Colgan et al. (2007: 606), in their study of organizational 'good practice' concerning equality and diversity, found that there were 'strong concerns about the ways in which organisations relied on LGB people to come forward with complaints before tackling problems'. Such 'organisational passivity' was also evident in our research as is illustrated by the following quote from a councillor in the South of England, which demonstrates the lack of understanding of effects of discrimination in interpreting the absence of grievance procedures as meaning there is no problem for staff who are lesbian, gay, bisexual and transgender.

> It's very important to me from the HR point of view to make sure that those people are not discriminated against, but I cannot think of any incidence where anyone has been discriminated about, against, and if they had been then surely I would have known because it would have come to me as a case . . . If we did receive a request from a group that said 'Look we feel that we're being discriminated against', then we would have to deal with that and act upon it and as far as I'm concerned that hasn't happened.
>
> (Councillor, Southern England)

The implication is that responsibility rests on LGBT people to raise awareness. A vicious circle is operating here as the following quote illustrates.

> I think sexual orientation is a different beast in their eyes and I suppose it is different, because it's much more subtle, and they say 'Well how can we

ensure services meet their needs if they don't come out?', it's this need to be out which is difficult, I think we can deal with visible difference.

(Manager, Wales)

This lack of visibility as compared to other equality strands is part of the argument for the introduction of monitoring schemes, in order to 'play the numbers game' and establish the presence of LGBT populations in particular locales (see Creegan and Keating 2010). However, even where such presence is established other processes of erasure may be in operation that relate to the question of 'Is there a need?' in a different sense. These are where historically and culturally specific concerns over the legitimacy of LGBT-related issues of discrimination and inequality are raised. For example, earlier chapters highlighted how stereotypes of lesbians, gay men and bisexuals as middle class and relatively affluent could mitigate against their being seen as facing discrimination (demonstrating a construction of inequality in terms of redistribution rather than recognition). As noted, contemporary cultural assumptions about sexualities, if not trans, as being about 'lifestyle choice' and a 'private matter' can add to this. Here the risk of erasure is connected with a lack of visibility of equalities issues affecting sexual and gender minorities, as well as LGBT people themselves.

Judgements around legitimate need and 'worthiness' leading to erasure are manifested also in relation to other equalities issues, the perceived hierarchy of equality strands discussed in Chapter 1, with the risk of sexualities and trans equalities initiatives being lost among a range of priorities especially in a climate of economic austerity. It is also the case that certain LGBT-related issues may be regarded as less legitimate and worthy of support, and more at risk of processes of resistance – including erasure – than others. We will come back to this later in the section on *Areas of resistance*.

Processes of erasure operate at both institutional and individual levels. At the institutional level, the discursive erasure of LGBT issues can be noticeable in policy documents, and in the ways in which equalities issues are discussed (or not) within local authorities (Monro 2005). Processes of erasure can occur in other ways. For example, although the introduction of an integrated approach to equality, discussed in Chapter 1, may be considered useful in driving forward the LGBT equalities agenda, there are risks in adopting such policies that the detail of LGBT equalities may be erased. Another example of organizational erasure mentioned by one or two participants was where local authority computer systems put firewalls in place resulting in people not being able to access information, including details of LGBT services and support groups.

A lot of library services block searches that include the words lesbian, gay or bisexual, and it's a blanket block because it assumes that they're all spam or porn. So people who are generally looking for support or advice or help can't actually find those services if they don't have their computer at home, and that quite often is these people who need it most, because they're likely to be the most economically deprived.

(Bi Community Representative, Wales)

Cultural norms and beliefs about sexuality and gender also inform such institutional forms of erasure. The institutionalization of heterosexuality within society and culture more generally has been a core theme of feminist and queer theory over the last two decades (see, for example, Warner 1993; Richardson 1996; Seidman 2009; Richardson et al. 2012). What this body of work highlights is that heterosexuality is normally an unquestioned assumption, 'deeply embedded in accounts of social and political participation, and our understandings of ourselves and the worlds we inhabit' (Richardson 1996: 1). In her discussion of 'inequality regimes' in organizations, Joan Acker (2006: 445) similarly argues that heterosexuality is assumed, unquestioned 'in many organizing processes and in the interactions necessary to these processes'. This was evident in our findings, several people who were interviewed commented on cultural assumptions within their organizations that everyone is or should be heterosexual.

This institutionalization of heterosexuality within society and culture is also linked to particular normative constructions of gender (Butler 1993; Jackson 2012). As Tam Sanger (2008) and others such as Monro (2005) have pointed out, the gender binary is an extremely influential discursive framework that connects sex, gender and sexuality together in particular ways (see also Richardson 2007), which can make it difficult for certain experiences and subjectivities to be intelligible. As a consequence, this can lead to the erasure of 'other' sexualities and genders. This is something a number of participants drew attention to, as is illustrated by the following quote from a gay employee working in the North East of England.

I wish more policies didn't just state in blanket terms, they just actually said who they apply to, because I think that there's [for] such a very long time now LGBT people have not been included, have been actively excluded, so that if you don't actually state that you mean us in your policy, there's an assumption that you don't, you know that this applies to whatever the general statement is...But if you don't say sexual orientation, people will assume that it means everybody but us, and I don't think enough organisations are getting their heads around that.

(Manager, North East England)

This form of institutional inequality often co-existed with a reduction of reporting of direct discrimination by lesbian, gay, bisexual and trans colleagues, giving a false impression of the level of LGBT inequalities experienced. Direct discrimination is still very real in some organizations and may affect particular groups within the LGBT acronym particularly strongly. Brett Chamberlain (2009) reports on UK research showing that bisexuals face substantial amounts of marginalization and bullying and harassment within the workplace. In the research on LGBT equality in local government examples of institutionalized heteronormativity and homophobic, biphobic and transphobic workplace cultures highlighted how it could be quite hard for LGBT employees to be out at work, reinforcing the invisibility of LGBT people as well as LGBT equalities issues. This was one area where it was recognized that erasure may impact differently on different strands within the LGBT cluster, with bisexual and trans communities seen as particularly vulnerable to high levels of erasure. For instance, commenting on visibility issues in relation to trans a senior equality and diversity officer in the South of England said:

> I think it's the whole transgender issue I think has not yet really emerged with any great clarity, just because I think that there's still, I think society in general is much more aware of and perhaps enlightened should we say about the gay and lesbian community, but I think in the transsexual, transgender community I think that they've still got a long way to go in terms of acceptance, in terms of understanding of the community as a whole, and as a consequence I think a lot of it is still very much underground and people are not, you know, prepared to 'come out'...
>
> (Manager, Southern England)

Active opposition: We don't really want to know, we oppose LGBT equalities

Despite the legislative and policy shifts that have occurred over the last decade there was evidence of resistance to change that went beyond ambivalence about LGBT equalities associated with lack of knowledge or feelings of discomfort, where people were 'still acting on very basic and clearly unsubstantiated prejudice' and being deliberatively obstructive. The kind of attitude expressed in the following quote: 'We don't really know anything about that and we don't really want to know anything about that.' Barriers that were seen as preventing or slowing down organizational change included lack of or poor leadership, underlying the importance placed on key individuals and personal characteristics. For instance, active resistance to change was frequently explained in psychological terms as the effects of 'discrimination' and 'prejudice', the latter term used more frequently in Northern Ireland, as well as 'homophobia' and, less so, transphobia (biphobia was referred to hardly at all and lesbophobia never). Although it has become a widely used term, 'homophobia' has been subject to various critiques within the literature (for example Adam 1998; Herek 2004), although more recently there have been attempts to rethink its utility (see, for example, Bryant and Vidal-Ortiz 2008). In particular, critiques have problematized the concept for its individualistic focus which, it is argued, draws attention away from the social and institutional aspects of LGBT inequality. In this sense, the increasing use of the term can be seen as part of a wider process of the depolitization of LGBT issues referred to elsewhere in this book.

Such concerns were borne out in the research findings, as indicated above, in so far as resistance to sexualities and transgender equalities was largely construed as a consequence of individual discriminatory practices. For example, a substantial number of research participants referred to the negative impact of certain managers and councillors who were unsympathetic to LGBT equality issues. Attitudinal resistance of this kind was sometimes seen as linked to political parties and faith communities that had in the past been unsympathetic to LGBT equalities, and where active resistance could be seen as a matter of 'pride', the 'acceptable face' of prejudice and discrimination. As one participant commented: ' I mean, it's the only prejudice I know where people can make a homophobic comment and at the same time make some kind of claim about their moral character '. (See Box 6.1.)

Box 6.1   Case study: Barriers to change in action

Where attempts are made to deliberately oppose the implementation of the equalities agenda, or block or slow it down through inaction, we refer to this as active resistance. Such forms of resistance can range from deliberate omission or erasure through to the active blocking of LGBT equalities initiatives, both administratively and politically, as is illustrated in the following quotes. In the first case of erasure all reference to sexualities is effectively removed by substituting the more 'diversity neutral' term 'different communities'. In the second quote resistance is through more direct blocking.

> **Interviewee:** I've had red lines through reports, where I've used the terminology, 'lesbian, gay, bisexual' (–)
> **Interviewer:** Right, so they want you to take out that?
> **Interviewee:** Yes.
> **Interviewer:** And use 'sexual orientation'?
> **Interviewee:** And just use 'different communities'.

(Equalities Manager, Wales)

> Initiatives were blocked, basically stopped above my head and didn't go any further within the council. I just remember sitting down with them [local voluntary sector organisation] and making a note of all their suggestions and then sending the memo to line management and it didn't go any further ... politically handcuffed.
> (LGB Community Member, Northern Ireland)

Resisting resistance

That local authorities now have a public duty to implement recent legislative and policy shifts that recognize the rights of LGBT people carries with it an expectation that staff will take such recognition into their public lives at work. However, it should be clear from the previous discussion that there were limits to this in terms of the kinds of barriers and resistance that were evident. Some writers have distinguished tolerance, as an attitude and 'virtue', from toleration, as forms of practice (see Brown 2006). In our study *overt* homophobia, which might include the expression of negative attitudes about sexual minorities, refusal to provide services and work with such groups and 'office banter', was generally considered to be no longer socially acceptable in the workplace, although overt biphobia for example stereotyping bisexuals as 'greedy' or 'indecisive' was quite apparent and is reported in other research (Chamberlain 2009). One contributor remarked that:

> you can't make homophobic comments in the workplace, because it counts as bullying and harassment . . . but they aren't necessarily aware that calling bisexual people greedy falls under that as well; and it tends to be, certainly in terms of anecdotal evidence and things I've heard from people it's more acceptable to make those comments about bisexual people and they won't be challenged as much by employers.
>
> (Bisexual Community Member, Wales)

It is clear from the research on LGBT equalities in local government that homophobic, biphobic and transphobic practices did still occur and could lead to LGBT staff feeling that it was 'unsafe' to come out at work. Other studies have also highlighted this. For example, Gavin Ellison and Briony Gunstone (2009), in their large-scale survey, found that many people working in key sectors and services – including education, the police and health services – feel that they cannot come out without fear of prejudice or discrimination.

Although many of those who were interviewed expressed desire for change through winning 'hearts and minds', it was recognized that one was often more likely to be dealing with *behavioural* change to be addressed through putting professional mechanisms in place, including training opportunities and personal performance management. In other words, 'acceptance' of LGBT equality was framed predominantly in behavioural terms rather than in terms of a person's attitudes and beliefs: what was considered acceptable behaviour in the public spheres of local authority work. However, it is important to acknowledge that some contexts of work could be regarded as less public and more 'off-duty' than others. These tensions were managed in some authorities through reference to professionalization. LGBT equalities work was framed as part of professional norms and duties, an ethic of public service and care that is typically associated with public sector organizations (Humphrey 1999; Cutcher 2009), regardless of a person's private beliefs. Related to this it was also, in part, about the management of prejudice through privatizing it. Several participants, for example, recognized that some staff may retain their prejudices to LGBT people despite the new public duties associated with the single Equality Act. However, they frequently emphasized a workplace culture modality that rejected prejudice being enacted or voiced publically with potential negative consequences for a person's career if this did occur. There were, then, acknowledged differences between public normalcy of LGBT equalities and private practice, as the following quotes illustrate.

> I think the council, you can't change people's minds necessarily but you can change their behaviour in terms of what you accept and what's acceptable behaviour and what's manageable... as an employer the council has an absolute role in doing everything it can to remove those issues from the workforce and from the delivery of services, but there's a reality to that in that you can't change an individual's personal view and thoughts, all you can do is determine what is acceptable behaviour on their part in those situations.
>
> (Manager, North East England)

> It's about people being given very clear parameters, you do that ever again I will sack you, I don't care what you think when you go home or what you say when you're down the pub, well I do but nevertheless I can't legislate against that but when it's reported to me [at work] that's a clear example.
>
> (Local Authority Officer, North East England)

What this suggests is that the increased public acceptability (if not acceptance) of LGBT individuals/issues also represents, in this context at least, a shift from a previously privatized tolerance to a privatization of intolerance. What we have referred to elsewhere as public duty occurring alongside private prejudice (see Richardson and Monro 2012).

This first section of the chapter has outlined a continuum of approaches or *narratives of resistance* to LGBT equalities, ranging from compliance to active resistance. However, as stated earlier, these are not conceptualized as 'fixed points' along a continuum, but rather discursive positions that organizations and individuals may draw upon in various policy and practice areas. It is also important to recognize that the process of describing these represents an artificial separating out of these different narratives, which may intersect and reinforce each other. For instance, one might consider the ways in which the perceived legitimacy of LGBT equalities intersects with levels of visibility, where visibility here refers to the degree of awareness of LGBT equalities. High legitimacy of inequality (*LGBT equality is wrong*) and low visibility (*low levels of understanding and awareness*) may interact in ways that enhance the possibilities for resistance (see Acker 2006). For example, the following quote from an officer in the South of England illustrates how practices of omission arising from the challenge of resourcing equality initiatives are likely to be underscored in workplace cultures where there is negative leadership and a lack of motivation to do such work that may manifest as minimal compliance, erasure or active resistance – or indeed all three in varying contexts. In terms of resisting such resistance, it is also important to acknowledge inequalities of power within organizations where professional hierarchies, especially at senior level, often mirror inequalities within society more generally. As other studies have found, this 'uneven strength and influence' means that those in more powerful institutional positions can block equality agendas (Cooper 2006: 933).

> I don't have the time if I'm honest, I don't have the time...I struggle to squeeze LGBT in, partly my fault because I need to start allocating more time for that, but partly because there's not much enthusiasm out there, and that's also from members [councillors] and I would also say from the existing county council.
>
> (Union LGBT Officer, Southern England)

It follows from this that we should be careful not to generalize about the likely effects of any of the approaches that have been outlined. Where resistance occurs in local authorities its impact can be considered in terms of specific areas or 'pockets of resistance' at a number of intersecting levels including:

- the type of LGBT equalities work that takes place within organizations
- differences within the LGBT cluster
- variations across different sections and levels within local authorities
- spatial aspects of resistance

In the next section of the chapter each of these are examined in turn.

Areas of resistance

Equality issues

There are specific issues associated with LGBT equalities initiatives, including, for example, violence, housing issues, provision of goods and services, employment rights, civil partnerships and adoption and fostering, that may lead to different forms of resistance being deployed unevenly. This relates to the discussion in Chapter 3 about how lesbian, gay, bisexual and trans citizenship is constituted and, also, the ways LGBT as imagined communities are constructed as deserving – or not – of services. For example, our research findings indicated that homophobic bullying was one issue considered 'difficult to argue with'. If active resistance was thought to be unlikely in this case, other areas of LGBT equalities work were perceived to be more at risk of being avoided or opposed. This was particularly apparent in relation to adoption and fostering. For instance:

> I think that with all equality issues there are extremes, there's a sort of a middle ground that a lot of people would buy into and fully support and then there are the aspects that people find more extreme and people aren't ready for,.... they just think that LGBT issues is about fostering and adoption and letting gay people adopt, which a lot of people feel really, really anti, but actually I think the main part of the agenda is about making sure school children aren't bullied and harassed and about making sure that people

aren't disadvantaged in getting employment, that they have services delivered properly and I know that you could say fostering and adoption is a service but that's sort of more at the outer reaches.

(Manager, Southern England)

These sorts of concerns about different areas of resistance mean that certain LGBT equalities issues are likely to be prioritized over others, in some instances, in a strategic manner as a step to fostering a culture of acceptance of LGBT equalities. This was seen as particularly important in previously inactive local authorities, or where there was thought to be opposition to LGBT equalities initiatives.

LGBT diversity

It is also important to recognize that different forms of resistance might be more or less specific to the discrete lesbian, gay, bisexual and trans communities as well as certain equalities issues. For instance, in a similar vein to the previous quote, a manager in a Welsh authority talked about how resistance can operate in the case of lesbians and gay men seeking to foster or adopt, ranging from compliance through to blocking, in ways that may be gendered as a consequence of prejudicial cultural stereotyping of gay men.

I think lesbians fare better than gay men do in that arrangement [fostering and adoption], you know, I think gay men still suffer very much from that view of predatory men, paedophiles you know...

(Manager, Wales)

In other ways gay men seem to fare rather better than other strands within the LGBT cluster, certainly in relation to visibility and access to resources which, as already outlined, are influential factors underlying practices of resistance such as omission and erasure. For example, responses to our interview questions and discussion within the ALS suggested few links with local lesbian, bisexual and trans community groups. Also, as has been discussed elsewhere in the book, many participants made no specific reference to bisexuality and there was very little evidence of equalities work being done specifically around bisexuality. This last point suggests that erasure is a particularly salient issue in delivering equalities to bisexual people, and also that bisexuality is marginalized within some of the community organizations that work in partnership statutory sector organizations, as the following quote indicates:

... trying to explain service delivery in a context where, bisexuality, identity is important in that service delivery is quite difficult to explain in a one-meet opportunity. So your sexual orientation is only ever relevant in the moment in which you're being served to be honest.... What needs to happen is, is in any service context, I need to be able to disclose the full aspects of my life and I need to have some indication that I'm able to do that; but if I am in a relationship with my husband and we've got three kids, but I personally identify as bisexual, housing provider don't need to get that right now; and all I need the housing provider to do is not treat the lesbian who comes next badly. So I can't mix her head up too much with too many different things.

[LGB Community Organisation Representative, England]

Although there was more discussion about transgender issues and the needs of trans people, it was clear that compared to lesbian and gay communities these issues and needs were much less well understood, which could also lead to erasure as well as omission. It is also important to recognize variation in forms of direct and indirect resistance within as well as across the different strands of the LGBT cluster. For example, the need to recognize diversity within trans populations, in terms of both individual subjectivities and identities and in government policies, has been highlighted by a number of recent studies (see, for example, Hines 2007; Monro 2007a; Stryker et al. 2008; Hines and Sanger 2010). As we also found, lack of visibility and the risk of erasure was much more apparent in the case of some trans people than others, particularly for transmen.

Organizational cultures

We can also think about areas of resistance in terms of variations across different sections and levels within local authorities. Previous studies have found that willingness of different services or directorates to respond to lesbian and gay equalities is variable. Davina Cooper, for instance, reported that 'housing, leisure and community services were usually more responsive than technical and direct labour departments' (Cooper 1994, 2006: 926). The research findings indicated that more traditional community service-based functions, such as neighbourhood services and environmental teams, were likely to be seen as the most resistant to change. In part this was understood in terms of specific institutional factors, including workplace cultures that exhibited 'old-fashioned' management styles and where there was a lack of professionalization and training that meant staff often did not understand or see the relevance of equalities issues to their work. For instance, the following quote from an elected member in the North East of England at a very senior level (Deputy Leader) expresses this sense of concern about certain 'pockets of resistance' within local authorities.

Our neighbourhood services team, you know environmental street services, are always the most difficult to shift we find, they've kind of got an old style command and control management thing to it, whereas children's services or adult services there's quite a bit of one to one working anyway, as opposed to you know, we provide a service for a street... There's not the same degree of professional development, you know what I mean, there's not part of their work where diversity would be a rather natural element of their work ... You know, you drive this machine to clean the streets, so we'll train you to drive this machine.

(Councillor, North East England)

In addition to certain organizational cultures making change more difficult to achieve, some participants also thought that it was about 'the kinds of people that are attracted to these jobs' being more likely to be resistant to LGBT equalities than staff working in other sectors of the authority. For example:

[I]t is partly their attitudes are more driven by the stuff at the club, and stuff they pick up from the tabloids, partly because their management are not flagging it up strongly enough about diversity in their work.

(Community and Voluntary Sector Project Worker, North East England)

This is discussed further later on in the chapter in the section on Agents of resistance.

Geographies of resistance

In thinking about areas of resistance it is important to consider how resistance to LGBT equalities may be spatially structured. Previous work has highlighted how LGBT equalities initiatives tend to be concentrated in urban areas and this was also the case in our research. However, one of the original aims of the study was to include rural as well as urban contexts for investigation in order to examine spatial aspects of LGBT equalities work in local government (see also the section on Space in Chapter 2, and Monro 2010b). This is important in a much wider sense. The focus on the metropolis has dominated ways of studying and theorizing LGBT lives, what Halberstam (2005) refers to as 'metronormativity' (see also Herring 2010).

The findings complement work by other researchers such as Moran and Skeggs (2004) on sexuality and violence, as well as developments in geographies of sexuality (for example Bell and Valentine 1995; Browne et al. 2007; Johnson and Longhurst 2009), in particular concerning rural and small town sexualities. Mary Gray, for example, in her ethnographic study of LGBT youth in rural Kentucky documents some of the issues connected with being 'out in the country' (see also Phillips et al. 2000; Little 2003 and, including work in an Australian context, Pini et al. 2012). In our research the importance of the spatial in shaping the cultures of the communities that local authorities represent was also evident, as will be illustrated by drawing on the findings from the Welsh case study and Action Learning Set.

The geographical dispersal of the Welsh population and attendant difficulties with communication and travel emerged as a major – in some instances a predominant – factor in the way that LGBT people's lives are structured and the local authority work that may (or may not) be taking place concerning LGBT equalities within Wales. A number of Welsh contributors from the case study (both local authority officers and community members) talked about the difficulties that LGBT people have accessing LGBT social spaces due to geographical barriers. The geographical characteristics of the country also pose a barrier to community organization, with one LGBT community organization representative discussing the obstacles to conducting community consultations in mid Wales: 'It is very difficult because mid Wales is very spread out, and has a lot of mountains in between major towns'. Many of the contributors to the research also discussed the ways in which Welsh LGBT people are socially excluded when they live in rural areas *and* are young, older, cannot drive or do not have access to private transport, or access to the internet, or are ill or disabled.

The research also highlighted how the geographical dispersal of people into small, close-knit communities often entails a lack of understanding of diversity and localized cultures of prejudice. The Welsh Action Learning Set, which included representatives from a range of southern and mid-Welsh authorities as well as two LGBT community representatives, raised issues concerning the importance of local communities, the church, in rural and small town settings in Wales, and the ways in which heterosexism constrains the lives of LGBT people who live in these localities. The town where the case study was conducted was described by both community members and local authority officers as having a 'laddish', homophobic culture (although across the study more generally there were also some indications that spatially defined (primarily heterosexual) rural communities could be supportive of local LGBT people.) Prejudice was structured in particular ways, with homophobic violence and displays of machismo serving to performatively shape heteronormative space (see Valentine 2002; Browne et al. 2007). For example, one of the (gay male) community members reported instances of violence against gay men and said that: 'fear is prevalent here, it really is among the gay community, and I think the bisexual community feel it more because you've got the gay community on one side that's hostile towards them and you've the straight community . . . they've got prejudices on both sides really'. This lack of understanding of sexual diversity was then reflected – and perpetuated by – local authority actors, for example:

[I]f those gay members of staff that are working in departments like Children and Young People are afraid of the stigmatisation of being predatory, not appropriate to work with children, all these other stereotypes that abound, that haven't gone away in Wales, that perhaps if you were working in Manchester, Brighton or elsewhere, you'd know that wasn't a sensible way of thinking, those stereotypes would have already been challenged, you know, you'd know that was an antiquated way of thinking, or completely wrong but here, there's no, there's only me I think sometimes who goes around challenging that, you know.

(Manager, Wales)

In the following section resistance to change at the level of the individual is examined in more detail.

Agents of resistance

The emphasis on the individual actor as an agent of change or resistance took a number of forms. The discussion in the first section of the chapter highlighted how affective issues, including embarrassment and levels of discomfort, as well as fears associated with lack of understanding and perceptions of personal and professional risk can lead to resistance to change. This section considers resistance at the level of the individual in further detail in terms of characteristics identified as potential barriers to change in relation to promoting equality for lesbian, gay, bisexual and trans people, including occupational position and level with organizations, political persuasion, gender, age, sexuality, class background, race and ethnicity, and faith and religious belief. As was outlined in Chapter 2, it is important to recognize that these are not discrete but rather intersecting categories. It is not however our intention here to discuss their interaction, nor debate the meanings associated with these categories, but rather to highlight what the participants in our research associated with being an agent of resistance.

There was a substantial amount of data that illustrated the perceived importance of leadership in understanding organizational change and resistance to change, both in terms of senior management roles within local authorities and from outside in particular via the public political support of elected members. The importance of party political support for the equalities agenda has been highlighted in earlier research (Monro 2006b). However, since then there has been a shift towards greater cross-party support for LGBT equalities, in England and Wales at least (see Chapter 7 for a discussion of the situation in Northern Ireland). That said, it remains to be seen what, if any, impact the ConDem coalition government formed in 2010 between the Conservatives and Liberal democrats will have. Concerns have already been expressed about the government's 'Red Tape Challenge', which invites the public to comment, amongst other things, on the Equality Act and its implementation. Such concern is perhaps not surprising given that the term 'red tape' is commonly associated with (in this case getting rid of) excessive regulation and beaurocracy.

Although some participants were generally positive about societal shifts that influence elected members, and felt that councillors are now aware of their responsibility to represent everybody from the 'widest possible spectrum of backgrounds', a significant number of those who took part in the research referred to older, white, male staff in senior positions as managers – as well as elected members – as being potentially, though not inevitably, unsympathetic to minority community issues. This is supported by other studies, which have found similar demographics in relation to people likely to hold discriminatory attitudes towards LGB people (see, for example, Mitchell et al. 2008).

There were, for instance, references to senior managers and councillors showing active resistance by attempting to block the LGBT equalities agenda or deliberately slow it down. Political resistance among local politicians was generally associated with being more 'right wing' and belonging to parties that had in the past been unsympathetic to LGBT issues. For instance:

> Interviewee: I think if you looked at the profile of elected members, where they are white, male, elderly, and dare I say it, Tory, right wing shall we say, the potential is there for them not to have [inaudible] to LGBT or the equality agenda is quite high...
>
> Interviewer: So am I right in thinking what you've referred to there is the potential for resistance, but in terms of putting subtle or not so subtle barriers?
>
> Interviewee: Yes but also...
>
> Interviewer: Slowing things down?
>
> Interviewee: Slowing things down, being deliberately obstructive.
>
> (Senior Manager, Southern England)

It was not only at the most senior levels of the occupational hierarchy in local authorities where the possibility of resistance was identified, the demographics of frontline workers in some services were also seen as predisposing them to resist LGBT equalities. The classed construction of this was very evident, with assumed occupational divisions between working-class and middle-class workers in relation to equality and diversity issues. For example, one community development worker in the North East of England described how she thought class was a predictor of tolerance and, as a consequence, forms of resistance arising from intolerance.

> I do feel in many parts of the council it is safe to do that [come out]. But I am sure that in, in maybe Neighbourhood Services, where you're employing more blue collared workers where it's, I mean this tolerance thing is quite a middle class thing and I wonder if there's as much tolerance, you know, in some of the depots and where people are doing manual work.
>
> (Community Development Worker, North East England)

If this is the case, how then are we to explain those in middle-class occupational positions within authorities resisting change? What other demographics of resistance were identified that might intersect with class? A significant number of those who took part in the research referred to older, male, heterosexual staff in general as being 'homophobic'. It is perhaps unsurprising that age was picked out as a significant factor, given the dramatic shifts in cultural understandings, attitudes and norms about sexuality and gender that have taken place over the last 50 years (Weeks 2008a). The meanings attached to sexuality and gender are differently organized according to their specific historical and cultural location (Richardson 2007). This is what Plummer (1995) refers to as the ever-changing stories of homosexuality and, one could add, bisexuality and transgender. As has been outlined in previous chapters, public recognition and valuing of (some) lesbians, gay, bisexual and transgender people do suggest that important shifts are taking place in what it means to be LGBT (as well as heterosexual, Richardson 2004). At the same time, 'old stories' about sexual and gender minorities are unlikely to simply disappear and continue to exert influence alongside these 'newer' stories. There may then be generational effects evident in forms of resistance to LGBT equalities that reflect the experience of having lived through different and competing discourses about sexuality in general, and sexual and gender diversity in particular.

The importance of temporal dimensions of resistance is supported by studies of organizational change. Such studies (for example McLoughlin et al. 2005; Randall and Proctor 2008) suggest that the extent to which a person is able to assimilate the meaning of change within their cultural values and norms, as well as their ability to refashion and re-define those aspects about which they are ambivalent, is important to their accepting change or, in the case of this not happening, change becoming a point of resistance. Following on from this, Leanne Cutcher (2009) argues that resistance is intertwined with 'worker subjectivity' and that this requires us to consider the temporal as well as the spatial (in terms of shared understandings of 'place') aspects of resistance. What she is highlighting is how individuals draw on understandings of themselves and their organizations in ways that are sedimented over time (see also Strangleman 2004). Workers may draw on discourses of the past as well as the present and their expectations of the future to make sense of organizational change, and where this threatens a person's sense of self-continuity, resistance may occur. Normalizing discourses can render this more or less 'acceptable' and such narratives of resistance may be drawn on as rationalizations or 'excuses' for resistance to change, for example where there is a dominant belief that a person's attitudes are hard to change later in life. For instance:

> I would say that young people are accepting gays and transsexuals in the workplace much better than they have in the past. I think that the young community are ... more willing to accept and work with these people, whereas, you know, people of my age and older, say pensioners, who have been brought up to, when I was a lad if a person was a homosexual it was 'Oh look, keep away from him, he's a homosexual'. Now that would not be the case, it's a person with a different way of life that we, that we accept ...
> (Councillor, Southern England)

Related to this, the changing age profile of the workforce, particularly at senior levels, was seen as likely to remove barriers to resistance within organizations in the future.

> [T]he blockers are the ones that are in the middle management, senior management, but they are getting towards the end of their service and

they'll be moving on soon, so you'll only get younger, more dynamic, more diversity-savvy people that are going to be moving into those roles.

(LGBT Community Representative, Southern England)

Constructions of agents of resistance were not only age-related, gendered and (hetero)sexualized, race and ethnicity were also seen as part of the demographics of resistance. Whiteness typically configured the resisting subject, although there was some reference to BME (black and minority ethnic) groups. This included, for example, discussion of homophobia within some sections of traveller communities and African-Caribbean communities (see also Chapter 2 on intersectionality).

Finally, the influence of religious beliefs was seen as particularly important in influencing how resistant or not particular authorities and individuals within them were to LGBT equalities. As an officer in the North East of England remarked: 'There are some people who have religious objections to it and that probably raises *the most vexing issue*, the conflict between religious and LGB issues' (our emphasis). While it is clear that there are tensions between these equality strands, contributors were also aware that this could be used strategically as a narrative of resistance that enables councils and individuals an 'opt out' of doing LGBT equalities work. For instance, a member of the South of England Action Learning Set talked about 'faith driven homophobia' still being accepted which 'can be used as a "smokescreen"'. Another contributor said that:

I think there is a really, really bigoted mindset still very common which is don't touch on sexuality because it might offend people who have strongly Christian religious views or might offend people with Muslim views... it's not even because the work has been done, we haven't researched 'Are people uncomfortable with it?' It's almost assuming that people will be uncomfortable with it.

(Local Authority Officer, Northern Ireland)

However, it is important to note that faith was not necessarily seen as a barrier to supporting LGBT equalities work and, in some instances, could be regarded as having positive effects. For example:

I'm not aware of people's religious beliefs getting in the way of how they behave in a place of work, I've not come across it. I've got some very strong Christians who work for me... and I've got some Muslims who work for me, I've got Hindus.... I'm not aware that's caused difficulties, actually thinking about those individuals they are probably more aware of equality issues because of their religious beliefs...

(Senior Manager, Southern England)

In the following chapter some of these complex dynamics between faith and sexuality are examined in more detail through a discussion of the implementation of LGBT equalities in Northern Ireland.

Summary

■ We can think of forms of resistance to change along a continuum ranging from compliance, omission, erasure, to active opposition.

■ These different forms of resistance are not discrete but may intersect with each other in particular ways that make resistance more or less likely.

■ The effects of different forms of resistance may be uneven across as well as within the LGBT communities.

■ There are a range of factors associated with sexualities and trans equalities work that make implementation of equalities initiatives difficult at both individual and organizational levels.

■ There are spatial aspects to understanding resistance.

■ Overcoming resistance at the individual level is largely perceived in terms of behavioural rather than attitudinal change, which can lead to a privatization of prejudice.

Lesbian, Gay, Bisexual and Transgender Equalities in Northern Ireland

7

> I would say though that our society here in general is pretty bi-polar in relation to sexuality, there's much increased acceptance of different sexualities in one regard but there is…bigotry towards people with minority sexualities or different sexualities hidden behind the face of religious freedom of expression.
>
> (Local Authority Officer)

How do the themes discussed in this book, such as democracy, citizenship and intersectionality, play out in relation to LGBT equalities in specific countries? This chapter seeks to ground and expand our analysis by examining LGBT equalities in a particular context: Northern Ireland. The story told in Northern Ireland is paralleled in various ways in other countries. Notably, homophobic discourses and activism are perpetuated by the Christian Right in the US and Northern Ireland in similar ways (see Wilson 2000, Burack and Josephson 2005) and party politics are influenced by matters of faith. There are also specific dynamics in Northern Ireland, for example the tensions that US authors such as Phelan (1989) have documented around assimilation into the 'mainstream' versus radical challenges to it (see Chapters 1 and 4) are somewhat different in Northern Ireland, because of the fracturing of the 'mainstream' by dynamics associated with sectarianism.

Northern Ireland consists of six counties with a population of almost 1.8 million in 2009 (Northern Ireland Statistics and Research Agency 2009). It has a very specific history of equal rights work, set within sharp dynamics associated with ethno-national conflict. The agenda is one of *rights and equality* (see, for example, The Equality Commission for Northern Ireland 2008b), rather than the *business case* for LGBT equality. Northern Ireland has in recent years leaned towards affirmative action regarding equalities, in comparison to other jurisdictions such as England. The model of equality is primarily an 'individual justice' one (individuals must seek legal redress if they are experiencing discrimination); although the specialist Equality bodies (such as the Equality Commission Northern Ireland – ECNI) play a role in supporting group justice models (ECNI 2008b).

Whilst a range of progressive legislation has been introduced in recent years, the Northern Irish situation continues to be structured by sectarianism, which plays out in complex ways in relation to sexuality and transgender. In this chapter, some of the key dynamics are explored. The chapter is structured as follows: context (LGBT people in Northern Ireland, historical background and terminology); equality infrastructure and legislation; the impact of recent legislation on LGBT equalities initiatives; and LGBT equalities in relation to the key themes of intersectionality and democracy. The focus is on intersectionality and democracy rather than other themes (such as organizational change) because of their importance to the Northern Ireland situation.

Context

Overall, our research indicates that there has been a cultural shift regarding LGB sexualities in Northern Ireland, with a movement towards greater tolerance in public attitudes and more positive media coverage, alongside the growth of a commercial gay scene in some urban areas and the development of LGB (and T) community organizations. Some of the developments are discussed in the following contrasting quotes from the research on LGBT equalities in local government:

> Twenty or thirty years ago they'd [LGBT people] have moved to England or gone somewhere and never come back.
>
> (Councillor)

> I think we've probably arrived at a stage where at least all people would be, you know, would recognise that there are gay people within our community, there are people that maybe don't conform to their notion of how, you know, in inverted commas a 'normal' society should be, but they accept fully that they still have a duty to help those people and support them without necessarily endorsing their lifestyle.
>
> (Mayor)

Despite a movement towards a somewhat more tolerant society, LGBT people in Northern Ireland face major challenges. Existing research reports high levels of homophobia and discrimination against LGB people (ECNI 2008a). For instance, one research project found that 31 per cent of a sample of 233 LGB people had been a victim of crime in the previous 12 months and over half of these thought that the crime was motivated by homophobia (Radford et al. 2006). Previously, a survey of 186 Northern Irish LGB people found that 82 per cent had experienced harassment and 55 per cent had been subjected to homophobic abuse (Jarman and Tennant 2003). There is less research about transgender people in Northern Ireland than there is about the LGB communities.

The trans community in Northern Ireland is much less developed than the US and the UK (see Currah et al. 2006 for a discussion of the US situation).

A Northern Irish survey with 31 respondents who identified as transgendered, transsexual, transvestite or 'other' reported that five had experienced verbal attack, four had been bullied, and two had experienced dismissal from employment as a result of their gender status (Hansson and Depret 2007). Although there is legislation in place, the survey showed that transgender people were reluctant to make a formal complaint due to fears of outing themselves and feelings that they would be ignored. Overall, trans people experienced difficulties in relation to employment, access to healthcare, harassment and abuse, and a lack of awareness about transgender amongst public service providers and the population in general. Whilst there was no data specifically available about bisexuals in Northern Ireland, the existing material about LGBT people in general indicates substantial levels of homophobia, biphobia and transphobia.

Northern Ireland: History and terminology

The Northern Irish LGBT equalities situation clearly needs to be framed within a much larger picture. Discussions of the Northern Irish political situation are sensitive, as sectarianism continues to be a major challenge in Northern Ireland. The 'troubles' are still quite recent. Between 1969 and 2000 nearly 2 per cent of the population were killed or injured (Dixon 2001) and there continues to be some sectarian violence (for example, the murder of Bobby Moffet in 2010; see McDonald 2010), although this has greatly reduced following the Belfast Agreement/Good Friday Agreement (GFA) in 1998. Academics have taken a range of approaches to analysis relating to Northern Ireland: openly partisan, unionist, nationalist (see below), those who claim to be neutral and those who take critical empirical stances (Miller 1998; see also Wolff 2007). The latter approach is adopted in this chapter in attempting to unravel some of the dynamics associated with the Northern Irish situation in relation to LGBT equality without falling into either unionist or nationalist positions (See Box 7.1).

Box 7.1   Northern Ireland: Background

It is important to understand the terms being used when discussing Northern Ireland and LGBT equalities. Who are the unionists and nationalists? In simple terms, unionists tend to see themselves as British and they want Northern Ireland to remain part of the UK. They are primarily Protestant, but there are some Catholic unionists. There is a subgroup of unionists, termed 'loyalists', who advocate paramilitary violence to achieve their political ends. Nationalists, who are overwhelmingly Catholic, tend to see themselves as Irish and aspire to a united Ireland. There is a paramilitary subgroup of nationalists termed 'republicans' (Dixon 2001). There has been a definitional slide between these ethno-nationalist identities and the use of religious labels, and hence 'Protestant' is commonly used in Northern Ireland to denote 'unionist' whilst 'Catholic' is used to mean 'nationalist' (Dixon 2001; see also Mitchell 2006). In addition:

- The term 'sectarianism' can be used to mean 'mutual dislike between Protestants and Catholics' (Clayton 1998: 40), or, rather, dislike between nationalists and unionists.
- The term 'ethno-sectarian' (see McAuley et al. 2010) is used to indicate the nexus of issues around which the tensions between the two main communities in Northern Ireland revolve: patterns of territorial conflict, group, class, and national identities, militarism, language, religious affiliation and political allegiance.
- We define 'ethnic groups' as groups of people with a subjective belief in common descent due to similarities of physical type, or customs, or both, which are related to shared memories of colonization and migration.
- The term 'racism' is sometimes used to mean prejudice that has a sectarian basis, as well as that based on perceived physiological type, when discussing Northern Ireland (McVeigh and Rolston 2007).
- The colour green is associated with nationalists, and orange with unionists.
- The term GLBT (gay, lesbian, bisexual and transgender) is sometimes used in Northern Ireland, and trans issues are often addressed separately to LGB ones; we use the term LGBT as a means of achieving consistency (unless we are speaking only about T or LGB people).

Northern Irish political history has been long and torturous, and it has been comprehensively discussed elsewhere (see, for example, Clayton 1998; Dixon 2001; Wolff 2007). Here, some key aspects are outlined, in order to explain the way in which contemporary Northern Irish society is structured and to set the scene for the exploration of LGBT equalities in Northern Ireland. As David Miller says:

> To understand and rethink Northern Ireland centrally involves recognising the economic, social, and cultural inequalities which underlie the conflict, which have their origins in colonisation and their current form as a result of that legacy and the actions of the participants in the conflict.
>
> (1998: xxiii)

The history of Northern Ireland is one of invasion and settler colonization, although accounts are contested and some unionist authors argue that the colonizers (English and Scottish Protestants) were in fact reclaiming land that earlier peoples had been driven from (see McAuley 1996). The conflict began when the Anglo Normans invaded Ireland in 1196, culminating in the Plantation of Ulster from 1610 (Holloway 2005), and hence ' ... the Plantation consisted in [sic] the brutal seizure of large tracts of land, and the removal of Irish inhabitants' (Clayton 1998: 48). There were further conflicts and land seizures by the British, and by 1661 Protestants held about 90 per cent of land across Ireland. Bloody conflicts continued during the 1661–1921 period, with a polarization of Irish identities forming around a unionist/nationalist dichotomy, the institutionalization of discrimination against Catholics, and the development of guerrilla-type organizations on both sides (see Holloway 2005). In 1921, following a war of independence, Ireland was partitioned. This created the Irish Free State (later the Republic of Ireland) as a self-governing territory, whilst Northern Ireland continued to be part of the UK (McVeigh and Rolston 2007; Wolff 2007). During the post Second World War period, a civil rights movement was started by Catholics who were influenced by the US civil rights movement. The development of this movement was a response to corruption of the political process, which ensured unionist control of nationalist majority areas and entrenched inequalities in housing and employment (Holloway 2005). However, conflicts continued, and the most recent period of sustained conflict in Northern Ireland began in the late 1960s and did not finish until the Belfast/Good Friday Agreement (hereafter known as the GFA) in 1998.

Overall, therefore, we can see that the roots of sectarianism go back a great many years, and hence 'political division [has] manifested in high levels of physical and social segregation and in an array of self-generating conflicting values, myths, and norms within each community' (McAuley 2004: 543). It is apparent that the fate of Northern Ireland is inextricably bound up with that of both the Irish Republic and the UK, although this is not examined further here. Importantly for our discussion of LGBT equalities, the roots of the civil rights movement in Northern Ireland stem from the nationalist civil rights movement. As Lisa Glennon suggests, 'Northern Ireland has a long pedigree in using rights-based strategies to tackle discrimination and inequality' (2006: 270) with anti-discrimination legislation on the grounds of religious belief and political orientation being in place since 1976. These roots and their subsequent growth into broader equal rights initiatives – manifested in particular in the GFA – are central to understanding the structuring of contemporary equalities work in Northern Ireland, although other drivers, in particular those coming from Westminster, are also important. In the next section, structures and legislation that underpin LGBT equalities in Northern Ireland are addressed.

Equality infrastructures in Northern Ireland

A range of equality initiatives were introduced in Northern Ireland during the early 1990s, notably the Policy Appraisal and Fair Treatment (PAFT) Guidelines which included sexual orientation. However, there were difficulties with the implementation of these initiatives (Hansson et al. 2007), and the then Standing Committee on Human Rights (SACRE) called for a strengthening of interventions. This call coincided with demands imposed by Europe via the European Union 2000 Framework Employment Equality Directive and:

> The ensuing Belfast Agreement [GFA] of April 1998 incorporated the new statutory obligations on public bodies to promote equality of opportunity

and good relations ... Under Section 75 (hereafter s75) of the 1998 Northern Ireland Act, public bodies have two statutory duties. The first is to have, in carrying out their functions, 'due regard' to provide equality of opportunity on the same nine grounds involved in the PAFT initiative *viz* religion and political opinion, gender, disability, race and ethnicity, sexual orientation, marital status and dependency. The second is to have 'regard' to the desirability of promoting 'good relations' between persons of different political opinions and race groups.

(Osborne 2003: 348)

The statutory duties concerning sexuality that were laid down in the GFA have been complemented by the introduction of a range of other legislation, including:

- The Civil Partnership Act 2004 which enables same-sex partnerships across the UK.
- The Equality Act (Sexual Orientation) Regulations Northern Ireland 2006 which support equality in the provision of goods, facilities and services, control of premises, education and the performance of public functions.
- The Sex Discrimination (Gender Reassignment) Regulations (Northern Ireland) 1999 which deals with employment discrimination against transsexuals.
- The Gender Recognition Act 2004 which provides various rights for transsexual people across the UK.
- The Criminal Justice (No. 2) (Northern Ireland) Order 2004 which addresses homophobic hate crime.

The GFA, which was signed by all of the major political parties in Northern Ireland on both sides of the sectarian divide, introduced 'a devolved administration in Northern Ireland and provided a framework for developing a pluralistic society in Northern Ireland, based on mutual recognition of opposing traditions' (McAuley 2004: 542). Devolved government post 1998 has entailed the reconfiguration of government departments, including the establishment of the Office of the First Minister and Deputy First Minister (OFMDFM) which has a Gender and Sexual Orientation Equality Unit, a Human Rights Commission (HRC) (see Osborne 2003), and the Equality Commission for Northern Ireland which amalgamated previous anti-discrimination bodies. The Equality Commission's role is varied and it has included issuing guidelines requiring public authorities to construct an Equality Scheme and to conduct Equality Impact Assessments (EQIA) on policies that are deemed to have an impact on equality of opportunity on the basis of the nine grounds listed in s75 (Osborne 2003). As demonstrated below, these have had important impacts on LGB equalities initiatives.

The Northern Irish devolved administration was established against a backdrop of the previous 'abuse of power in the execution of public services' (Knox and Carmichael 2006: 97), in the sense that prejudice against Catholics was institutionalized in the statutory sector in terms of both service provision and employment within that sector. Equal rights legislation has helped to substantially remedy the inequalities experienced by Catholics, and now Protestants are under-represented in some areas of the public sector and affirmative action has sought to remedy this (Osborne 2003). However, as a result of their earlier role in supporting institutionalized sectarianism, local authorities have been stripped of most of their powers and roles since the early 1970s. Services such as housing have been provided by a raft of other bodies, and hence a plethora of public or quasi-public bodies emerged in Northern Ireland and the 'complex edifice that is the Northern Ireland public sector has led to charges that it is both over-governed and over-administered' (Knox and Carmichael 2006: 98).

Northern Ireland is underpinned by structures that include designated state machinery such as the Equality Commission and implementation mechanisms, notably those associated with s75. In contrast to countries where most services are provided by private companies (such as the US), in Northern Ireland there is a large, complex public sector and quasi-public sector, and this complexity may have implications for LGBT equalities. In the next section the ways in which aspects of these developments have facilitated LGBT equalities work are examined.

The impact of LGBT equalities legislation

The changes that were instigated by the new legislation, beginning with PAFT in the early 1990s and then with the more hard hitting s75 in 1998 and the Sex Discrimination (Gender Reassignment) Regulations (Northern Ireland) 1999, marked a new era for LGBT people in Northern Ireland. At the level of government and the organizations working closely with government, there was a marked shift towards support for equality, supported by an implementation framework including positive actions and mechanisms for individuals to tackle discrimination and harassment. This section explores the main changes, first providing a general overview and then looking at the developments within local government, drawing on the research findings from the LGBT Equalities in Local Government project.

As has been outlined, strong legislative and administrative structures aimed at supporting a pluralist and equal society have developed in Northern Ireland since the 1990s. LGB equalities work in Northern Ireland is underpinned by these structures. Existing literature suggests that 'the liberal framework of equality, human rights and non-discrimination is gradually helping to deliver practical change [regarding gay and lesbian rights]' (Glennon 2006: 272). Our research found that considerable work had been done in developing the infrastructures and mechanisms needed to effect change, particularly the growth of partnership work around the LGBT equalities agenda, and work concerning particular agendas of importance to sexual and transgender equality, such as hate crime and civil partnerships. Contributors to the research discussed the development of case law supporting LGBT equalities, and a related increase in awareness around sexual orientation and employment-related issues such as discrimination and harassment. Northern Irish LGBT equalities work is wrapped up together with the broader civil rights agenda that has been pronounced in Northern Ireland since the early 1990s. Sometimes LGBT equalities work is explicitly included within 'good relations' initiatives and this forms a strategy for dealing with what is seen as a 'sensitive topic' by many people.

There is support for LGBT equalities initiatives amongst statutory players in some localities in Northern Ireland. This support has included providing some funding for a Pride event, the display of large billboard posters against hate crime regarding sexual identity in one city, support from prominent statutory sector representatives for a major public launch of an anti-homophobic hate crime initiative, and development of a leaflet tackling prejudice. Cultures that were somewhat gay-affirmative were apparent in at least one local authority:

> ... he [colleague] organised a civil partnership and he had a big celebration and a lot of his colleagues went to it ... you know people know him, it's not what I mean I mean, you know, I know exactly who he is as a person and it's maybe accepted, he doesn't experience any sort of homophobia from colleagues.
>
> (Local Authority Officer)

Why has there been a shift towards support for LGBT equalities, or at least tolerance and the prevention of hate crime, in Northern Ireland? The legislation concerning LGBT equalities, which is recognized to have been externally imposed on Northern Ireland, appears to have substantially driven recent changes. S75 has had a marked impact because of the obligations it places on public authorities to do equality impact assessments regarding sexual orientation, to provide regular reports to the ECNI, to monitor sexual orientation, to consult with user groups including LGBT people, and to train staff concerning equalities issues, include sexual orientation and transgender. In some cases, legislation is used as a lever to deal with resistance against the LGBT equalities agenda, for example:

> We've done some work with councils through the Equality Officers and through the Chief Executives to explain that 'You aren't condoning it, if you like, the [civil partnership] ceremony, but the council is legally required to carry out this ceremony.'
>
> (National Organisation Representative in ALS)

Whilst legislation is clearly central to the implementation of LGBT equalities in Northern Ireland, the research showed that there are other factors driving LGBT equalities work. These include:

■ The growth of active LGB and T community organizations who are engaged with statutory sector organizations.

- The influence of community activists and people who are now working in statutory sector arenas who come from community activist backgrounds.
- Changes within the police force (there is now a Gay Police Association within the Police Service Northern Ireland (PSNI)).

Examples of developments include (in one locality) statutory and community sector organizations such as churches, universities, police, ambulance and fire services working together to tackle homophobic hate crime and to develop an interagency agreement about how to address broader issues affecting the LGBT community, such as suicide and domestic violence. In another locality, a training package about hate crime (including homophobic hate crime) was developed for schools, community groups and hate crime perpetrators, as part of partnership work. One contributor in this authority said that:

> Five years ago we would have found it very difficult to include homophobia as an issue when we were teaching them in schools; some of the schools would have said 'OK' openly, 'No problem doing sectarianism and racism but we don't want the [pause] we don't want representatives of the GLBT community coming into our schools, we don't want that to be the focus of our project', and this year when we brought all the schools together basically after the six week programme all the schools, each class from the schools comes together for one day and the pupils present their learning and these are thirteen and fourteen year olds, great fun coordinating about 350 of them [laughs]. And for the first time this year I would say that actually in loads of those presentations that the pupils did, they did proactively talk about sexual orientation.
>
> (Local Authority Officer)

Overall, we can see that there has been a substantial shift in Northern Ireland regarding LGBT equalities over the last two decades, and in particular since the GFA. LGBT rights claims have gained legitimacy, at least within some sections of local and central government and related organizations. The changes are particularly noticeable with regard to the implementation mechanisms associated with the GFA, and the partnership work that has developed in some localities regarding issues such as homophobic hate crime. These changes are taking place alongside broader cultural shifts towards greater acceptance of LGBT people. However, the changes appear primarily top-down (driven via legislation and state mechanisms), and there are still major difficulties with achieving LGBT equality in Northern Ireland.

Challenges to the implementation of LGBT equalities

Despite the developments that have been outlined there is a substantial implementation gap regarding LGBT equalities in Northern Ireland. The legislation and the frameworks that are in place to implement it are very progressive, but challenges remain concerning change on the ground across the equalities strands. Robert Osborne remarked in 2003 that whilst the procedural elements of the generic equalities initiatives have been met, public organizations had not at that time reconsidered their policies and procedures in any wholesale way. Looking now at LGBT equalities in particular, the literature indicates that: 'To the extent that a statutory duty may ultimately be judged by its enforcement, the inclusion of sexual orientation in section 75 has had very little impact (Hansson et al. 2007: 1). In practice, discrimination complaints on the grounds of sexual orientation have been reported to be low although there have been a number of key tribunal decisions and settlements (ECNI 2008a). Our research showed that some contributors felt that LGBT equalities work is not in evidence in some localities. There was evidence of high levels of erasure of LGBT issues overall (see also the previous chapter), as illustrated in this section of an interview with a local councillor.

> **Interviewee:** Quite honestly it's not really, it [LGBT issues] doesn't really come to the surface at all.
> **Interviewer:** No.
> **Interviewee:** It would be, erm, I've only been on the council [for a couple of years], but at the same time, a debate of that nature has never come to council.
> **Interviewer:** No. Do you think it's just, do you think it would just be seen as inappropriate as council business or is it? I mean what are the, I mean, can you explain why?
> **Interviewee:** I think the traditional, erm, [short pause], erm, the whole tradition of this part of the world, with things like that were swept under the carpet, this type of thing just weren't mentioned. And that just comes, you know, it's the same in the council.

The B and T parts of the LGBT equalities agenda were especially underdeveloped in Northern Ireland. There was no evidence of any equalities work being done specifically around bisexuality in statutory organizations, although one community organization representative reported that their organization had done work to tackle biphobia within the gay community some years previously. The only statutory sector discussions about transgender related to the practicalities of people undergoing gender reassignment surgery, and very limited understanding of trans issues was shown by statutory sector actors.

What are the barriers to the implementation of LGBT equalities in Northern Ireland? Some of the impediments are similar to those found in other UK contexts, for example the amount of equalities-related initiatives that public authorities are now required to support (see Osborne 2003), deficient community engagement and support, the perceived sensitivity of the agenda (see Monro and Richardson 2010), and fear of victimization if LGB people complain of discrimination (ECNI 2008a). Some barriers concern the mechanisms that have been put in place to support LGBT equality, for instance inadequate financial compensation for successful legal settlements (ECNI 2008a). Others are specific to Northern Ireland – the impact of sectarianism and faith, which will be discussed in the following section on intersectionality, and the apparent bigotry of some key political parties, which will be addressed in the section on democracy. Other impediments of particular importance in the Northern Irish context include the 'conservative' nature of Northern Irish society, with LGBT people not being accepted in some sections of the local community – or being accepted only if they are 'discreet' about their sexual identity (of course, this phenomena is common elsewhere, for example the Southern US (Wilson 2000)). In the research on Northern Ireland, one ALS member said that 'people are still acting on very basic and unsubstantiated prejudice, and that's another sign that we are really in the very early stages of dealing with sexual orientation effectively'. Other contributors said that:

> ... it is potentially difficult [for someone working within the local authority] to be seen supporting LGBT groups ...
>
> (Action Learning Set Member)

> There's probably quite a lot of people who are personally uncomfortable with talking, working and developing good practice around sexualities because you know we're not long out of a period in Irish society where you couldn't have said the word without blushing ... Sexual equalities are absolutely not mainstream within the work of the council, absolutely not I mean even in my own work I mean I'm saying that it's good for me talk about how bad everyone else is [but] I am that bad person too. There is no, there is no regard to sexual, sexuality and equality in our work at present if there is it's all very much equality commission led or responses you know we are not proactive in that area ...
>
> (Local Authority Officer)

There are also broader dynamics at play in Northern Ireland which may work against the LGBT equalities agenda. For example, a councillor argued that pushing legislation (LGBT equalities legislation and other forms of legislation) was likely to impede progress and create a backlash. Whilst this is also the case in other countries, the fact that equalities legislation has been imposed by Westminster onto Northern Ireland may increase the possibility of a back-lash. Another important issue more generally is that, as McAuley (2004) argues (in relation to young people in Northern Ireland), the long-term conflict in Northern Ireland has resulted in an enormous credibility gap regarding the state. This credibility gap is likely to make it harder for public bodies to be effective in relation to LGBT equalities work. This is because if a substantial proportion of the general population are alienated from statutory sector orga-nizations and parts of the state, then they will tend to ignore or resist anything that these organizations do, regardless of what it is.

Overall, there have been big advances in the LGBT equalities agenda in Northern Ireland over the past period, but advances at the legislative and state infrastructure levels have outstripped developments amongst statutory sector organizations and in the local communities. There are some impediments which are likely to be common across different countries, concerning both the difficulties with implementing progressive change in a top-down fashion and the nature of discrimination against LGBT people. There are also barriers that are particularly important in the Northern Irish context: the 'traditional' nature of Northern Irish society, the impact that the 'troubles' have had on state infrastructures, and the structuring role of sectarianism and religion. The next section will explore sectarianism and religion in relation to LGBT equalities in Northern Ireland.

Intersectionality

As has been shown, the roots of Northern Irish movements for equality – including LGB equality – can be found in the nationalist civil rights movement that grew out of the injustices that Catholics experienced in Northern Ireland during the twentieth century. This civil rights movement drew its inspiration from developments in the US, perhaps partly because of Irish people's links with the Irish American communities. The GFA, which incorporated both unionist and nationalist concerns, forms part of the foundation for the changes that have taken place since 1998. There are of course other factors influencing the development of LGB equalities in Northern Ireland, including in particular the legislation that was initially imposed by Europe and then subsequently by Westminster, as discussed above. The push for transgender equality in Northern Ireland is driven by this legislation, as transgender was not included in the s75 equality grounds, and it is noticeable that transgender equalities work is considerably less developed in Northern Ireland than it is in the rest of the UK.

This section of the chapter will bring an intersectional analysis to the exploration of LGBT equalities work in Northern Ireland. As outlined in Chapter 2, intersectionality concerns the ways in which social characteristics and forces are routed through each other; such forces can include race and ethnicity, gender, socio-economic class, ability and age. In Chapter 2, there was some discussion of how intersectionality works at the individual level (every individual has different aspects of their identity); here the focus is on the operation of intersectionality at the group or community level. Intersectional difference is apparent when looking at the differences between the lesbian, gay, bisexual and transgender communities amalgamated under the acronym LGBT. As has already been indicated, bisexuality is heavily erased in Northern Ireland generally; it could be imagined that this relates to a tendency to stay closeted where possible when homophobia and biphobia are severe. Trans is less evident than elsewhere in the UK (both in wider society and in terms of equalities initiatives) and there is a tendency to separate LGB from T because 'the fact is LGB is a sexual orientation issue whereas the T is a gender issue' (community worker).

There were some indications of prejudice against trans people within the LGB communities that were linked to the impact of homophobia, for example an LGB community representative reported that some gay men were anxious about trans women using a venue that they used, because they thought that this would perpetuate the stereotype that 'all gay men like to dress as women'.

The hierarchy of equalities strands that we described earlier in this book is structured in a particular way in Northern Ireland, because s75's three grounds for promoting good relations include at its core only religious belief, political opinion and racial group (McVeigh and Rolston 2007) and sexual orientation was seen by a number of contributors as being very low down the hierarchy. However, intersectional equalities work has taken place since the development of PAFT and this was evident in the findings, for instance one local authority contributor discussed the way that sexual identities are crosscut by other identities such as being a carer or a single parent. There are a range of other important intersectional dynamics at play in Northern Ireland, including those relating to age (specifically, a number of contributors talked about young people generally being more progressive regarding LGBT equalities), recent patterns of immigration (including an influx of homophobic immigrants), the traveller community, the rural/urban divide and the structuring effects of the economic downturn and high levels of deprivation generally. The focus here is on ethno-sectarianism, including religion. This is because intersectionality takes a very particular and complex form in Northern Ireland, with the ethno-sectarian divide forming an important structuring factor.

Robbie McVeigh and Bill Rolston (2007) argue that there has been a trend for the Northern Irish state machinery to focus on diversity, specifically minority ethnic groups, in Northern Ireland and that this overlooks the issue of ethno-sectarianism. They state, 'Increasingly, state intervention has moved away from the subject at all. To even mention sectarianism or inequality or injustice becomes anathema to "good relations" ' (2007: 15), but that '...there is no area of social life in Northern Ireland which is not sectarianised, or structured in some way by sectarianism' (2007: 16). The idea that sectarianism, and religion, have become something of a taboo was supported by some of the contributors to our research. This sense of taboo acts as an impediment to open discussion of the relationship between faith and sexuality. For instance, an ALS member suggested that the push to 'neutrality' has stifled discussions about gay rights, and race, with broader fears about a backlash from political, community-based and Christian organizations impeding work in this field.

As noted above, ethno-sectarianism includes divides around religion, identity, territorial claims, political affiliation, and patterns of violence, brutality and community violation (see Clayton 1998; McAuley et al. 2010). There are some forces that cut across the ethno-sectarian divide as well as becoming sedimented within this divide, including class (the paramilitary subsections of the unionists and loyalists are disproportionately from working-class communities (Dixon 2001)), gender (see Coulter 1998) and violence. It appears that ethno-nationalist identities shape patterns of prejudice against LGBT people – and support for LGBT equalities – in specific ways in Northern Ireland.

In what ways is sectarianism gendered and sexualized? There is some literature about the gendering of sectarianism. For example, Dixon (2001) describes the way in which, for nationalists, Irish history is interpreted as a tale of (mostly) masculine heroism against British oppression. The unionist marching season, which takes place every year from mid-July to mid-August (Dixon 2001), can also be interpreted as a demonstration of (mostly) masculine commemoration of victories over Catholics. The rigid gender demarcation that is implied by the masculinization of nationalism is of course hugely problematic for many transgender people. Gender traditionalism causes difficulties for LGB people as well, because of the inherent assumptions that people should be in heterosexual relationships. For example, a councillor talked about the way in which heterosexual marriage and traditional gendered roles (the man going out to do paid work, the woman taking the unpaid homemaker role) have been central to Irish culture historically, although this is now changing.

There is also some analysis of the way in which heterosexuality works through sectarianism in Northern Ireland. Glennon (2006) reviews literature about the way in which the rise of nationalism acted to erase sexual difference, with a link being made in some nationalist discourses between homosexuality and enfeebled masculinity. Similarly, focusing on the Irish Republic, Kathryn Conrad (2004) describes Irish nationalist discourse as heteronormative, placing the Irish man at the centre of the family and the nation. Conrad also identifies a nationalist trend towards keeping divergences from heterosexuality hidden within the family. This trend may be due to historical experiences of having to keep many things hidden in order to avoid being subject to discipline by people associated with the colonial state. This process of history of communal closeting seems to be echoed in our research findings about the social erasure of LGBT identities in Northern Ireland.

There was a sense from the research about LGBT equalities in local government that the combination of religious and political forces that support sectarianism overrides LGBT equalities concerns to a large degree, despite the movement towards neutrality noted above. For example, a community worker talked about the way in which homophobia was not tackled in a strong way in a particular locality, and that 'there is probably a rationale for it, political parties probably thought "let's not upset the bigger apple cart here", which is working relationships between the Protestants and Catholics or the nationalist and the unionist communities'. Another contributor rather pointedly noted that:

> ... you have to look at the political background, you know if someone has been shot or there was [sic] buildings being blown up and there really wasn't much time for people to be sitting thinking about their sexual orientation.
>
> (Local Authority Manager)

This contributor then went on to indicate that there is now space to consider issues such as sexuality because of the decrease in sectarian violence. A third contributor, a member of the ALS, discussed having to respond to the tensions around the summer marching period and not wanting to have to deal with anything else, illustrating in a clear way how sectarian concerns remain paramount in Northern Ireland, although such concerns may remain unspoken.

The religious component of sectarianism is rather hard to tease out from the broader patterns, but it is worth exploring religion a little, as impediments regarding the faith/ethno-nationalist intersection appear to be the biggest barrier to LGBT equalities in Northern Ireland. This is indicated in the literature, for instance Glennon (2006) discusses the way in which the Democratic Unionist Party (DUP) attempted (and failed) to invoke common Christian values amongst nationalists and unionists as a means of blocking progress on the Civil Partnership Bill. On a related note, there are some religious exemptions to the Equality Act (Sexual Orientation) Regulations Northern Ireland 2006 (see ECNI 2008b). There was a considerable amount of evidence in our research findings about the role of religion in maintaining heterosexism and gender binarism in Northern Irish society. For example:

> ...there is a very solid barrier there and its religiously based and has great political influence erm, and that is a barrier that I don't actually see us being able to shift any time soon, if ever. You know, so again when the barrier has been, is being presented by the largest political party in the region it's a serious barrier.
>
> (Community Worker)

> ...you could in this organisation very easily get away with being bigoted toward homosexual people by saying that it was your religious, it was your freedom of religious expression that allowed you to hold those thoughts.
>
> (Local Authority Officer)

The picture is, however, a complex one in relation to religion and LGBT equalities. For a start, there are differences between the Catholic church and the various parts of the Protestant church in the way LGB issues are dealt with. It appears that there may be more tolerance overall towards LGB people by the Catholic church in Northern Ireland, and that this is bound up with the experiences of oppression, conflict and civil rights activism that the Catholic communities have experienced. For instance, a councillor who is a practising Catholic said that 'there's a quiet acceptance of it, you know, whatever way people are born'. This contributor then went on to say, however, that tolerance is not just present within the Catholic communities. Another contributor pointed out how important it is not to paint a picture in which Protestants are seen as more prejudiced towards LGBT people in general. There are several branches of the Ulster Protestant church, and contributors said that:

... the Democratic Unionist Party is linked to the Free Presbyterian church, who [sic] take, you know, [sighs] I'm sure this [inaudible], take quite a fundamental approach to the whole thing, you know.

(Councillor)

... evangelical Christianity or that type of thing, erm it probably varies from church to church I'm sure that there are still tensions there around the, well all Christian churches and the perceptions erm basically different interpretations in Biblical teaching...

(Local Authority Officer)

Another aspect of the picture regarding religion and LGBT equalities in Northern Ireland is that there is evidence of change. In particular, some religious figures in Northern Ireland are now actively and positively engaged with the LGBT communities.

One of the really odd things that developed out of this homophobia, anti-homophobia protocol launch, both Bishops attended, to get the Church of Ireland Bishop there we thought was a major success but to have the Catholic Bishop attending as well left us slightly shell-shocked... even today the Bishop, the Anglican Bishop, the Church of Ireland Bishop might call in for a cup of coffee and a chat. Very few gay centres [in Northern Ireland] where you will call in and find the local Anglican Bishop having a coffee and a chat...

(Community Worker)

Alliance building between churches and LGBT community groups is linked to broader developments such as the growth of partnership work with different communities, but seems to also be related to changes within both Protestant and Catholic churches. The councillor who was quoted earlier in this section discussed the way in which the church has 'mellowed' and noted a shift so that 'people now practise their own form of Catholicism or Protestantism or whatever. So they're not prepared to accept that "this is wrong" '. This does not so much indicate a shift towards secularism, but rather that people are demonstrating agency regarding the way in which they interpret religion. This is likely to make space for LGBT people to rework religious doctrine in a more LGBT-positive way, in a similar fashion to the processes taking place within other religions such as Islam (see the chapter on intersectionality).

To summarize, it is clear that whilst some intersectional patterns are shared across the UK, several powerful intersecting forces in Northern Ireland create a particular situation for LGBT equalities in that locality. In particular, nationalism, religion and prejudice against LGBT people combine in an especially obstructive way. However, the way that sectarianism structures the situation for LGBT people in Northern Ireland reveals the contradictions inherent in faith-based prejudice, because it appears unevenly spread across the sectarian divide for reasons other than religious doctrine. Faith-based prejudice has, for the fundamentalist sections of the unionist parties as well as elsewhere, become welded to a sense of ethno-national identity in which there is little room for sexual and gender diversity. Despite this trend, there is evidence of movement within the church and elsewhere, framed within the context of broader shifts towards a more participatory and open democracy. It is to these developments concerning democracy and LGBT people that the chapter now turns.

Political parties and democracy

The chapter on democracy explored a number of themes that are relevant to LGBT equalities, including LGBT democracy in a global context, representative democracy and LGBT people, and LGBT participative democracy. Now, the discussion addresses key aspects of Northern Irish democratic processes in relation to LGBT equalities. It will focus on two types of democracy, representative and participative, whilst noting that global issues such as climate change are of course relevant to democracy in Northern Ireland, as elsewhere (for example, the water crisis in Northern Ireland in late 2010 (Press Association 2010) may have been linked to broader processes of climate change). As we noted in the chapter on democracy, if people do not have access to basic amenities they are not likely to be able to participate in normal democratic processes.

The broad picture in Northern Ireland is one of a postconflict democracy in which there are some signs of LGBT inclusion in democratic processes, as well as very substantial barriers at both national and local levels. These barriers can be cross-party, and they may be tied to concerns about LGBT equalities being perceived to be an electoral liability. The following quote indicates some of the difficulties at a local level:

> A number of councils said they wouldn't do it [hold civil partnerships] ... the elected members rather than the officers ... there are certainly issues, and civil partnership is one of them, where elected members feel they have to take a stand, and while in a training programme or a closed meeting they will be very committed to equality, whenever there are public events and they have to go out and say what they feel the electorate wants them to say ...
>
> (National Stakeholder)

The democratic structures to support LGBT equalities are in place in Northern Ireland, but this does not necessarily translate into LGBT people's voices being heard in the political arena. As has already been explained, party politics in Northern Ireland are structured by sectarianism, as demonstrated in the following table, and this has important implications for LGBT equalities in Northern Ireland.

Table 7.1 Political parties in Northern Ireland

Nationalist	Unionist	Cross Community
Sinn Fein (SF)	Democratic Unionist Party (DUP)	Alliance Party of Northern Ireland
Social Democrat and Labour Party (SDLP)	Ulster Unionist Party (UUP)	
	Progressive Unionist Party (PUP)	

Source: (http://www.ark.ac.uk/elections/gparties.htm accessed 06 January 2011)

As indicated earlier in the chapter, the Northern Irish equalities agenda has historically been associated with the nationalists and the civil rights movement, and this association has continued post GFA. The politics of LGB equality are inextricably linked up with those of the GFA, because pro-GFA parties find it hard not to support LGB rights, given the way in which sexual orientation is written into the GFA remit (see Glennon 2006). Nationalist parties fully embraced the GFA, and have subsequently remained broadly supportive of LGB equalities policies. The Democratic Unionist Party (DUP) stayed anti-Agreement; 'The DUP has led those sections of unionism that have formulated the strongest opposition to the GFA, based around the discourse that "the Union is under threat" ' (McAuley 2004: 536). The Ulster Unionist Party (UUP) includes both anti- and pro-Agreement opinion. Sections of the UUP emphasize an attachment to UK citizenship that is multicultural, with some support for LGB equalities within the party (see Glennon 2006). The only Unionist party that is generally supportive of gay and lesbian rights is the Progressive Unionist Party (PUP) (McAuley 2004).

The sectarian nature of party political support for LGBT equalities is evident at the level of party publicity, for instance at the time of writing the DUP website (http://www.dup.org.uk/ accessed 06 January 2011) did not mention sexual orientation or the word 'gay' at all. In comparison, the Sinn Fein website had 68 references, referring for instance to a presidential speech made by Gerry Adams in 2003 which included the following statement: 'The rights and entitlements of citizens, regardless of creed, colour, race, gender, age, sexual orientation, disability, or political opinion is non-negotiable' (http://www.sinnfein.ie/contexts/312 accessed 06 January 2011). The association of the equalities and the rights agenda with nationalism was also substantiated in our research, as illustrated by the following quotes:

> We had a difficulty here [in Northern Ireland], I suppose historically, that a lot of matters to do with equality, a lot of matters to do with rights, for some reason ended up being associated with one section of the community. I remember at the time the Human Rights Commission was established and politicians referring to it as 'Oh not another green elephant...' I think one of the interesting things would be the Bill of Rights for Northern Ireland,

the proposed Bill of Rights for Northern Ireland, and I know that hasn't made the progress that we would have liked it to have made, again because it's become a bit of a political football.

(Mayor)

…in recent years it [sexuality equalities] has been a key element in the manifesto of at least two, but really significantly one political party and that would be Sinn Fein. As I say, very very high profile. Everything we do now, Sinn Fein will examine every element to make sure equality has been mainstreamed.

(Local Authority Officer)

It is important to point out that our research showed that opinion about the support of the major political parties for LGBT equalities was somewhat divided. Also, a community representative noted that 'I'm left then in a dangerous position of again generalising that somehow nationalists are much nicer towards gay people rather than unionists which is a road I do not want to go down…there are [also] extremists on the Catholic side of the divide'. However, opposition to the LGBT equalities agenda is particularly marked amongst the main unionist parties, and it is to this opposition that the chapter now turns.

There is some discussion of unionist party political homophobia in the literature. Glennon (2006) reviews the way in which the extension of civil partnerships to Northern Ireland forced reactions from the mainstream political parties; the DUP tried several times to prevent the extension, citing 'the distinctive cultural and moral values of people within this jurisdiction' (2006: 269) (in other words, invoking particular ethnic identities as a means of consolidating a homophobic ideology). The UUP also opposed civil partnerships.

Our research demonstrated the extent to which the DUP is publically homophobic along a number of lines. Fundamentalist Christianity is one major touchstone, but contributors also discussed the medical pathologization of same-sex sexualities and resistance to the implementation of s75, for example '…the DUP would be very, very much you know that basically "these people can be corrected, give them the right tablet and they can be corrected"' (councillor). The impact of key political figures, notably the DUP's Ian Paisley and former DUP politician Iris Robinson, in publically promoting homophobic views, is also marked in Northern Ireland. Iris Robinson made homophobic statements to the media in the summer of 2008 (Ashe 2009), which were discussed by a number of contributors to our research as having a very negative impact on public attitudes to LGB people at the time of the research (2008–9). For example, as one contributor said:

…their [DUP] views are religiously based yet at the same time they're very clear with their equality statements and have no problem, for example, with the Minister for Equality Ian Paisley Junior making viciously homophobic comments. Could you imagine an equality minister in Westminster or in

Scotland or in Wales getting away with the same? It shows you the power of that block.

(Community Project Worker)

Homophobia has had the effect of directly impeding LGBT people's access to representative democratic processes in Northern Ireland. There is a dearth of politicians who are out as LGBT in Northern Ireland. Homophobia is clearly institutionalized within the DUP and – because of majoritarian representative democratic processes – more broadly within the legislature. Contributors said, for example:

> In a conversation with Martin McGuiness regarding the Shared Futures document we were very much pushing to ensure we're included, and we were told in no uncertain terms that the Reverend Ian Paisley was not having it [laughs] and that it was going to be a battle for another day, both in vetoes. So we found ourselves actually campaigning at Stormont earlier this year...
>
> (LGBT Community Organisation Representative)

> Often councils, particularly very strong DUP councils, will not do anything on equality unless they are forced to do it, so rather than section 75 being a very positive piece of legislation, it's regarded as 'We'll do as little as we can to meet the requirements'... they'll drag their feet ... they would probably be quite proud of the fact that they were the last ones...
>
> (National Stakeholder)

> ...maybe there is a widening gap between the explicit commitment to the new equality agenda between all parties, and indeed in recent times we've seen an increasing frustration from DUP and SDLP about Sinn Fein's beating of the equality drum...
>
> (Local Authority Officer)

As demonstrated, there are very substantial party political barriers to the LGBT equalities agenda amongst the main unionist parties. However, there were also indications in our research that the picture is far from homogenous, and that change is taking place concerning support for LGBT equalities amongst party politicians. There has been considerable support for the LGBT equalities agenda from some local and national politicians generally, for instance one community member discussed support from Social Democrat and Labour Party politicians at a national LGBT event. Importantly, there is also change starting to take place amongst unionist politicians. Recent journalistic coverage suggests that changes within the DUP may be linked to a reaction to the Iris Robinson sex scandal in which Robinson 'rang down the curtain on her political career by conducting an affair with a teenager 41 years her junior' (http://www.u.tv/News/Irish-Robinsons-homophobia-inspires-play/ accessed 06 January 2011, see also Fidelma Ashe's 2009 analysis). Contributors to our research said, for instance, that:

We were looking at using a council facility, and there were objections within the council to homosexuals [sic] using council premises, these were actually voiced quite openly by people that claim to belong to the Socialist parties [laughs], one of the arguments being that decent people would have to use the conveniences after us, that sort of thing. The councillors, or the majority of councillors, responded with horror at what they were hearing and the festival went ahead, with the Mayor and many councillors actually adjourning a meeting and crossing the square to join us, so [we] were dealing with, you know, a powerful statement by the politicians.

(Community Organisation Representative)

Dawn Purvis the co-sponsor of the event in the long gallery, [she was at the time from] the Progressive Unionist Party, actually Dawn Purvis has in the past launched the foreign Pride festival. So we again we're starting to see that change within unionism ... had a lot of Ulster unionist persons attending the [LGBT] event and some of them subsequently went on the Gay Pride march in Belfast, so we're seeing a change that change is not simply part of the nationalist community.

(Community Project Worker)

Overall, therefore, the LGBT equalities agenda has been structured by sectarian party politics over the past period, and that homophobia is institutionalized within the powerful DUP, where prejudice is justified on the basis of faith, medicalized models of sexuality, and an ethno-nationalist resistance to the GFA. However, discrimination against LGBT people does appear to cut across the sectarian party political divide to a degree, as does support for LGBT equalities, or at least tolerance. Importantly, there are some indications of unionist support for the LGBT equalities agenda, both amongst the PUP and amongst some individuals within the main unionist parties.

What other forms of democratic engagement are available to LGBT people in Northern Ireland, in addition to (or instead of) representative democracy? Participative democracy is important for the LGBT equalities agenda in Northern Ireland. The GFA obliges public authorities to consult with their communities, and this is one means by which LGBT people can potentially have influence. LGBT people's participation may also be facilitated by a broader factor, civil society. Civil society – the networks and structures that support participatory democracy – are particularly well developed in Northern Ireland, and there are generally high levels of political awareness and awareness of equalities issues. For instance, one local authority contributor suggested that the general public are very well informed about the political process and equalities legislation, whilst a mayor said that 'we had a very strong voluntary sector here that evolved as a result of the troubles, the conflict, because of the absence of direction from government centrally the people basically organised at community level'.

Overall, participative democratic processes are taking place regarding LGBT equalities, for instance contributors to the research reported:

- An overall growth in influence of LGBT community groups, and increased efforts by councils and other statutory bodies to engage with them.
- A mayor speaking at an LGBT support group's launch, which resulted in lobbying work, such as a Good Relations officer advising and supporting councillors.
- Conserving resources by bringing key voluntary and community sector LGBT representatives together with representatives from councils for consultation and partnership work.
- Some councils setting up consultative panels with representatives from the nine s75 groups that meet a few times a year and that are properly resourced.

In Northern Ireland, as elsewhere in the UK, the development of participative democratic processes regarding LGBT people is patchy in practice; overt homophobia, biphobia and transphobia, a lack of LGBT community trust in local authorities, a lack of 'real' engagement out in the LGBT communities, and weak LGBT community capacity all form impediments. There are also aspects of the Northern Irish situation that are problematic for LGBT equalities and participatory democracy. High levels of civic engagement can result in LGBT equalities being blocked. There was some indication of this in Northern Ireland, for example one local authority contributor said that the level of demonstrations, and questioning of council actors, can act as an impediment to decisions being made. In addition, the issue of the loudest voices discussed in the chapter on democracy is apparent in Northern Ireland. The situation is particularly difficult for 'silent groups of people who don't come though the LGBT channel' (local authority officer) such as men who have sex with men; these groups are more hidden and therefore harder to engage. One contributor reported that the section of the population who speak Irish would be afraid of contacting the council generally, and hence particularly marginalizing intersection is apparent regarding being Catholic (so having a history of difficult experiences with the statutory sector), LGBT (particularly as many LGBT people are not generally 'out') and speaking Irish. Violence as a structuring factor (including homophobic hate crime) also appears to be particularly striking in Northern Ireland, and this is likely to negatively affect participatory democratic engagement, as illustrated in the following quote:

> There was something that the Staff Commission tried to arrange, you know at regional level, for local government officers to meet the [LGB umbrella group] in their offices, and as I say I was struck by the big steel door on the place and all the rest, it was like a prison inside there basically, you know it was keeping them safe from the outside world and they did explain that the building had been attacked and stuff.
>
> (Local Government Manager)

To summarize, in Northern Ireland the democratic process is structured by sectarianism, because the equal rights agenda, as encapsulated in the

GFA, is supported primarily by the main nationalist parties, with virulently homophobic opposition from some sections of the DUP and from some other unionist politicians. The equalities agenda also seems to have become a political football, taking on meaning beyond a concern with equality, due to its association with one side of the sectarian divide. However, this is not the whole story, with some indications of support for a more tolerant position amongst politicians on both sides of the sectarian divide. There are also participative democratic structures in place, which whilst not unproblematic, offer an alternative route into the democratic process.

Discussion

This chapter has explored some of the key themes from this book – in particular intersectionality and democracy – in relation to LGBT equalities in a particular locality, Northern Ireland. In doing so, it has demonstrated the way in which socio-political context shapes LGBT equalities, and provided insight into specific aspects of this, such as the relationship between sexuality, religion and party politics. The chapter provided a snapshot of the situation of LGBT people in Northern Ireland, and then described the history of the locality, before outlining the ways in which equalities work has developed there.

An intersectional analysis is important when addressing LGBT equalities in Northern Ireland, whether the term 'intersectional' is used or not. This is because sectarianism, which forms such a significant force in the country, is formed from a combination of different forces and characteristics, including national allegiance, ethnic affiliations and religion. Sectarianism is gendered and sexed in particular ways, reflecting both the traditionalism found in Northern Ireland and the way in which the civil rights movement and the subsequent shift towards equal rights has stemmed from nationalist roots.

In Northern Ireland, processes of democracy in relation to LGBT equalities are structured by sectarianism, with the LGBT equalities agenda being associated with the nationalist side because of the broader political history of the civil rights movement and the GFA. The LGBT equalities agenda has therefore evolved in a particular way: the association with Sinn Fein and nationalism has on the one hand opened opportunities for advancement of the agenda (it could be imagined that some nationalists have ended up supporting the agenda because it is associated with the GFA, even if they are not personally pro sexualities equalities), whilst on the other hand it has reinforced institutionalized homophobia amongst the unionists because an anti-equality ethno-nationalist and religious intersection has become sedimented. It would be a mistake, however, in this chapter, to overstate the sectarian split, and we would not wish to discursively reinforce it. There are certainly signs of change regarding all the parties, as demonstrated in the findings from our research. The participative structures that have evolved at the grass roots and in relation to the GFA are also broadly facilitative of LGBT equalities, although, as with electoral politics, there are problems with majoritarianism.

Summary

■ There has been significant movement towards LGB, and to a lesser extent T, equalities in Northern Ireland over the last 20 years, driven by externally imposed legislation, and well-developed implementation structures.

■ Tradition, and faith-related homophobia, biphobia and transphobia form hefty barriers to LGBT equalities in Northern Ireland, although there is a sense that attitudes are changing and that people are reinterpreting faith in more LGBT-friendly ways.

■ Sectarianism plays a major role in structuring LGBT equalities in Northern Ireland.

■ Religious prejudice is particularly noticeable amongst the more evangelical sections of the Protestant church, which are associated with the main unionist political parties, but there was evidence of diversity in stances towards LGBT people across different parts of the church.

■ LGBT equalities and other forms of equalities are very sensitive in electoral terms, an issue that is of course not limited to the Northern Ireland context.

■ Intersectional analysis regarding sexuality and gender is particularly useful in Northern Ireland because it provides a means of teasing out the dynamics associated with faith and religion, nationalism, territorialism and ethnicity, and the ways that these shape LGBT equalities.

Conclusion

The aim of this book has been to explore sexuality and trans in relation to diversity and equality, through an examination of how equalities policy does, or does not, get implemented. In so doing, the book has contributed to broader debates concerning citizenship, intersectionality, organizational processes and democracy. It is in the context of growing awareness of social and cultural diversity being a fact of life, especially in the west, that the discussion is framed. In critically assessing the state of equality and diversity among LGBT populations in the UK and elsewhere, the analysis draws on a wide range of research and an empirical case study to concretize the discussion. There has been a shift towards the increased visibility of bisexual and transgender issues in some countries, a shift which is substantially overlooked in the literature. This book has woven in analysis of trans and bisexual issues alongside that of lesbian and gay issues, paying attention to the divergences in agendas as well as the alliances.

Overall, the book deals with some of the key theoretical debates that have contributed to changing understandings of sexuality and sexual politics over the last 20 years or so in this new era of LGBT normalization. A central concern is to understand how models of citizenship are constructed by marginalized groups (such as sexual/gender minorities) as new democratic moments emerge, and where we see evidence of new citizenship subjectivities emerging alongside 'older stories' of forms of intolerance, stigma and discrimination. In the UK, equality initiatives have been rolled out under neoliberal forms of governance, where decentralization to local government has occurred. Apparent tensions exist between a shift towards a politics of individual rights and an emphasis on collective rights of specific groups (for example 'gay rights'), and between equality and diversity. Through an analysis of an empirical case study the book addresses a number of interlinked themes, including the relation between cultural and material aspects of recognition, and the limits to the articulation of a notion of sexual or intimate citizenship. However, it also offers new insights into these developments in its consideration of the production of new citizen subjects, including the issue of the paradox of sexuality being both relevant and irrelevant, a group feature and an individual characteristic, and a focus on being not doing.

The language of citizenship has in recent years been mobilized, sometimes controversially, to articulate a wide range of claims and demands. However, this is a particular historical moment where we are witnessing a major 'jolt' in how people are contesting citizenship rights and to which upheavals in the world are linked. A moment where nascent movements, inspired by, but not necessarily wanting to replicate western democracy and models of citizenship, are demanding social and political transformation. This means that the outcomes of these transformations are not necessarily going to look like neoliberal models of citizenship and associated understandings of the individual and their (human) rights. These jolts reverberate and unsettle social scientific explanations of citizenship, demanding that we ask new questions about how we theorize these key concepts. The answers to these questions are complex and play out differently in different societies. The categories of lesbian, gay, bisexual and trans are themselves western constructs, and southern rights movements may use these categories, or other categories (or both) when mobilizing for the rights of gender and sexual minorities.

We live in a moment where we are seeing contestations leading to the making of new citizens alongside contexts where other people remain or are made invisible in citizenship terms. This at the same time as questions are being raised about the conceptual and political utility of citizenship, especially in a context where there has been a strong emphasis by policy makers and researchers on the question of citizenship in increasingly diverse societies. The concept of citizenship draws attention to the rights and responsibilities that accrue to individuals on the basis of their membership in a community, typically understood to be that of the nation-state. In recent times, however, the concept has come under significant interrogation, prompting new definitions of citizenship such as cosmopolitan citizenship, ecological citizenship and – a key focus of this book – sexual citizenship. In extending theoretical frameworks in citizenship studies, a number of important questions have been raised. Should we be thinking 'beyond citizenship'? How does the concept of citizenship deal with power, inequality and difference? What are the problems of framing struggles over belonging in terms of citizenship in a globalizing world? How can we bring together the concept of going beyond citizenship or 'post citizenship' and hold this in tension with the fact that in many parts of the world lots of people are non-citizens; thereby helping to generate new understandings and research approaches to citizenship. Such questioning is not merely of academic interest, it is of central importance to developing critiques of norms of citizenship formed under conditions of injustice.

In its use of intersectionality theory to explore the theme of equality and diversity the book also broadens understandings of the link between equality and diversity. First, it makes the point that diversity is not simply a matter of recognizing different identities such as lesbian, white, working class and so on Rather, we need to understand that such identities are themselves diversified through their complex intersections. It follows from this that equality has to be considered not simply in terms of discrete categories, but in terms of these differences. That is, what counts as equality for white, middle-class lesbians may very different for working-class black lesbians for whom economic and racial equality intersect with sexual equality in particular ways.

Secondly, it draws attention to how equality is not just a matter of rights, but also a matter of capabilities and equal access to institutions and resources that allow for equal participation in social and political life. The book points to the importance of the global context and global processes (including international LGBT rights networks), in understanding localized issues of sexualities and trans equality. It examines some of the issues concerning different forms of democratic engagement (representative and participatory), including the issue of majoritarian prejudice and the way in which this can impede the equality of LGBT people. Furthermore, in considering the rationales that are often used to resist equality measures in institutions and organizations the book offers important insights for public policy and organizational studies. More broadly, these ideas serve as a reminder that alongside the positive changes that have occurred in relation to LGBT equality there is a need to be critical of what this may mean in practice. The attendant consequences of greater public recognition and normalization of the idea of LGBT equality may be the privatization of intolerance and prejudice.

One of the important aspects of the book is that the empirical research it draws on was carried out at a crucial period of legislative and policy change. In this sense the analysis is located in a postlegislative equality era where the kind of changes earlier writers debated have now come about. It therefore offers an interesting comparison with earlier research to show how the contemporary situation is different or similar (or, perhaps, differently similar) from before. For instance, earlier research (for example Cooper 1997; Cooper and Monro 2003; Browne 2007) suggested that developing sexualities equalities would be much easier with legislative and institutional backing. Although to some extent this does seem to be the case, it is clear that implementing equality is very complex and involves a broadening of perspectives on resistance and change at different intersecting levels. This represents an important contribution to the literature where in debates about recognition the link between diversity and equality has often been neglected. Indeed, a number of significant differences from the earlier research are apparent, for instance in the UK there appears to be greater cross party recognition of the case for LGBT equality and a shift towards regarding LGBT people as 'ordinary citizens'. However, many of the issues identified in earlier research still seem to be pertinent. This includes, for example, the importance of affective aspects of sexualities and trans equality strands, such as the perception of LGBT issues as 'sensitive', the low status accorded such work, and the recognition that 'private prejudice' is still prevalent. To an extent, in countries such as the UK, the boundaries of 'normalcy' have shifted, and certain types of lesbian and gay citizen (for example, those in monogamous relationships, and those who work and pay taxes) are now more socially accepted, whilst other people (including bisexuals who are not in monogamous relationships, people in polyamorous relationships, those who engage in public sex or sex work) are now framed as socially marginal or 'unacceptable'. A similar trajectory can be observed with respect to trans issues; trans people who have had gender reassignment surgery (or intend to do so) have greater claims to social legitimacy and acceptability than those who identify as gender-fluid or diverse.

Overall, there are substantial shifts taking place regarding the equality of sexual and gender minorities, but these are fractured by structuring processes relating to nationality and national identity, race and ethnicity, socio-economic differences and dynamics, and a range of other factors. Individual adherence (or not) to localized norms concerning lifestyle and identity (these could include, for example, dress codes, work ethics, publically demonstrated relationship structures) play an important role concerning the extent to which sexual and gender minorities have equal access to social and material resources. The group-based identity politics which has played such an important role in the lesbian, gay and transgender movements continues to be relevant, but increased diversity concerning identity (both within sexual and gender minority groupings and elsewhere) calls for increasingly flexible, nuanced understandings of equality. In making its conceptual points and illustrating them empirically, this book will hopefully make a significant contribution to this process of rethinking perspectives on diversity and equality.

Notes

5 Organizational Change

1. Kirklees council was aspiring to level 5 of the Equalities Standard at the time of the production of the strategy.
2. http://www.kirklees.gov.uk/you-kmc-policies/equalitydiversity.EDS_Actionplan.pdf (accessed 15 May 2010)

References

Acker, J. (2006) 'Inequality Regimes: Gender, Class, and Race in Organizations', *Gender and Society*, 20(4): 441–464.

Adam, B. (1987) *The Rise of the Gay and Lesbian Movement*. Boston: Twayne Publishers.

Adam, B. (1997) *The Rise of a Gay and Lesbian Movement*. Revised Edition. Boston: Twayne Publishers.

Adam, B. (1998) 'Theorizing Homophobia', *Sexualities*, 1(4): 387–404.

Adam, B., Duyvendak, J.W. and Krawel, A. (eds) (1998) *The Global Emergence of Gay and Lesbian Politics: National Imprints of a Worldwide Movement*. Philadelphia: Temple University Press.

Ahmed, S. (2007) 'You end up doing the document rather than doing the doing': Diversity, Race Equality and the Politics of Documentation', *Ethnic and Racial Studies*, 30(4): 590–609.

Ahmed, S. (2011) *On Being Included: Racism and Diversity in Institutional Life*. Durham: Duke University Press.

Aizura, A.Z. (2006) 'Of Borders and Homes: The Imaginary Community of (Trans)sexual Citizenship', *Inter-Asia Cultural Studies*, 7(2): 289–309.

Ajutament de Barcelona (2010) *Municipal Plan for LGBT People in Barcelona: 2015*. Barcelona: Ajutament de Barcelona (translated from Catalan).

Altman, D. (1993) *Homosexual Oppression and Liberation* (1st edn. 1971). New York: New York University Press.

Altman, D. (2001) *Global Sex*. Chicago, IL: University of Chicago Press.

Amnesty (2001) *Crime of Hate, Conspiracy of Silence: Torture and Ill-Treatment Based on Sexual Identity*. London: Amnesty International.

Andolina, R., Laurie, N. and Radcliffe, S. (2009) *Indigenous Development in the Andes. Culture, Power and Transnationalism*. Raleigh, Durham: Duke University Press.

Andrews, J., Cameron, H. and Harris, M. (2008) 'All Change? Managers' Experience of Organizational Change in Theory and Practice', *Journal of Organizational Change Management*, 21(3): 300–314.

Andrucki, M.J. (2007) 'Locating the State in Queer Space: GLBT Non-Profit Organizations in Vermont, USA', *Social and Cultural Geography*, 8(1): 89–104.

Anetzberger, G.J., Ishler, K.J., Mostade, J. and Blatt, M. (2004) 'Gay and Grey', *Journal of Lesbian and Gay Social Services*, 17(1): 23–45.

Angelides, S. (2001) *A History of Bisexuality*. Chicago: University of Chicago Press.

Ashe, F. (2009) 'Iris Robinson's Excitable Speech: Sexuality and Conflict Transformation in Northern Ireland', *Politics*, 29(1): 20–27.

Ault, A. (1994) 'Hegemonic Discourse in an Oppositional Community: Lesbian Feminist Stigmatization of Bisexual Women', *Critical Sociology*, 20(3): 107–122. Reprinted in B. Beemyn and M. Eliason (eds) *Queer Studies. A Lesbian, Gay, Bisexual and Transgender Anthology*. New York: New York University Press.

Badgett, M.V.L. (2001) *Money, Myths and Change: The Economic Lives of Lesbians and Gay Men*. Chicago: University of Chicago Press.

Badgett, M.V.L. (2010) *When Gay People Get Married: What Happens When Societies Legalize Same-Sex Marriage*. New York: New York University Press.

Bagilhole, B. (1997) *Equal Opportunities and Social Policy Issues of Gender, Race, and Disability*. London: Longman.

Barber, B. (1984) *Strong Democracy: Participatory Politics for a New Age*. Berkeley: University of California Press.

Barker, N. (2006) 'Sex and the Civil Partnership Act: The Future of (Non)Conjugality', *Feminist Legal Studies*, 14(2): 241–259.

Barrett, M. and Davidson, M.J. (eds) (2006) *Gender and Communication at Work*. Aldershot: Ashgate Publishing.

Barth, J. and Parry, J. (2009) 'Political Culture, Public Opinion, and Policy (Non)Diffusion: The Case of Gay- and Lesbian-Related Issues in Arkansas', *Social Science Quarterly*, 90(2): 309–325.

Bawer, B. (1993) *A Place at the Table: The Gay Individual in American Society*. New York: Poseidan Press.

Bech, H. (1997) *When Men Meet: Homosexuality and Modernity*. Cambridge: Polity Press.

Beckett, C. (2004) 'Crossing the Border: Locating Heterosexuality as a Boundary for Lesbian and Disabled Women', *Journal of International Women's Studies*, 5(3): 44–52.

Beckett, C. and Macey, M. (2001) 'Race, Gender and Sexuality: The Oppression of Multiculturalism', *Women's Studies International Forum*, 24(3–4): 309–319.

Beetham, D. (1999) *Democracy and Human Rights*. Cambridge: Polity Press.

Bell, D.A. (2006) *Beyond Liberal Democracy: Political Thinking for an East Asian Context*. Princetown and Oxford: Princetown University Press.

Bell, D. and Binnie, J. (2000) *The Sexual Citizen: Queer Politics and Beyond*. Cambridge: Polity Press.

Bell, D. and Binnie, J. (2002) 'Sexual Citizenship: Marriage, the Market and the Military', in D. Richardson and S. Seidman (eds) *The Handbook of Lesbian and Gay Studies*. London: Sage.

Bell, D. and Binnie, J. (2004) 'Authenticating Queer Space: Citizenship, Urbanism and Governance', *Urban Studies*, 41(9): 1807–1820.

Bell, D. and Valentine, G. (eds) (1995) *Mapping Desire: Geographies of Sexualities*. London: Routledge.

Bendl, R. and Fleischmann, A. (2008) 'Diversity Management Discourse Meets Queer Theory', *Gender and Management: An International Journal*, 23(6): 382–394.

Benhabib, S. (2010) *The Claims of Culture: Equality and Diversity in the Global Era*. Princeton: Princeton University Press.

Berlant, L. (1997) *The Queen of America Goes to Washington City: Essays on Sex and Citizenship*. Durham and London: Duke University Press.

Berry, C., Martin, F. and Yue, A. (eds) (2003) *Mobile Cultures: New Media in Queer Asia*. Raleigh, Durham: Duke University Press.

Bhavnani, K. (1997) 'Women's Studies and its Interconnections with 'Race', Ethnicity and Sexuality', in V. Robinson and D. Richardson (eds) *Introducing Women's Studies: Feminist Theory and Practice*, 2nd edn. Basingstoke: Macmillan, New York: New York University Press.

Binnie, J. (2004) *The Globalization of Sexuality*. London: Sage.

Blasius, M. (ed) (2001) *Sexual Identities, Queer Politics*. Princetown: Princetown University Press.

Blasius, M. and Phelan, S. (eds) (1997) *We Are Everywhere: A Historical Sourcebook of Gay and Lesbian Politics*. New York: Routledge.

Borger, J. (2010) 'Commonwealth has "Abandoned" Human Rights Role', *The Guardian*, 9 October 2010.

Bornstein, K. (1994) *Gender Outlaw: On Men, Women, and the Rest of Us*. London: Routledge.

Bornstein, K. (1998) *My Gender Workbook*. London: Routledge.

Botcherby, S. and Creegan, C. (2009) *Moving Forward: Putting Sexual Orientation in the Public Domain*. Manchester: Equality and Human Rights Commission, Research Summary No. 40.

Bowditch, J.L., Buono, A.F. and Stewart, M.M. (2007) *A Primer on Organizational Behavior*. Hoboken, NJ: John Wiley & Sons.

Bowleg, L. (2008) 'When Black + Lesbian + Woman ≠ Black Lesbian Woman: The Methodological Challenges of Qualitative and Quantitative Research', *Sex Roles*, 59: 312–325.

Bowring, M. and Brewis, J. (2009) 'Truth and Consequences: Managing Lesbian and Gay Identity in the Canadian Workplace', *Equal Opportunities International*, 28(5): 361–377.

Brah, A. and Phoenix, A. (2004) 'Aint I a Woman? Revisiting Intersectionality', *Journal of International Women's Studies*, 5(3): 75–86.

Breitenbach, E. (2004) *Researching Lesbian, Gay, Bisexual and Transgender Issues in Northern Ireland*. Edinburgh: University of Edinburgh, Belfast: Office of the First Minister and Deputy First Minister.

Bristow, J. and Wilson, A. (1993) *Activating Theory: Lesbian, Gay, and Bisexual Politics*. London: Lawrence and Wishart.

Brown, G., Browne, K. and Lim, J. (2007) 'Introduction, or Why Have a Book on Geographies of Sexualities?', in K. Browne, J. Lim, and G. Brown (eds) *Geographies of Sexualities*. Aldershot: Ashgate.

Brown, M. (1997) *RePlacing Citizenship: AIDS Activism and Radical Democracy*. New York: The Guildford Press.

Brown, S. (2002) 'Con Discriminacion y Repression no Hay Democracia' The Lesbian and Gay Movement in Argentinia', *Latin American Perspectives*, 29(2): 119–138.

Brown, W. (2006) *Regulating Aversion. Tolerance in the Age of Identity and Empire*. Princeton and Oxford: Princeton University Press.

Browne, K. (2007) *Count Me in Too: Academic Findings Report*. Brighton: University of Brighton and Spectrum. Available at: http://www.spectrum-lgbt.org/cmiToo/downloads/CMIT_AcademicReport_final_June07.pdf.

Browne, K., Lim, J. and Brown, G. (2007) *Geographies of Sexualities*. Farnham, UK; Burlington, USA: Ashgate.

Browne, K. (2011) ' "By Partner We Mean...": Alternative Geographies of "Gay Marriage" ', *Sexualities*, 14(1): 100–122.

Brunni, A. (2006) 'Have you Got a Boyfriend or are You Single? On the Importance of Being "Straight" in Organizational Research', *Gender, Work and Organization*, 13(3): 299–316.

Bryant, K. and Vidal-Ortiz, S. (2008) 'Introduction to Retheorizing Homophobias', *Sexualities*, 11(4): 387–396.

Bryant, K. and Pini, B. (2011) *Gender and Rurality*, Newyork and London: Routledge.

Burack, C. and Josephson, J.J. (2005) 'Origin Stories: Same-Sex Sexuality and Christian Right Politics', *Culture and Religion,* 6(3): 369–392.

Burawoy, M. (2000) 'Introduction: Reaching for the Global', in M. Burawoy, J.A. Blum, S. George, Z. Gillie, M. Thayer, T. Gowan, L. Haney, M. Klawiter, S.H. Lopez and S. Riain (eds) *Global Ethnography: Forces, Connections and Imaginations in a Postmodern World*. Berkeley: University of California Press.

Burrell, G. and Hearn, J. (1989) 'The Sexuality of Organization', in J. Hearn, D.L. Sheppard, P. Tancred-Sheriff and G. Burrell (eds) *The Sexuality of Organization*. London, Newbury Park, New Delhi: Sage Publications.

Butler, J. (1990) *Gender Trouble: Feminism and the Subversion of Identity*. London: Routledge.

Butler, J. (1993) *Bodies that Matter: On the Discursive Limits of 'Sex'*. London: Routledge.

Butler, J. (1997) *The Psychic Life of Power*. Stanford: Stanford University Press.

Butler, J. (2004) *Undoing Gender*. London: Routledge.

Butler, S. (2004) 'Gay, Lesbian, Bisexual and Transgender (GLBT) Elders', *Journal of Human Behavior and the Environment,* 9(4): 24–44.

Butt, R. (2011) Protect Gay Asylum Seekers, Rowan Williams Urges. *The Guardian,* 29 January 2011: 20.

Cahill, S. (2004) *Same-Sex Marriage in the United States: Focus on the Facts*. New York: Lexington Books.

Cahill, S. and Tobias, S. (2007) *Policy Issues Affecting Lesbian, Gay, Bisexual and Transgender Families*. Ann Arbor, MI: University of Michigan Press.

Calhoun, C. (1994) 'Social Theory and the Politics of Identity', in C. Calhoun (ed) *Social Theory and the Politics of Identity*. Cambridge, MA, Oxford: Blackwell Publishers Ltd.

Canaday, M. (2009) *The Straight State: Sexuality and Citizenship in Twentieth-Century America*. Princetown and Oxford: Princetown University Press.

Carabine, J. and Monro, S. (2004) 'Lesbian and Gay Politics and Participation in New Labour's Britain', *Social Politics: International Studies in Gender, State & Society*, 11(2): 312–327.

Carbido, D.W. (1999) *Black Men and Race, Gender and Sexuality: A Critical Reader*. New York, London: New York University Press.

Carnevale, D.G. (2003) *Organizational Development in the Public Sector*. Boulder: Westview Press.

Carver, T. and Mottier, V. (eds) (1998) *Politics and Sexuality: Identity, Gender, Citizenship*. London and New York: Routledge. Reprinted 2005, London: Taylor and Francis.

Casey, M.E. (2004) 'De-Dyking Queer Space(s): Heterosexual Female Visibility in Gay and Lesbian Spaces', *Sexualities*, 7(4): 446–461.

Casey, M.E. (2007) 'The Queer Unwanted and Their Undesirable Otherness', in K. Browne, J. Lim and G. Brown (eds) *Geographies of Sexualities*. Aldershot: Ashgate.

Chamberlain, B. (2009) *Bisexual People in the Workplace: Practical Advice for Employers*. London: Stonewall.

Chasin, A. (2000) *Selling Out. The Gay and Lesbian Movement Goes to Market*. New York: St. Martin's Press.

Chemers, M.M. and Murphy, S.E. (1995) 'Leadership and Diversity in Groups and Organizations', in M.M. Chemers, S. Oskamp, and M.A. Costano (eds) *Diversity in Organizations: New Perspectives for a Changing Workplace*. London: Sage.

Clayton, P. (1998) 'Religion, Ethnicity and Colonisation as Explanations of the Northern Ireland Conflict', in D. Miller (ed) *Rethinking Northern Ireland*. Harlow, Essex: Addison Wesley Longman Limited.

Cock, J. (2002) 'Engendering Gay and Lesbian Rights: The Equality Clause in the South African Constitution', *Women's Studies International Forum*, 26(1): 35–45.

Coleman-Fountain, E. (2011) *Making Sexual Selves: A Qualitative Study of Lesbian and Gay Youth*. Unpublished PhD thesis, Newcastle upon Tyne: Newcastle University, UK.

Colgan, F., Creegan, C., McKearney, A. and Wright, T. (2006) *Lesbian, Gay and Bisexual Workers: Equality, Diversity and Inclusion in the Workplace?*, Comparative Organisation and Equality Research Centre, London Metropolitan University. Available at: www.workinglives.org/docs/ESF_LGB_Report_5_June_2006.pdf.

Colgan, F., Creegan, C., McKearney, A. and Wright, T. (2007) 'Equality and Diversity Policies and Practices at Work: Lesbian, Gay and Bisexual Workers', *Equal Opportunities International*, 26(6): 590–609.

Colgan, F., Wright, T., Creegan, C. and McKearney, A. (2009) 'Equality and Diversity in the Public Services: Moving Forward on Lesbian, Gay and Bisexual Equality?', *Human Resource Management Journal*, 19(3): 280–301.

Colgan, F. and Wright, T. (2011) 'Lesbian, Gay and Bisexual Equality in a Modernising Public Sector: Opportunities and Threats', *Gender, Work & Organization*, 18(6): 548–570.

Collins, A. (2004) 'Sexuality and Sexual Services in the Urban Economy and Socialscape: An Overview', *Urban Studies*, 41(9): 1631–1641.

Collins, D. (1998) *Organizational Change, Sociological Perspectives*. London, New York: Routledge.

Connell, R.W. (1995) *Masculinities*. Cambridge: Polity Press.

Connell, R.W. and Messerschmidt, J.W. (2005) 'Hegemonic Masculinity: Rethinking the Concept', *Gender and Society*, 19(6): 829–859.

Conrad, K.A. (2004) *Locked in the Family Cell: Gender, Sexuality and Political Agency in Irish Nationalist Discourse*. Madison, WI: University of Wisconsin Press.

Cook, J.A. (2000) 'Sexuality and People with Psychiatric Disabilities', *Sexuality and Disability*, 18(3): 195–206.

Cooper, D. (1994) *Sexing the City. Lesbian and Gay Politics within the Activist State*. London: Rivers Oram Press.

Cooper, D. (1995) *Power in Struggle: Feminism, Sexuality and the State*. Buckingham: Open University Press.

Cooper, D. (1997) 'Governing Troubles: Authority, Sexuality and Space', *British Journal of Sociology of Education*, 18(4): 501–517.

Cooper, D. (2002) 'Imagining the Place of the State: Where Governance and Social Power Meet', in D. Richardson and S. Seidman (eds) *Handbook of Lesbian and Gay Studies*. London: Sage.

Cooper, D. (2004) *Challenging Diversity: Rethinking Equality and the Value of Difference*. Cambridge: Cambridge University Press.

Cooper, D. (2006) 'Active Citizenship and the Governmentality of Local Lesbian and Gay Politics', *Political Geography*, 25: 921–943.

Cooper, D. and Monro, S. (2003) 'Governing from the Margins: Queering the State of Local Government', *Contemporary Politics*, 9: 229–255.

Corbett, J. (1994) 'A Proud Label: Exploring the Relationship between Disability Politics and Gay Pride', *Disability and Society*, 9(3): 343–357.

Correa, S., Petchesky, R. and Parker, R. (2008) *Sexuality, Health and Human Rights*. Oxon, New York: Routledge.

Cossman, B. (2007) *Sexual Citizens. The Legal and Cultural Regulation of Sex and Belonging*. Stanford, CA: Stanford University Press.

Coulter, C. (1998) 'Feminism and Nationalism in Ireland', in D. Miller (ed) *Rethinking Northern Ireland*. Harlow, Essex: Addison Wesley Longman Limited.

Council of Europe (2011) *Discrimination on Grounds of Sexual Orientation and Gender Identity in Europe*. Strasberg, Cedex: Council of Europe Publishing.

Creegan, C. and Keating, M. (2010) *Improving Sexual Orientation Monitoring*. Manchester: Equality and Human Rights Commission.

Crenshaw, K.W. (1991) 'Mapping the Margins: Intersectionality, Identity Politics, and Violence against Women of Colour', *Stanford Law Review*, 43(6): 1241–1299.

Crenshaw, K.W. (1997) 'Intersectionality and Identity Politics: Learning from Violence against Women of Colour', in M. Stanley and V. Naryan (eds) *Restructuring Feminist Political Theory: Feminist Perspectives*. Cambridge: Polity Press.

Cronin, A. and King, A. (2010) 'Power, Inequality and Identity: Exploring Diversity and Intersectionality Amongst Older LGB Adults', *Sociology*, 44(5): 876–892.

Croucher, S. (2006) 'South Africa's Democratisation and the Politics of Gay Liberation', *Journal of South African Studies*, 28(2): 315–330.

Cruz-Malavé, A. and Manalansan IV, M.F. (eds) (2002) *Queer Globalizations. Citizenship and the Afterlife of Colonialism*. New York: New York University Press.

Cunningham, F. (2002) *Theories of Democracy: A Critical Introduction*. London, New York: Routledge.

Currah, P., Juang, R.M., and Minter, S. (eds) (2006) *Transgender Rights*. Minneapolis: University of Minnesota Press.

Cutcher, L. (2009) 'Resisting Change from Within and Without the Organization', *Journal of Organizational Change Management*, 22(3): 275–289.

Cvetkovich, A. (2003) *An Archive of Feelings: Trauma, Sexuality, and Lesbian Public Cultures*. Durham and London: Duke University.

Daly, M. (1984) *Pure Lust: Elemental Feminist Philosophy*. London: The Women's Press.

Daunton, M. and Hilton, M. (eds) (2001) *The Politics of Consumption: Material Culture and Citizenship in Europe and America*. Oxford: Berg.

Davies, D. (2000) 'Sharing Our Stories, Empowering Our Lives: Don't Dis Me!', *Sexuality and Disability*, 18(3): 179–186.

Davis, A. (1981) *Women, Race and Class*. New York: Random House.

Davis, K. (2009) 'Intersectionality as Buzzword: A Sociology of Science Perspective on What Makes a Feminist Theory Successful', *Feminist Theory*, 9(1): 67–85.

Delanty, G. (2000) *Citizenship in a Global Age. Society, Culture, Politics*. Buckingham: Open University Press.

D'Emilio, J. (2000) 'Cycles of Change, Questions of Strategy, the Gay and Lesbian Movement After Fifty Years', in C.A. Rimmerman, K.D. Walld and C. Wilcox (eds) *The Politics of Gay Rights*. Chicago: University of Chicago Press.

D'Emilio, J. and Freedman, E. (1988) *Intimate Matters. A History of Sexuality in America*. New York: Harper and Row Publishers.

Denscombe, M. (2003) *The Good Research Guide*, 2nd edn. Buckingham: Open University Press.

Dilworth, R.L. (1998) 'Action Learning in a Nutshell', *Performance Improvement Quarterly*, 11(1): 28–43.

Dixon, P. (2001). *Northern Ireland: The Politics of War and Peace*. Basingstoke: Palgrave Macmillan.

Dower, N. (2003) *An Introduction to Global Citizenship*. Edinburgh: Edinburgh University Press.

Dreger, A.D. (2000) *Intersex in the Age of Ethics*. Maryland: University Publishing Group.

Duggan, L. (1995) 'Queering the State', in L. Duggan and N. Hunter (eds) *Sex Wars: Sexual Dissident and Political Culture*. New York: Routledge.

Duggan, L. (2002) 'The New Homonormativity: The Sexual Politics of Neoliberalism', in R. Castronova and D.D. Nelson (eds) *Materializing Democracy: Toward a Revitalized Cultural Politics*. Durham, NC: Duke University Press.

Dunphy, R. (2000) *Sexual Politics: An Introduction*. Edinburgh: Edinburgh University Press.

Durose, C., Gains, F., Richardson, L., Combs, R., Bromme, K. and Eason, C. (2011) *Pathways to Politics*. Manchester: Equality and Human Rights Commission. EHRC Research Report No. 65.

Eaklor, V.L. (2011) *Queer America: A People's GLBT History of the United States*. New York: The New Press.

Egan, P.J. and Sherrill, K. (2005) 'Marriage and the Shifting Priorities of a New Generation of Lesbians and Gays', *PS: Political Science and Politics*, 38(2): 229–232.

Elliott, R.D. (2005) 'International Lesbian and Gay Law Association', in H. Graupner and P. Tahminjis (eds) *Sexuality and Human Rights: A Global Overview*. New York, London, Victoria: Harrington Park Press.

Ellison, G. and Gunstone, B. (2009) *Sexual Orientation Explored: A Study of Identity, Attraction, Behaviour and Attitudes in 2009*. Manchester: Equality and Human Rights Commission. Research Report No. 35.

Engel, S. (2002) 'Making a Minority: Understanding the Formation of the Gay and Lesbian Movement in the United States', in D. Richardson and S. Seidman (eds) *Handbook of Lesbian and Gay Studies*. London: Sage.

Epstein, S. (1987) 'Gay Politics, Ethnic Identity: The Limits of Social Constructionism', *Socialist Review*, 17(3–4): 9–54.

Epstein, S. (1999) 'Gay and Lesbian Movements in the United States: Dilemmas of Identity, Diversity, and Political Strategy', in B.D. Adam, J.W. Duyvendak and A. Krouwel (eds) *The Global Emergence of Gay and Lesbian Politics: National Imprints of a Worldwide Movement*. Philadelphia: Temple University Press.

ECNI (2008a) *The Changing Face of Prejudice in Northern Ireland*. Belfast: The Equality Commission for Northern Ireland.

ECNI (2008b) *Eliminating Sexual Orientation Discrimination in Northern Ireland: A Guide to the Provision of Goods, Facilities, Services, and Premises. The Equality Act (Sexual Orientation) Regulations (Northern Ireland) 2006*. Belfast: The Equality Commission for Northern Ireland.

EHRC (2009) *Beyond Tolerance: Making Sexual Orientation a Public Matter*. Manchester: Equality and Human Rights Commission.

EHRC (2011) *How Fair is Britain?* Manchester: Equality and Human Rights Commission.

Essig, L. (1999) *Queer in Russia: A Story of Sex, Self, and Other*. Durham and London: Duke University Press.

Evans, D. (1993) *Sexual Citizenship: The Material Construction of Sexualities*. London: Routledge.

Faderman, L. (1981) *Surpassing the Love of Men: Romantic Friendships and Love between Women from the Renaissance to the Present*. London: The Women's Press.

Farnham, D. and Horton, S. (1996) *Managing People in the Public Services*. Houndmills: Macmillan.

Feinberg, L. (1996) *Transgender Warriors: Making History from Joan of Arc to Dennis Rodman*. Boston: Beacon Press.

Fine, R. (2007) *Cosmopolitanism*. Abingdon: Routledge.

Fish, J. (2008) 'Navigating Queer Street: Researching the Intersections of Lesbian, Gay, Bisexual and Transgender (LGBT) Identities in Health Research', *Sociological Research Online*, 13(1) http://www.socresonline.org.uk/13/1/12.html. Last accessed on 10/12/2010.

Fleming, P. (2007)' Sexuality, Power and Resistance in the Workplace', *Organization Studies*, 28(2): 239–256.

Foucault, M. (1979) *The History of Sexuality. vol. 1: An Introduction*. London: Allen Lane.

FRA (2010) *Homophobia, Transphobia and Discrimination on Grounds of Sexual Orientation and Gender Identity – 2010 Update (Comparative Legal Analysis)*. Available at: http://fra.europa.eu/fraWebsite/lgbt-rights_en.htm. Last accessed on 04/02/2011.

Franke, K.M. (2006) 'The Politics of Same-Sex Marriage Politics', *Columbia Journal of Gender and Law*, 15(1): 236–248.

Fraser, N. (1995) 'From Redistribution to Recognition? Dilemmas of Justice in a 'Post-Socialist Age', *New Left Review*, 1(212): 68–93.

Fraser, N. (2003) *Redistribution or Recognition? A Political-Philosophical Exchange*. London: Verso.

Fraser, N. (2008) *Scales of Justice: Reimagining Political Space in a Globalizing World*. New York: Columbia University Press.

Fredrickson, G.M. (2003) *The Historical Construction of Race and Citizenship in the United States*. Geneva: United Nations Research Institute for Social Development.

Fuss, D. (1990) *Essentially Speaking: Feminism, Nature and Difference*. London: Routledge.

Gagen, E.A. (2000) 'Playing the Part: Performing Gender in America's Playgrounds', in S.L. Holloway and G. Valentine (eds) *Children's Geographies: Playing, Living, Learning*. London, New York: Routledge.

Gagnon, J. and Simon, W. (eds) (1967) *Sexual Deviance*. New York: Harper Row.

Gagnon, J. and Simon, W. (1973) *Sexual Conduct*. London: Hutchinson.

Gamson, J. (1995) 'Must Identity Movements Self-destruct? A Queer Dilemma', *Social Problems*, 42(3): 390–407.

Garnet, L., and Peplau, L.A. (2006) Sexuality in the Lives of Aging Lesbian and Bisexual Women, in D. Kimmel, T. Rose, and S. David (eds) *Lesbian, Gay, Bisexual and Transgender Aging*, 2nd edn. New York: Columbia University Press.

George, S. (1993) *Women and Bisexuality*. London: Scarlett Press.

Gerstmann, E. (2004) *Same-Sex Marriage and the Constitution*. New York: Cambridge University Press.

Giddens, A. (1991) *Modernity and Self-Identity*. Cambridge: Polity.

Glenn, E. N. (2002) *Unequal Freedom: How Race and Gender Shaped American Citizenship and Labour*. Cambridge, MA: Harvard University Press.

Glennon, L. (2006) 'Strategizing for the Future through the Civil Partnership Act', *Journal of Law and Society*, 33(2): 244–276.

Goetz, A. M. and Hassim, S. (2003) *No Shortcuts to Power*. London, New York: Zed and Cape Town: David Philip.

Goldblatt, B. (2006) 'Case Note: Same-Sex Marriage in South Africa – The Constitutional Court's Judgement', *Feminist Legal Studies*, 14: 261–270.

Gould, C.C. (2004) *Globalizing Democracy and Human Rights*. Cambridge: Cambridge University Press.

Grabham, E. (2007) 'Citizen Bodies, Intersex Citizenship', *Sexualities*, 10(1): 29–48.

Grabham, E., Cooper, D., Krishnadas, J. and Herman, D. (eds) (2009) *Intersectionality and Beyond. Law, Power and the Politics of Location*. London: Routledge-Cavendish.

Grant, D., Mechelson, G., Oswick, C. and Wailes, N. (2005) 'Guest Editorial: Discourse and Organizational Change', *Journal of Organizational Change*, 18(1): 6–15.

Graupner, H., and Tahmindjis, P. (eds) (2005) *Sexuality and Human Rights: A Global Overview*. New York, London, Victoria: Harrington Park Press.

Guasp, A. (2007) *The Teacher's Report: Homophobic Bullying in Britain's Schools*. London: Stonewall.

Gunkel, H. (2010) *The Cultural Politics of Female Sexuality in South Africa*. New York: Routledge.

Hacker, H. (2007) 'Developmental Desire and/or Transnational Jouissance: Re-Formulating Sexual Subjectivities in Transnational Contact Zones', in K. Browne, J. Lim and G. Brown (eds) *Geographies of Sexualities*. Famham, UK; Burlington, US: Ashgate.

Halberstam, J. (2005) *In a Queer Time and Place: Transgender Bodies, Subcultural Lives*. New York: New York University Press.

Hancock, A.M. (2007) 'Intersectionality as a Normative and Empirical Paradigm', *Politics and Gender*, 3(2): 248–252.

Hansson, U. and Depret, H.M. (2007) *Equality Mainstreaming: Policy and Practice for Transgender People*. Belfast: Institute for Conflict Research.

Hassard, J., Holliday, R. and Wilmott, H. (eds) (2000) *Body and Organization*. London, Thousand Oaks, New Delhi: Sage Publications.

Hassim, S. (2006) *Women's Organisations and Democracy in South Africa Contesting Authority*. Wisconsin: The University of Wisconsin Press.

Hatch, M. J. (1997) *Organization Theory*. New York: Oxford University Press Inc.

Heaphy, B. (2008) 'The Sociology of Lesbian and Gay Reflexivity or Reflexive Sociology?', *Sociological Research Online* 13(1) Unpaginated. http://www.socresonline.org.uk/13/1/9.html, accessed 10 December 2010.

Hearn, J. and Parkin, W. (1995) *'Sex' at 'Work': The Power and Paradox of Organizational Sexuality*. Englewood Cliffs, NJ: Prentice Hall.

Hearn, J. and Parkin, W. (2001) *Gender, Sexuality and Violence in Organizations*. London: Sage.

Held, D. (1995) *Democracy and the Global Order: From Modern State to Cosmopolitan Governance*. Cambridge: Polity Press.

Held, D. (2010) *Cosmopolitanism: Ideals and Realities*. Cambridge: Polity Press.

Hemmings, C. (2002) *Bisexual Spaces: A Geography of Sexuality and Gender*. London: Routledge.

Herek, G.M. (2004) ' "Beyond Homophobia": Thinking About Sexual Prejudice and Stigma in the Twenty-First Century', *Sexuality Research and Social Policy: Journal of NRSC*, 1(2): 6–24.

Herring, S. (2010) *Another Country: Queer Anti-Urbanism*. New York: New York University Press.

Highleyman, L.A. (2001) *A Brief History of the Bisexual Movement*. Boston, MA: Bisexual Resource Centre. Available at: http://www.biresource.org, accessed 17 June 2010.

Hill Collins, P. (2000) *Black Feminist Thought: Knowledge, Consciousness and the Politics of Empowerment*. New York: Routledge.

Hines, S. (2007) *Transforming Gender: Transgender Practices of Identity, Intimacy and Care*. Bristol: The Policy Press.

Hines, S. (2009) 'A Pathway to Diversity? Human Rights, Citizenship and Politics of Transgender', *Contemporary Politics*, 15(1): 87–102.

Hines, S. and Sanger, T. (2010) *Transgender Identities: Towards a Social Analysis of Gender Diversity*. London: Routledge.

Hirst, P. (1993) 'Associational Democracy', in D. Held (ed) *Prospects for Democracy: North, South, East, West*. Cambridge: Polity Press.

Holloway, D. (2005) *Understanding the Northern Ireland Conflict: A Summary and Overview of the Conflict and Its Origins*. Belfast: The Community Dialogue Critical Issues Series. Volume 3.

Honneth, A. (1996) *The Struggle for Recognition: The Moral Grammar of Social Conflicts*, Cambridge: Polity Press.

Honneth, A. (2002) 'Grounding Recognition: A Rejoinder to Critical Questions', *Inquiry - an Interdisciplinary Journal of Philosophy*, 45(4): 499–519.

Honneth, A. (2004) 'Recognition and Justice – Outline of a Plural Theory of Justice', *Acta Sociologica*, 47(4): 351–364.

hooks, b. (1984) *Feminist Theory: From Margin to Centre*. Boston: South End Press.

Hubbard, P. (2001) 'Sex Zones: Intimacy, Citizenship and Public Space', *Sexualities*, 4(1): 51–71.

Hull, K.E. (2006) *Same-Sex Marriage: The Cultural Politics of Love and Law*. Cambridge: Cambridge University Press.

Humphrey, J. (1999) 'Organizing Sexualities, Organized Inequalities: Lesbians and Gay Men in Public Service Occupations', *Gender, Work and Organization*, 6(3): 134–151.

Humphrey, J. (2002) *Towards a Politics of the Rainbow: Self-Organization in the Trade Union Movement*. Aldershot: Ashgate.

Hunter, S. (2011) *Power Politics Emotions: Impossible Governance*. London: Routledge-Cavendish.

Hurtado, A. and Sinha, M. (2008) 'More than Men: Latino Feminist Masculinities and Intersectionality', *Sex Roles*, 59: 337–349.

Hutchins, L. and Kaahumanu, L. (eds) (1991) *Bi Any Other Name: Bisexual People Speak Out*. Boston: Alyson Publications Inc.

ILGA (International Lesbian and Gay Association) (2010) International Lesbian, Gay, Bisexual, Trans and Intersex Association, http://ilga.org/ (home page), accessed 11 May 2011.

ILGA-Europe, Marriage and Partnership Rights for Same Sex Partners: Country by Country in Europe, http://www.ilga-europe.org/home/issues/families/recognition_of_relationships/legislation_and_case_law/marriage_and_partnership_rights_for_same_sex_partners_country_by_country, accessed 1 February 2011.

Jackson, S. (2008) 'Families, Domesticity and Intimacy: Changing Relationships in Changing Times', in D. Richardson and V. Robinson (eds) *Introducing Gender and Women's Studies*, 3rd edn. Basingstoke: Palgrave Macmillan.

Jackson, S. (2012) 'Heterosexuality, Sexuality and Gender: Re-thinking the Intersections', in D. Richardson, J. McLaughlin and M.E. Casey (eds) *Intersections Between Feminist and Queer Theory*. 2nd edn. Basingstoke: Palgrave Macmillan.

Jackson, S. and Scott, S. (eds) (1996) *Feminism and Sexuality: A Reader*. Edinburgh: Edinburgh University Press.

Jackson, S. and Scott, S. (2010) *Theorizing Sexuality*. Maidenhead: Open University Press.

Jarman, N. and Tennant, A. (2003) *An Acceptable Prejudice? Homophobic Violence and Harassment in Northern Ireland*. Belfast: Institute for Conflict Research.

Johnson, L. and Longhurst, R. (2009) *Space, Place and Sex: Geographies of Sexualities*. Lanham, Maryland: Rowman and Littlefield, Inc.

Josephson, J. (2005) 'Citizenship, Same-Sex Marriage, and Feminist Critiques of Marriage', *Perspectives on Politics*, 3(2): 269–281.

Kandaswamy, P. (2008) 'State Austerity and the Racial Politics of Same-Sex Marriage in the US', *Sexualities*, 11(6): 706–725.

Kaplan, M.B. (1997) *Sexual Justice: Democratic Citizenship and the Politics of Desire*. New York: Routledge.

Katz, J.N. (1992) *Gay American History: Lesbians and Gay Men in the U.S.A.* New York: Penguin Books Ltd. Revised edition.

Kidd, J.D. and Witten, T.M. (2008) 'Understanding Spirituality and Religiosity in the Transgender Community: Implications for Aging', *Journal of Religion, Spirituality and Aging*, 20(1): 29–62.

Kimmel, D., Rose, T. and David, S. (eds) (2006) *Lesbian, Gay, Bisexual and Transgender Aging*, 2nd edn. New York: Columbia University Press.

Kirk, K. and Heath, E. (1984) *Men in Frocks*. London: Gay Men's Press.

Kirsch, M.H. (2000) *Queer Theory and Social Change*. London: Routledge.

Klesse, C. (2007) *The Spectre of Promiscuity: Gay Male and Bisexual Non-Monogamies and Polyamories*. Aldershot: Ashgate.

Koenig, M. and de Guchteniere, P. (eds) (2007) *Democracy and Human Rights in Multicultural Societies*. Aldershot: Ashgate and United Nations Educational, Scientific, and Cultural Organization (UNESCO).

Kollman, K. and Waites, M. (2009) 'The Global Politics of Lesbian, Gay, Bisexual and Transgender Human Rights: An Introduction', *Contemporary Politics*, 15(1): 1–17.

Knox, C. and Carmichael, P. (2006) 'Improving Public Services: Public Administration in Northern Ireland', *Journal of Social Policy*, 35(1): 97–120.

Larner, W. and Craig, D. (2005) ' "After Neoliberalism?": Community Activism and Local Partnerships in Aotearoa New Zealand', *Antipode*, 37(3): 402–424.

Laurie, N., Poudel, M., Richardson, D. and Townsend, J. (2011) 'Crossing back over the open border: geographies of post trafficking citizenship in Nepal', Working Paper, Newcastle University, available download at www.posttraffickingnepal.co.uk.

Leach, S. and Wingfield, M. (1999) 'Public Participation and the Democratic Renewal Agenda: Prioritisation or Marginalisation?', *Local Government Studies*, 25(4): 46–59.

Lehring, G. (1997) 'Essentialism and the Political Articulation of Identity', in S. Phelan (ed) *Playing with Fire: Queer Politics, Queer Theories*. New York: Routledge.

Levine, M.P. (1979) 'Employment Discrimination against Gay Men', *International Review of Modern Sociology*, 9: 151–163.

Lewin, E. (1993) *Lesbian Mothers: Accounts of Gender in American Culture*. Ithaca, NY: Cornell University Press.

Lewis, G. (2005) 'Same-Sex Marriage and the 2004 Presidential Election,' *PS: Political Science and Politics*, 38: 195–199.

Lim, J. and Browne, K. (2009) 'Senses of Gender', *Sociological Research Online*, 14(1) http://www.socresonline.org.uk/14/1/6.html. Last accessed on 10/12/2010.

Linstead, S., Brewis, J. and Linstead, A. (2005) 'Gender in Change: Gendering Change', *Journal of Organizational Change*, 18(6): 542–560.

Lister, R. (2003) *Citizenship: Feminist Perspectives*, 2nd edn. London: Palgrave Macmillan.

Little, J. (2003) 'Riding the Rural Love Train: Heterosexuality and the Rural Community', *Sociologica Ruralis*, 43(4): 401–417.

Lloyd, M. (2005) *Beyond Identity Politics: Feminism, Power and Politics*. London: Sage Publications Ltd.

Lofgren-Martenson, L. (2009) 'The Invisibility of Young Homosexual Women and Men with Intellectual Disabilities', *Sexuality and Disability*, 27: 21–26.

Long, S. (2005) 'Raped by the State', *Index on Censorship,* 34(3): 122–129.

Lupton, D. (1999) *Risk*. London: Routledge.

Lustiger-Thaler, H., Nederveen-Pietevse, J. and Roseneill, S. (eds) (2011) *Beyond Citizenship: Feminism and the Transformation of Belonging*. Basingstoke: Palgrave Macmillan.

MacGillivray, I.K. (2000) 'Educational Equity for Gay, Lesbian, Bisexual, Transgendered and Queer/Questioning Students: The Demands of Democracy and Social Justice for America's Schools', *Education and Urban Society*, 32(3): 303–323.

Mackay, F., Monro, S. and Waylen, G. (2009) 'The Feminist Potential of Sociological Institutionalism', *Politics and Gender*, 5(2): 253–262.

Maeckelbergh, M. (2009) *The Will of the Many: How the Alterglobalisation Movement is Changing the Face of Democracy*. London: Pluto Press.

Marshall, T.H. (1950) *Citizenship and Social Class*. Cambridge: Cambridge University Press.

Massad, J. (2002) 'Re-Orienting Desire: The Gay International and the Arab World', *Public Culture*, 14(2): 361–385.

Mbeki, T. (2004) 'Proceedings at the Joint Sitting of Parliament', Cape Town, South Africa, 21 May.

McAuley, J.W. (1996) 'From Loyal Soldiers to Political Spokespersons: A Political History of a Loyalist Paramilitary Group in Northern Ireland', *Etudes Irlandes,* 21, 165–182.

McAuley, J.W. (2004) 'Peace and Progress? Political and Social Change Among Young Loyalists in Northern Ireland', *Journal of Social Issues*, 60(3): 541–562.

McAuley, J.W., Tongue, J. and Shirlow, P. (2010) 'Conflict Transformation, and Former Loyalist Paramilitary Prisoners in Northern Ireland', *Terrorism and Political Violence*, 22: 22–40.

McCall, L. (2005) 'The Complexity of Intersectionality', *Signs*, 30(3): 1771–1800.

McClintock, A. (1995) *Imperial Leather: Race, Gender and Sexuality in the Colonial Contest*. London, New York: Routledge.

McDonald, H. (2010) 'Ulster Loyalist Dawn Purvis Resigns from Party over UVF Killing', 3 June 2010, http://www.guardian.co.uk/politics/2010/jun/03/Ulster-loyalist-dawn-purvis-resigns-uvf-killing accessed 8th of January 2011.

McIntosh, M. (1968) 'The Homosexual Role', *Social Problems*, 16(2): 182–192.

McLaughlin, J., Phillimore, P. and Richardson, D. (2011) 'Introduction', in J. McLaughlin, P. Phillimore and D. Richardson (eds) *Contesting Recognition*. Basingstoke: Palgrave Macmillan.

McLoughlin, I., Badham, R. and Palmer, G. (2005) 'Cultures of Ambiguity: Design, Emergence and Ambivalence in the Introduction of Normative Control', *Work, Employment and Society*, 19(1): 67–89.

McNiff, J. (2001) *Action Research: Principles and Practice*, 2nd edn. London: Routledge.

McNulty, A., Richardson, D. and Monro, S. (2010) *Lesbian, Gay, Bisexual and Trans (LGBT) Equalities and Local Governance: Research Report for Practitioners and Policy Makers*. Newcastle upon Tyne: Newcastle University, UK. Available at: http://research.ncl.ac.uk/selg/documents/Broadeninghorizonsshortreport.pdf.

McRuer, R. (2006) *Crip Theory. Cultural Signs of Queerness and Disability*. New York: New York University Press.

McVeigh, R. and Rolston, B. (2007) 'From Good Friday to Good Relations: Sectarianism, Racism and the Northern Ireland State', *Race and Class*, 48(4): 1–23.

Meeks, C. and Stein, A. (2012) 'Refiguring the Family: Towards a Post-Queer Politics of Gay and Lesbian Marriage', in D. Richardson, J. McLaughlin and M.E. Casey (eds) *Intersections Between Feminist and Queer Theory*. 2nd edn. Basingstoke: Palgrave Macmillan.

Miles, N. (2008) *The Double-Glazed Glass Ceiling: Lesbians in the Workplace*. London: Stonewall.

Miller, D. (1993) 'Deliberative Democracy and Social Change', in D. Held (ed) *Prospects for Democracy: North, South, East, West*. Cambridge: Polity Press.

Miller, D. (ed) (1998) *Rethinking Northern Ireland*. Harlow, Essex: Addison Wesley Longman Limited.

Miller, T. (2007) *Cultural Citizenship: Cosmopolitanism, Consumerism, and Television in a Neoliberal Age*. Philadelphia: Temple University Press.

Minton, H.L. (2002) *Departing from Deviance: A History of Homosexual Rights and Emancipatory Science in America*. Chicago: University of Chicago Press.

Mitchell, C. (2006) 'The Religious Content of Ethnic Identities', *Sociology*, 40(6): 1135–1152.

Mitchell, M., Howarth, C., Kotecha, M. and Creegan, C. (2008) *Sexual Orientation Research Review 2008*. Manchester: Equality and Human Rights Commission.

Monro, S. (2005) *Gender Politics: Activism, Citizenship and Sexual Diversity*. London: Pluto Press.

Monro, S. (2006a) 'Sexualities Initiatives in Local Government: Measuring Success', *Local Government Studies*, 32(1): 19–39.

Monro, S. (2006b) 'Transgender Youth: Stories of an Excluded Population', in C. Leccardi and E. Ruspini (eds) *A New Youth*. Aldershot: Ashgate Publishers.

Monro, S. (2007a) 'Transgender: Destabilising Feminisms?', in V. Munro and C. Stychin (eds) *Sexuality and the Law: Feminist Engagements*. London: Glasshouse Press.

Monro, S. (2007b) 'New Institutionalism and Sexuality at Work in Local Government', *Gender, Work and Organisation*, 14(1): 1–19.

Monro, S. (2010a) 'Gender Diversity: The Indian and UK Cases', in S. Hines and T. Sanger (eds) *Transforming Sociology: Towards a Social Analysis of Gender Diversity*. London, New York: Routledge.

Monro, S. (2010b) 'Sexuality, Space, and Intersectionality: The Case of Lesbian, Gay and Bisexual Equalities Initiatives in UK Local Government', *Sociology*, 44(5): 996–1010.

Monro, S. (2011) 'Introducing Transgender Citizenship', in E. Oleksy, D. Golanska and J. Hearn (eds) *The Limits of Gendered Citizenship: Contexts and Contradictions*. London, New York: Routledge.

Monro, S. and Richardson, D. (2010) 'Intersectionality and Sexuality: The Case of Sexualities and Transgender Equalities Work in UK Local Government', in Y. Taylor, S. Hines and M. Casey (eds) *Theorizing Intersectionality and Sexuality*. Basingstoke: Palgrave Macmillan.

Monro, S. and Warren, L. (2004) 'Transgendering Citizenship', *Sexualities*, 7(3): 345–362.

Moore, A. (2010) ' "I" and "We" Identities – an Eliasian Perspective on Lesbian and Gay Identities', *Sociological Research Online*, 15(4) http://www.socresonline.org.uk/ 15/4/10.html. Last accessed on 10/12/2010.

Moran, L. and Skeggs, B. (2004) *Sexuality and the Politics of Violence*. London: Routledge.

Morgan, R., Marais, C. and Wellbeloved, J.R. (2009) *Trans: Transgender Life Stories from South Africa*. Auckland Park: Fanele.

Mouffe, C. (2000) *The Democratic Paradox*. London: Verso.

Mouffe, C. (2005) *The Democratic Paradox. On the Political (Thinking in Action)*. London, New York: Routledge.

Murray, S. and Roscoe, W. (eds) (1998) *Boy-Wives and Female Husbands: Studies of African Homosexualities*. New York: St. Martin's Press.

Nava, M. and Davidoff, R. (1995) *Created Equal: Why Gay Rights Matter to America*. New York: St Martin's Press.

Nichols, A. (2010) 'Dance Ponnaya, Dance! Police Abuses Against Transgender Sex Workers in Sri Lanka', *Feminist Criminology*, 5: 195.

Nilan, P. and Feixa, C. (2006) 'Introduction: Youth Hybridity and Plural Worlds', in P. Nilan and C. Feixa (eds) *Global Youth? Hybrid Identities, Plural Worlds*. London, New York: Routledge.

Nkoana, T. (2008) Ancestors Calling: Experiences of a South African Trans-Man. Available at: http://www.genderdynamix.co.za/content/view/355/204/, accessed 1 February 2011.

Noel, M. J. (2006) 'Progressive Polyamory: Considering Issues of Diversity', *Sexualities*, 9(5): 602–620.

Northern Ireland Statistics and Research Agency (2009) *Population and Migration Estimate 2009: Statistical Report*. Belfast: Northern Ireland Statistics and Research Agency.

Nussbaum, M. (1999) *Sex and Social Justice*. Oxford: Oxford University Press.

O'Byrne, D.J. (2003) *The Dimensions of Global Citizenship: Political Identity Beyond the Nation-State*. London: Frank Cass and Co.

Ochs, R. (1996) 'Biphobia: It Goes More than Two Ways', in B.A. Firestein (ed) *Bisexuality: The Psychology and Politics of an Invisible Minority*. London: Sage.

Olesky, E.H. (ed) (2009) *Intimate Citizenships. Gender, Sexualities, Politics*. London: Routledge.

Ong, A. (1996) 'Cultural Citizenship as Subject-Making: Immigrants Negotiate Racial and Cultural Boundaries in the United States', *Current Anthropology*, 37(5): 737–762.

Osborne, R.D. (2003) 'Progressing the Equality Agenda in Northern Ireland', *Journal of Social Policy*, 32(3): 339–360.

Ozgilbin, M.F. and Tatli, A. (2008) *Global Diversity Management: An Evidence-Based Approach*. Houndmills: Palgrave Macmillan.

Pakulski, J. (1997) 'Cultural Citizenship', *Citizenship Studies*, 1(1): 73–86.

Pant, B. and Standing, K. (2011) 'Citizenship rights and womens's roles in development in post-conflict Nepal, *Gender & Development*, 19(3): 409–421.

Parekh, B. (1994) 'Cultural Diversity and Liberal Democracy', in G. Parry and M. Moran (eds) *Democracy and Democratization*. London: Routledge.

Parish, J.T., Cadwaller, S. and Busch, P. (2008) 'Want to, Need to, Ought to: Employee Commitment to Organizational Change', *Journal of Organizational Change Management*, 21(1): 32–52.

Parkes, G., Hall, I. and Taylor, S.J. (2006) 'Gender Dysphoria and Cross-Dressing in People with Intellectual Disability: A Literature Review', *Mental Retardation*, 44(4): 260–271.

Pateman, C. (1988) *The Sexual Contract*. Palo Alto, CA: Stanford University Press.

Paternotte, D. and Kollman, K. (2010) 'Regulating Intimate Relationships in the European Polity: Same-Sex Unions and Policy Convergence', Paper presented at the Political Studies Association (UK) Women and Politics International Conference, University of Manchester, 19 February 2010.

Pellegrini, A. (2002) 'Consuming Lifestyle: Commodity Capitalism and Transformations in Gay Identity', in A. Cruz-Malavé and M.F. Manalansan IV (eds) *Queer Globalizations. Citizenship and the Afterlife of Colonialism*. New York: New York University Press.

Petchesky, R. (2000) 'Sexual Rights: Inventing a Concept, Mapping an International Practice', in R. Parker, R.M. Barbosa and P. Aggleton (eds) *Framing the Sexual Subject: The Politics of Gender, Sexuality and Power*. Berkeley and Los Angeles: University of California Press.

Phelan, S. (1989) *Identity Politics: Lesbian-Feminism and the Limits of Community*. Philadelphia: Temple University Press.

Phelan, S. (1994) *Getting Specific: Postmodern Lesbian Politics*. Minneapolis: University of Minnesota Press.

Phelan, S. (1995) 'The Space of Justice: Lesbians and Democratic Politics', in A.R. Wilson (ed) *A Simple Matter of Justice? Theorizing Lesbian and Gay Politics*. London: Cassell.

Phelan, S. (2001) *Sexual Strangers. Gays, Lesbians and Dilemmas of Citizenship.* Philadelphia: Temple University Press.

Phillips, A. (1991) *Engendering Democracy.* Cambridge: Polity Press.

Phillips, A. (2006) *Which Equalities Matter?* Cambridge: Polity Press.

Phillips, R., Shuttleton, D. and Watt, D. (eds) (2000) *De-Centering Sexualities. Politics and Representations Beyond the Metropolis.* London: Routledge.

Pidd, H. (2010) 'From Section 28 to a Home Office Float – Tories Come Out in Force at Gay March', *The Guardian*, 3 July 2010: 17.

Pinello, D.R. (2006) *America's Struggle for Same-Sex Marriage.* New York: Cambridge University Press.

Plummer, K. (1975) *Sexual Stigma: An Integrationist Account.* London: Routledge and Kegan Paul.

Plummer, K. (1995) *Telling Sexual Stories. Power, Change and Social Worlds.* London: Routledge.

Plummer, K. (2003) *Intimate Citizenship. Private Decisions and Public Dialogues.* Seattle, London: University of Washington Press.

Plummer, K. (2005) 'Intimate Citizenship in an Unjust World', in M. Romero and E. Margolis (eds) *The Blackwell Companion to Social Inequalities.* Oxford: Wiley Blackwell.

Plummer, K. (2006) 'Rights Work: Constructing Lesbian, Gay, and Sexual Rights in Late Modern Times', in L. Morris (ed) *Rights.* London, New York: Routledge.

Pollitt, C., Birchall, J. and Putnam, K. (1998) *Decentralising Public Service Management.* Houndmills: Macmillan.

Press Association (2010) Water Rationed in Northern Ireland as Engineers Battle Leaks, 29 December 2010, http://www.guardian.co.uk/uk/2010/dec/28/water-rationed-northern-ireland-leaks, accessed 5 February 2011.

Prosser, J. (1998) *Second Skins: The Body Narratives of Transsexuality.* New York: Columbia University Press.

Puar, J.K. (2002) 'Circuits of Queer Mobility: Tourism, Travel and Globalization', *GLQ: A Journal of Lesbian and Gay Studies*, 8(1/2): 101–138.

Puar, J.K. (2007) *Terrorist Assemblages: Homonationalism in Queer Times.* Durham: Duke University Press Books.

Pullen, A. and Knights, D. (2007) 'Editorial: Undoing Gender: Organizing and Disorganizing Performance', *Gender, Work and Organization,* 14(6): 505–511.

Radford, K., Betts, J. and Ostermeyer, M. (2006) *Policing, Accountability and the Lesbian, Gay, and Bisexual Community in Northern Ireland.* Belfast: Institute of Conflict Research.

Rahman, M. (2000) *Sexuality and Democracy: Identities and Strategies in Lesbian and Gay Politics.* Edinburgh: Edinburgh University Press.

Rahman, M. (2004) 'The Shape of Equality: Discursive Deployments During the Section 28 Repeal in Scotland', *Sexualities*, 7(2): 150–166.

Rahman, M. (2010) 'Queer as Intersectionality: Theorizing Gay Muslim Identities', *Sociology*, 44: 944–951.

Randall, J. and Proctor, S. (2008) 'Ambiguity and Ambivalence. Senior Manager's Accounts of Organizational Change in a Restricted Government Department', *Journal of Organizational Change Management*, 21(6): 686–700.

Raymond, J. (1980) *The Transsexual Empire: The Making of the She-Male.* London: The Women's Press. (2nd edn. 1994, New York: The Teacher's Press).

Rayner, G. (2010) 'William Hague: The Rumours of a "Gay Past" ', *The Daily Telegraph*, 3 September 2010. www.telegraph.co.uk/. Last accessed on 04/09/2010.

Rayside, D. (1998) *On the Fringe: Gays and Lesbians in Politics*. Ithica: Cornell University Press.

Reason, P. and Bradbury, H. (2001) *The Handbook of Action Research, Participative Inquiry and Practice*. London: Sage.

Reddy, V. (2009) 'Queer Marriage: Sexualising Citizenship and the Development of Freedoms in South Africa', in M. Steyn and M. Van Zyl (eds) *The Prize and the Price: Shaping Sexualities in South Africa*. Cape Town: HSRC Press.

Rembis, M.A. (2010) 'Beyond the Binary: Rethinking the Social Model of Disabled Sexuality', *Sexuality and Disability*, 28: 51–60.

Richardson, D. (1996) 'Heterosexuality and Social Theory', in D. Richardson (ed) *Theorising Heterosexuality*. Buckingham: Open University Press.

Richardson, D. (1998) 'Sexuality and Citizenship', *Sociology*, 32(1): 83–100.

Richardson, D. (2000a) *Rethinking Sexuality*. London: Sage.

Richardson, D. (2000b) 'Constructing Sexual Citizenship: Theorizing Sexual Rights', *Critical Social Policy*, 20(1): 105–135.

Richardson, D. (2000c) 'Claiming Citizenship? Sexuality, Citizenship and Lesbian/Feminist Theory', *Sexualities*, 3(2): 271–288.

Richardson, D. (2004) 'Locating Sexualities: From Here to Normality', *Sexualities*, 7(4): 393–413.

Richardson, D. (2005) 'Desiring Sameness? The Rise of a Neoliberal Politics of Normalisation', *Antipode*, 37(3): 515–553.

Richardson, D. (2007) 'Patterned Fluidities: (Re)Imagining the Relationship Between Gender and Sexuality', *Sociology*, 41(3): 457–474.

Richardson, D. (2008) 'Conceptualizing Gender', in D. Richardson and V. Robinson (eds) *Introducing Gender and Women's Studies*, 3rd edn. Basingstoke: Palgrave Macmillan.

Richardson, D. (2010) 'Youth Masculinities: Compelling Male Heterosexuality', *The British Journal of Sociology*, 61(4): 737–756.

Richardson, D. (2012) 'Bordering Theory', in D. Richardson, J. McLaughlin and M.E. Casey (eds) *Intersections Between Feminist and Queer Theory*, 2nd edn. Basingstoke: Palgrave Macmillan.

Richardson, D., McLaughlin, J. and Casey, M.E. (eds) (2012) *Intersections Between Feminist and Queer Theory*, 2nd edn. Basingstoke: Palgrave Macmillan.

Richardson, D. and Monro, S. (2012) 'Public Duty and Private Prejudice: Sexualities Equalities and Local Government', *The Sociological Review*, forthcoming.

Richardson, D., Poudel, M. and Laurie, N. (2009) 'Sexual Trafficking in Nepal: Constructing Citizenship and Livelihoods', *Gender, Place and Culture*, 16(3): 257–276.

Richardson, D. and Seidman, S. (2002) 'Introduction', in D. Richardson and S. Seidman (eds) *Handbook of Lesbian and Gay Studies*. London: Sage.

Richardson, E. H. and Turner, B.S. (2001) 'Sexual, Intimate or Reproductive Citizenship?', *Citizenship Studies*, 5(3): 329–338.

Riggle, E.D.B. and Tadlock, B.L (eds) (1999) *Gays and Lesbians in the Democratic Process: Public Policy, Public Opinion, and Political Representation*. New York, Chichester: Columbia University Press.

Riggle, E.D.B., Rostosky, S.S. and Horne, S.G. (2009) 'Marriage Amendments and Lesbian, Gay, and Bisexual Individuals in the 2006 Election', *Sexuality Research & Social Policy*, 6(1): 80–89.

Rimmerman, C.A. (2001) *From Identity to Politics: The Lesbian and Gay Movements in the United States*. Philadelphia: Temple University Press.

Rimmerman, C.A. (2005) *The Lesbian and Gay Movements: Assimilation or Liberation?* Boulder: Westview Press.

Rimmerman, C.A. and Wilcox, C. (2007) *The Politics of Same-Sex Marriage*. Chicago: University of Chicago Press.

Rollins, J. and Hirsch, H.N. (2003) 'Sexual Identities and Political Engagements: A Queer Survey', *Social Politics,* 10(3): 290–313.

Rosaldo, R. (1994) 'Cultural Citizenship in San Jose, California', *Polar,* 17: 57–63.

Rose, N. (1999) *Powers of Freedom*. Cambridge: Cambridge University Press.

Rose, N. (2001) 'The Politics of Life Itself', *Theory, Culture and Society,* 18(6): 1–30.

Rosenfeld, D. (2003) 'Identity Careers of Older Gay Men and Lesbians', in J. Gubrium and J.A. Hostein (eds) *Ways of Aging*. Oxford, Melbourne, Berlin: Blackwell Publishers Limited.

Rostosky, S.S., Riggle, E.D.B., Gray, B.E. and Hatton, R.L. (2007) 'Minority Stress Experiences in Committed Same-Sex Couple Relationship', *Professional Psychology: Research and Practice,* 38(4): 392–400.

Rouhani, F. (2007) 'Religion, Identity and Activism: Queer Muslim Diasphoric Identities', in K. Browne, J. Lim, and G. Brown (eds) *Geographies of Sexualities*. Aldershot: Ashgate.

Rumens, N. (2007) 'Working at Intimacy: Gay Men's Workplace Friendships', *Gender, Work and Organization,* 15(1): 9–30.

Ryan-Flood, R. (2009) *Lesbian Motherhood. Gender, Families and Sexual Citizenship*. Basingstoke: Palgrave Macmillan.

Ryrie, I., McDonnell, S.M. and Allman, K. (2010) *Experiences of and Barriers to Participation in Public and Political Life for Lesbian, Gay, Bisexual and Transgender People*. Report to the Government Equalities Office. London: Office for Public Management.

Sandbrook, R., Edelman, M., Heller, P. and Teichman, J. (2007) *Social Democracy in the Global Periphery: Origins, Challenges, Prospects*. Cambridge: Cambridge University Press.

Sandilands, C. (2002) 'Lesbian Separatist Communities and the Experience of Nature: Towards a Queer Ecology', *Organization Environment,* 15: 131–163.

Saner, E. (2010) 'Pride and Prejudice', *The Guardian,* 17 July 2010.

Sanger, T. (2008) 'Trans Governmentality: The Production and Regulation of Gendered Subjectivities', *Journal of Gender Studies,* 17(1): 41–53.

Schilt, K. (2006) 'Just One of the Guys? How Transmen Make Gender Visible at Work', *Gender and Society,* 20(4): 465–490.

Sedgewick, E. (1991) *Epistemology of the Closet*. Hemel Hempsted: Harvester Wheatsheaf.

Seidman, S. (1993) 'Identity and Politics in "Postmodern" Gay Culture: Some Historical and Conceptual Notes', in M. Warner (ed) *Fear of a Queer Planet: Queer Politics and Social Theory*. Minneapolis: University of Minnesota Press.

Seidman, S. (ed) (1996) *Queer Theory/Sociology*. Oxford: Blackwell.

Seidman, S. (1997) *Difference Troubles: Queering Social Theory and Sexual Politics*. Cambridge: Cambridge University Press.

Seidman, S. (2002) *Beyond the Closet: The Transformation of Gay and Lesbian Life*. New York and London: Routledge.

Seidman, S. (2009) 'Critique of Compulsory Heterosexuality', *Sexuality Research and Social Policy: Journal of NSRC*, 6(1): 18–28.

Sen, A. (2009) *The Idea of Justice*. London: Penguin.

Shakespeare, T., Gillespie-Sells, K. and Davies, D. (1996) *The Sexual Politics of Disability: Untold Desires*. London: Cassell.

Shields, S.A. (2008) 'Gender: An Intersectionality Perspective', *Sex Roles*, 59: 301–311.

Smith, A-M. (1994) *New Right Discourse on Race and Sexuality: Britain, 1968–90*. Cambridge: Cambridge University Press.

Smith, M. (2005) 'Resisting and Reinforcing Neoliberalism: Lesbian and Gay Organizing at the Federal and Local Levels in Canada', *Policy and Politics*, 33(1): 75–93.

Smith, M. (2008) *Political Institutions and Lesbian and Gay Rights in the United States and Canada*. New York, Oxon: Routledge.

Soper, K. and Trentmann, F. (eds) (2007) *Citizenship and Consumption*. Basingstoke: Palgrave Macmillan.

Spivak, G. (1988) 'Can the Subaltern Speak', in K. Grossberf and C. Nelson (eds) *Marxism and the Interpretation of Culture*. Chicago: Chicago University Press.

Spruill, J. (2004) 'Ad/Dressing the Nation', *Journal of Homosexuality*, 46(3): 91–111.

Spurlin, W.J. (2006) *Imperialism within the Margins: Queer Representation and the Politics of Culture in Southern Africa*. Basingstoke: Palgrave MacMillan.

Stacey, J. and Davenport, E. (2002) 'Queer Families Quack Back', in D. Richardson and S. Seidman (eds) *Handbook of Lesbian and Gay Studies*. London: Sage.

Stein, E. (1993) *Forms of Desire: Sexual Orientation and the Social Constructionist Controversy*. London and New York: Routledge.

Stevenson, N. (ed) (2001) *Culture and Citizenship*. London: Sage.

Stevenson, N. (2003) *Cultural Citizenship: Cosmopolitan Questions*. Buckingham: Open University Press.

Stonewall (2010) What We Do, Research and Policy, Health and Healthcare, http://www.stonewall.org.uk/what_we_do/research_and_policy/health_and_healthcare/3477.asp, accessed 28 February 2011.

Strangleman, T. (2004) *Work Identity at the End of the Line? Privatisation and Culture Change in the UK Rail Industry*. London: Palgrave Macmillan.

Stryker, S. (2008) *American Transgender History*. Berkeley, CA: Seal Press.

Stryker, S. and Whittle, S. (eds) (2006) *The Transgender Studies Reader*. New York: Routledge.

Stryker, S., Currah, P. and Moore, L.J. (eds) (2008) 'Special Issue', *Women's Studies Quarterly*, 36(3/4): 1–336.

Stychin, C. (2003) *Governing Sexuality. The Changing Politics of Citizenship and Law Reform*. Oxford and Portland, Oregon: Hart Publishing.

Stychin, C. (2004) 'Same-Sex Sexualities and the Globalization of Human Rights Discourse', *McGill Law Journal*, 49: 951–968.

Sullivan, A. (1995) *Virtually Normal: An Argument about Homosexuality*. New York: Alfred A. Knopf.

Sullivan, N. (2003) *A Critical Introduction to Queer Theory*. Edinburgh: Edinburgh University Press.

Swarr, A.L. (2004) 'Moffies, Artists, and Queens', *Journal of Homosexuality*, 46(3): 73–89.

Taylor, C. (1994) 'The Politics of Recognition', in A. Gutmann (ed) *Multiculturalism: Examining 'The Politics of Recognition'*. Princeton, NJ: Princeton University Press.

Taylor, Y. (2007) *Working Class Lesbian Life: Classed Outsiders*. Basingstoke: Palgrave Macmillan.

Taylor, Y. (2009) *Lesbian and Gay Parenting: Securing Social and Educational Capital*. Basingstoke: Palgrave Macmillan.

Taylor, Y. (2011) 'Lesbian and Gay Parents' Sexual Citizenship: Recognition, Belonging and (Re) Classification', in J. McLaughlin, P. Phillimore and D. Richardson (eds) *Contesting Recognition*. Basingstoke: Palgrave Macmillan.

Taylor, Y., Hines, S. and Casey, M. (2010) *Theorizing Intersectionality and Sexuality*. Basingstoke: Palgrave Macmillan.

Teppo, A. (2009) 'A Decent Place? Space and Morality in a Former "Poor White" Suburb', in M. Steyn and M. van Zyl (eds) *The Prize and the Price: Shaping Sexualities in South Africa*. Cape Town: HSRC press.

Terry, J. (1999) *An American Obsession. Science, Medicine and Homosexuality in Modern Society*. Chicago: University of Chicago Press.

Thomas, C., Aimone, J.O. and MacGillivray, C.A.F. (eds) (2000) *Straight with a Twist: Queer Theory and the Subject of Heterosexuality*. Champaign, IL: University of Illinois Press.

Thornton, H.B., Potocnik, F.C.V. and Muller, J.E. (2009) 'Sexuality in Later Life', in M. Steyn and M. van Zyl (eds) *The Prize and the Price: Shaping Sexuality in South Africa*. Cape Town: HSRC Press.

Turner, B. (1993) 'Contemporary Problems in the Theory of Citizenship', in B.S. Turner (ed) *Citizenship and Social Theory*. London: Sage.

Turner, B. (1999) 'Cosmopolitan Virtue: Citizenship, Reactive Nationalism and Masculinity'. Paper presented at the Rethinking Citizenship: Critical Perspectives for the 21st Century conference, University of Leeds, 29–30 June 1999.

Turner, B.S. (2008) 'Citizenship, Reproduction and the State: International Marriage and Human Rights', *Citizenship Studies*, 12(1): 45–54.

ukblackpride (2010) http://www.ukblackppride.org.uk/ (home page), accessed 16 July 2010.

Vaid, U. (1995) *Virtual Equality: The Mainstreaming of Gay and Lesbian Liberation*. New York: Doubleday.

Valentine, G. (2002) 'Queer Bodies and the Production of Space', in D. Richardson and S. Seidman (eds) *The Handbook of Lesbian and Gay Studies*. London: Sage.

Valentine, G. (2007) 'Theorizing and Researching Intersectionality: A Challenge for Feminist Geography', *The Professional Geographer*, 59(1): 10–21.

Valentine, G., Vanderbeck, R.M., Anderson, J., Sadgrove, J. and Ward, K. (2010) 'Emplacements: The Event as Prism for Exploring "Intersectionality": A Case Study of the Lambeth Conference', *Sociology*, 44: 925–943.

Vincent, L. and Camminga, B. (2009) 'Putting the "T" in South African Human Rights: Transsexuality in the Post-Apartheid Order', *Sexualities*, 12: 678–700.

Voronov, M. (2009) 'From Marginalization to Phronetic Science: Towards a New Role for Critical Management Studies', *Journal of Organizational Change Management*, 22(5): 549–566.

Waites. M. (2003) 'Equality at last? Homosexuality, Heterosexuality and the Age of Consent in the United Kingdom', *Sociology*, 37(4): 637–655.

Walby, S. (1997) *Gender Transformations*. London: Routledge.

Walby, S. (2007) 'Complexity Theory, Systems Theory, and Multiple Intersecting Social Inequalities', *Philosophy of the Social Sciences*, 37(4): 449–470.

Walby, S. (2011) *The Future of Feminism*. Cambridge: Polity Press.

Ward, J. (2008) *Sexualities, Work and Organizations: Stories by Gay Men and Women in the Workplace at the Beginning of the Twenty-First Century*. London and New York: Routledge.

Ward, J. and Winstanley, D. (2006) 'Watching the Watch: The UK Fire Service and Its Impact on Sexual Minorities', *Gender, Work and Organization*, 13(2): 193–219.

Ward, L. and Carvel, J. (2008) 'Goodbye Married Couples, Hello Alternative Family Arrangements', *The Guardian*, 23 January 2008.

Warner, M. (ed) (1993) *Fear of a Queer Planet: Queer Politics and Social Theory*. Minneapolis: University of Minnesota Press.

Warner, M. (1999) *The Trouble with Normal: Sex, Politics and the Ethics of Queer Life*. Cambridge, MA: Harvard University Press.

Watney, S. (1994) *Practices of Freedom: Selected Writings on HIV/AIDS*. London: Rivers Oram Press.

Weeks, J. (1990) *Coming Out: Homosexual Politics in Britain from the Nineteenth Century to the Present*. Revised and updated edition. London: Quartet.

Weeks, J. (1995) *Invented Moralities: Sexual Values in an Age of Uncertainty*. Cambridge: Polity Press.

Weeks, J. (1998) 'The Sexual Citizen', *Theory, Culture and Society*, 15(3–4): 35–52.

Weeks, J. (2000) *Making Sexual History*. Cambridge: Polity Press.

Weeks, J. (2008a) *The World We Have Won. The Remaking of Erotic and Intimate Life*. London: Routledge.

Weeks, J.(2008b) 'Regulation Resistance, Recognition', *Sexualities*, 11(6): 787–792.

Weeks, J. (2009) *Sexuality*, 3rd edn. London: Routledge.

Weeks, J., Heaphy, B. and Donovan, C. (2001) *Same Sex Intimacies: Families of Choice and other Life Experiments*. London: Routledge.

Weldon, A.L. (2008) 'The Structure of Intersectionality: A Comparative Politics of Gender', *Politics and Gender*, 2: 235–248.

Werum, R. and Winders, B. (2001) 'Who's "In" and Who's "Out": State Fragmentation and the Struggle over Gay Rights, 1974–1999', *Social Problems*, 48(3): 386–410.

White, J.A. (2007) 'The Hollow and the Ghetto: Space, Race and the Politics of Poverty', *Politics and Gender*, 3(2): 271–280.

Whittle, S. (2002) *Respect and Equality: Transsexual and Transgender Rights*. London: Cavendish Publishing Ltd.

Whittle, S. (2006) 'The Opposite of Sex is Politics – The UK Gender Recognition Act and Why It Is Not Perfect, Just Like You and Me', *Journal of Gender Studies*, 15(3): 267–271.

Whittle, S. and Turner, L. (2007) ' "Sex Changes"? Paradigm Shifts in "Sex" and "Gender" Following the Gender Recognition Act?', *Sociological Research Online*, 12(1) unpaginated http:// www.socresonline.org.uk/12/1/whittle.html, accessed 10 December 2010.

Whittle, S., Turner, L. and Al-Alami, M. (2007) *Engendered Penalties: Transgender and Transsexual People's Experiences of Inequality and Discrimination*. London: The Equalities Review.

Wilchins, R.A. (1997) *Read My Lips: Sexual Subversion and the End of Gender*. Ann Arbor, MI: Firebrand Books.

Wilkerson, A. (2002) 'Disability, Sex Radicalism, and Political Agency', *NWSA Journal*, 14(3): 33–57.

Wilkinson, R. and Hughes, S. (eds) (2002) *Global Governance: Critical Perspectives*. London, New York: Routledge.

Williams, C.L. and Dellinger, K. (2010) *Gender and Sexuality in the Workplace*. Bingley: Emerald Group Publishing Ltd.

Wilson, A.R. (2000) *Below the Belt: Sexuality, Religion and the American South*. London: Cassell.

Wilson, A.R. (2007) 'With Friends Like These: The Liberalization of Queer Family Policy', *Critical Social Policy*, 27(1): 50–76.

Wilson, A.R. (2009) 'The "Neat Concept" of Sexual Citizenship: A Cautionary Tale for Human Rights Discourse', *Contemporary Politics*, 15(1): 73–85.

Wilson, A.R. and Burgess, S. (2007) 'Sexuality and the Body Politic: Thoughts on the Construction of an APSA Sexuality and Politics Section', *PS: Political Science and Politics*, 40: 377–381.

Wilson, F.M. (2003) *Organizational Behaviour and Gender*, 2nd edn. Aldershot: Ashgate Publishing Ltd.

Wolff, S. (2007) 'Conflict Management in Northern Ireland', in M. Koenig and P. de Guchtneire (eds) *Democracy and Human Rights in Multicultural Societies*. Aldershot: Unesco Publishing/Ashgate.

Woodward, K. and Woodward, S. (2009) *Why Feminism Matters: Feminism Lost and Found*. Basingstoke: Palgrave Macmillan.

Wright, T. (2011) 'Exploring the Intersections of Gender, Sexuality and Class in the Transport and Construction Industries', in G. Healy, G. Kirton and M. Noon (eds) *Equality, Inequalities and Diversity: Contemporary Challenges and Strategies*. Basingstoke, New York: Palgrave MacMillan.

Yip, A. (2004) 'Negotiating Space with Family and Kin in Identity Construction: The Narratives of British Non-Heterosexual Muslims', *The Sociological Review*, 52(3): 336–350.

Yu, B.T.W. and Ming, T.W. (2008) 'Effects of Control Mechanisms on Positive Organizational Change', *Journal of Organizational Change Management*, 21(3): 385–404.

Yuval-Davis, N. (1997) *Gender and Nation*. London: Sage.

Yuval-Davis, N. (2006) 'Intersectionality and Feminist Politics', *European Journal of Women's Studies*, 13(3): 193–210.

Zanoni, P., Janssens, M., Benschop, Y. and Nkomo, S. (2010) 'Unpacking Diversity, Grasping Inequality: Rethinking Difference through Critical Perspectives', *Organization*, 17(1): 9–29.

Index